D0409029

The Rise of the
Working-Class Shareholder

The Rise of the

Working-Class Shareholder

LABOR'S LAST BEST WEAPON

David Webber

 Harvard University Press

Cambridge, Massachusetts
London, England
2018

Second Printing

Library of Congress Cataloging-in-Publication Data

Names: Webber, David (David H.), author.
Title: The rise of the working-class shareholder : labor's last best weapon /
    David Webber.
Description: Cambridge, Massachusetts : Harvard University Press, 2018. |
    Includes bibliographical references and index.
Identifiers: LCCN 2017045239 | ISBN 9780674972131 (alk. paper)
Subjects: LCSH: Pension trusts—Investments—United States. |
    Working class—United States—Economic conditions—21st century. |
    Stockholders—Political activity—United States. | Labor economics—
    United States. | Industrial relations—United States. | Labor unions—
    United States.
Classification: LCC HD7105.35.U6 W43 2018 | DDC 331.25/
    240973—dc23
LC record available at https://lccn.loc.gov/2017045239

For Irit

Then Saul dressed David in his own tunic. He put a coat of armor on him and a bronze helmet on his head. David fastened on his sword over the tunic and tried walking around, because he was not used to them.

"I cannot go in these," he said to Saul, "because I am not used to them." So he took them off. Then he took his staff in his hand, chose five smooth stones from the stream, put them in the pouch of his shepherd's bag and, with his sling in his hand, approached the Philistine.

—1 Samuel 17:38–40 (NIV)

Contents

Preface

Organized labor in America has never been closer to extinction. In the 1960s, more than one-third of the American workforce was unionized. Today, that number has dropped to 10 percent, mostly concentrated in state and local government jobs. Loss of unionization has not only led to lower compensation and job security for workers but has weakened unions themselves. One-party control of the American government makes this grim picture even worse. As this book comes to press in 2018, the Republicans control the White House, the Senate, the House of Representatives, thirty-four governorships, thirty-four state senates, and thirty-two state house chambers. With the appointment of Justice Neil Gorsuch, the Supreme Court's majority is as conservative as ever and seems set to deliver sharp legal blows to unions. The political marginalization of the Democrats, labor's traditional partner, has left labor exposed to unprecedented levels of political, legal, and economic attack.

In the face of this bleak backdrop, a group of ingenious, committed, and canny labor activists has quietly developed a formidable new source of power for labor: shareholder activism. These activists have taken advantage of the only decisively positive trend affecting labor in recent decades: the massive growth of worker pension funds, which amount to somewhere between $3 and $6 trillion, depending on how one does the math. These pension funds—sometimes called "labor's capital"—are invested in corporations, hedge funds, and private equity funds. And they are a tremendous source of power for labor.

As this book shows, this pension fund power has been used in several different ways. Some of it has been employed to thwart self-serving and entrenched corporate managers and directors. Some has been used directly against hedge funds and private equity funds that take working-class shareholder money and direct it against workers' interests. Some has been put to benefit labor directly: to fend off attacks on pensions, push back against job losses, and create jobs—jobs that can strengthen pensions by increasing contributions to them. And some has been used to find common ground with other investors. These investors include anyone with a retirement account, as well as mutual funds, foundations, and socially responsible investors who may share labor's long-term investment focus and sympathize with its broader social goals. This book tells the story of the activists who have fought for these developments, and the accompanying legal and political challenges they have faced.

What analysis of their activism reveals is that the power of labor's capital operates along two dimensions: advancing workers' interests as workers, and advancing workers' interests as long-term shareholders saving for retirement. These interests are rarely considered together. They are studied in different parts of the academy, covered by different bodies of law, and serviced by different professionals and businesses who often show little awareness or understanding of the other dimension. On the rare occasion when these interests are discussed together, they are portrayed as being in conflict. Although that's sometimes true, they can also be highly compatible, and mutually reinforcing. Neither interest can be understood properly without reference to the other.

In addition to telling the stories of some of the activists who are looking out for workers' interests, this book articulates a legal and policy framework for navigating this dual set of concerns. I offer a structure for assessing how workers should balance their interests in their jobs with their interests as pension fund investors in a way that best advances their economic well-being overall. Sometimes, that means directly promoting their interests as workers. Other times, it means directly advancing their interests as shareholders. Sometimes, it means finding common ground with other investors. And sometimes it means going it alone. To help guide workers through this maze, I propose a worker-centric legal and policy vision that provides for taking into account the full range of workers' real interests when determining how their powerful pension funds make investment decisions.

Finally, I also explore the well-funded and forceful backlash against labor's capital. In particular, the Koch brothers' political advocacy group Americans for Prosperity and the Laura and John Arnold Foundation, among others, are funding pension "reform" efforts that are ostensibly aimed at solving an alleged pension crisis, one whose existence is debatable. These pension reform efforts, if fully implemented, will destroy labor's ability to continue its shareholder activism. Just as unfavorable congressional legislation or an unfavorable Supreme Court decision could undercut unions themselves, these efforts by the Kochs, the Arnolds, and others could undercut labor's pensions, undermining both worker retirement security and shareholder power. These efforts amount to a form of economic voter suppression—a reduction in the economic voice of working- and middle-class people—paralleling voter suppression efforts in the political sphere. Still, there are reasons to remain optimistic that labor's capital can withstand these challenges, not least because these funds are primarily concentrated in Democratic states and cities with large public sectors and relatively friendly politicians and laws.

It is ironic that much of what may survive of the labor movement in the twenty-first century is its capital. Labor is clearly going to have to adapt to an even more hostile legal and business environment in the near term. There are many calls for reconstituting labor in newer, more sustainable forms, forms that are better adapted to the twenty-first-century workplace. Recent activist campaigns, like the Fight for $15, a movement for a sustainable minimum wage, are examples of the kinds of street power in which labor must continue to invest. Other policy initiatives, like a universal basic income, should be explored. But these initiatives are not enough. While the future of the American labor movement cannot be built on shareholder activism alone, it cannot be built without it. The reason for that is simple. For far too long, labor and its progressive sympathizers have sought to transform the market from outside the market: from courts, from legislatures, from regulators, from street protests, from strikes. These tools are important. But ultimately, it is not possible to transform the market from the outside. It must be transformed from within.

The activists you will meet here have proven that labor can, through pension-based stock ownership, project power straight into the heart of American capitalism, into its corporate boardrooms, into Wall Street, into banks, hedge funds, and private equity funds, as well as into the halls of Congress and state capitals. Many of the activists who have developed and refined these weapons are still in their thirties and forties and have decades of fight left. They have the skills and the expertise, the networks and the tactics, to continue to fight between elections and between financial crises, when public attention drifts away and business as usual returns. But they will only be able to go on doing so if they have the support of the broader labor movement and of others interested in workers' welfare.

At a time that is rightfully dispiriting for workers, I hope that readers will take inspiration, as I have, from the passion and skill of these activists, who are formidable strategists and tacticians. To date, their successes have been completely invisible. There are two main reasons for that. One is that the American left—particularly the segment that is focused on worker issues—is viscerally uncomfortable with labor wielding shareholder power, a capitalist weapon. The failure of virtually the entire left-of-center political spectrum to adequately defend these pensions and the power they exert—the failure to even understand how these pensions function—is a profound strategic, tactical, and moral blunder. That failure has left these pensions and their shareholder power deeply vulnerable to counterattacks by the Kochs and others. And it is one reason why, despite all the heroics you will read about in these pages, shareholder activism remains a large stick lying on the ground, waiting to be picked up. In contrast, the American right pounces on these activists anytime they exhibit even a hint of concern for workers, an entirely cynical exercise in which special interests accuse labor's capital of being a special interest. This combination of progressive neglect and conservative hostility has kept this form of activism in the shadows. But the dire situation faced by workers in this country makes it crucial to bring it into the light.

I hope that this book will enlighten readers about the important work that is being done by labor's shareholder activists. And I hope that it will convey in the starkest terms what would be lost if this power were eliminated. Regardless of who occupies the White House, the Congress, or, for that matter, the Supreme Court, protecting labor's pensions and labor's shareholder power is one fight that isn't quite over.

The Rise of the
Working-Class Shareholder

1

Safeway

Changing the Math

If the strike I'm about to describe had followed the typical, late twentieth-century pattern, it would have proceeded like this: First, the CEO would announce a steep pay cut for workers. The cut would be so sharp that it would be too demoralizing to return to work without a fight. Although the union leadership would fear failure, it would decide it had to take a chance at success. So the workers would strike. For weeks or more, they would march, and sing, and pump their fists in the air. The CEO would wait and wait, knowing exactly what the strike would cost his workers—more than it would cost him. That's how he would play it, by the numbers, by the math, the dreaded math that was spreading throughout the body of American labor like a blight. The unions needed something to change the math and couldn't see what that was. When was the last time labor had the math on its side? The 1950s? Maybe the 1960s? Not anymore. That's why the CEO would be so confident. In time, the workers would vote to accept his offer and get back to work before things got even worse, to agree to some face-saving concessions and move on with their lives. The forgotten California supermarket strike of 2003–4 played out almost exactly like this, with one critical difference, a difference that lies at the heart of this book. Spontaneously, and almost by accident, that strike revealed a bold way for workers to change the math.

In 2003, Safeway Inc., a unionized supermarket chain facing competition from nonunion workplaces like Wal-Mart, sought to boost profits by cutting benefits for workers. At the time, Safeway operated more than 1,700 stores across the United States and Canada and employed 172,000 people. The company had been paying its workers in Southern and Central California twelve dollars an hour plus health benefits, while capping them at thirty-two hours per week, less than fulltime employment. Workers prized these benefits, which were the primary attraction of a Safeway job, given the low wages and the income cap created by the hour limit. But then the company proposed freezing worker wages and dramatically increasing the percentage of health insurance premiums employees paid, undercutting the main reason to work there. Safeway also sought to shift workers to a health plan that would place much of the risk of future medical-cost inflation on employees and set lower-tier wages for new hires. In October 2003, shortly after Safeway announced these cuts, 97 percent of the company's employees, represented by the United Food and Commercial Workers union (UFCW), voted to go on strike.[1]

At the time, Steven Burd was Safeway's CEO. Burd took charge of Safeway in the 1990s on behalf of the private equity firm Kohlberg Kravis Roberts & Company (KKR), which had bought the business in 1986. But after KKR took Safeway public, Burd promptly went on a shopping spree, paying $3.6 billion from the company's treasury to acquire three regional supermarket chains,

Dominick's in Illinois, Randall's in Texas, and Genuardi's in Pennsylvania, adding more than three hundred stores.[2] The acquisitions were catastrophic. Burd paid far more for the chains than they were worth, burdening the company with debt. Sales fell, and the company lost $828 million in 2002 alone, almost all of it driven by these failed acquisitions.[3] Burd now faced a crisis of his own making. To get out of it, he hoped to make Safeway's workers atone for his sins by cutting their pay.

But before making public his intent to cut worker pay, Burd quietly prepared to defend himself and his executive allies from the strike that would certainly follow. In retrospect, his preparations make him look like a medieval king using state-of-the-art techniques to defend against an attack on land without realizing that an attack was also coming by sea. Here, the attack on land was a traditional strike, for which Burd prepared ably. Ironically, these preparations made him even more vulnerable to the attack by sea that followed, a wholly unexpected labor-led shareholder revolt, devised by a combative and innovative union leader named Sean Harrigan.

Burd's first move was to cash in on his own shareholdings. Upon announcing the strike-triggering pay cut, Safeway's stock price would certainly fall. Beginning weeks before the strike, and continuing up until one week before he announced the cuts, Burd personally sold $21.4 million of Safeway stock after executing stock options. The company claimed that Burd's transactions were planned long before the strike, and therefore not barred by insider trading laws. The government apparently agreed, because no insider trading investigation took place.[4] Not surprisingly, Safeway's stock price dropped after the strike was announced. Thus, Burd used a legal loophole to sell his shares just before announcing the strike-triggering raid on worker benefits, thereby avoiding the hit to his shares that all other Safeway shareholders would incur.[5]

Also, Burd did not ask Safeway's executives to take the same pay cut he asked of its other workers. Quite the opposite—in December 2003, two months into what would become a five-month strike by Safeway workers, Burd granted eleven of the company's top executives stock options worth $10 million. Following standard operating procedure, Burd and Safeway justified these grants by arguing that the company would not be able to function without these 11 crucial employees, though the company struggled mightily to function without the 59,000 striking employees who actually ran the 852 California stores affected by the strike. Steve Westly, the California state controller at the time, offered this understated description of the stock options: "[They were] the wrong message to send workers and shareholders."[6]

Burd's preparations for a showdown with Safeway's workers went beyond announcing the benefits cuts after he completed selling his shares, or buying the loyalty of his management team with stock options. He also entered into a revenue-sharing agreement among Safeway subsidiaries Vons, Albertsons, and the Kroger Company's store Ralphs, all of which were facing the same strike. The firms agreed to share costs and revenue to cushion the blow of the impending UFCW walkout. The agreement prompted a lawsuit by then California attorney general Bill Lockyer, who argued that it violated antitrust laws.[7]

Most importantly, Burd faced the strike knowing that he could count on Safeway's board of directors to back him through a long, bitter, and extremely costly fight. His confidence was well-placed because the board was not the least bit independent.[8] Today, thanks to working-class shareholder activists and others, no publicly held company listed on the New York Stock Exchange (NYSE)—as Safeway was at the time—would be allowed to employ a board like Burd's; it would flunk the NYSE's independence requirements. Because business relationships between directors and the company can corrupt and compromise a board's ability to independently oversee and assess the CEO, the NYSE in 2004 finally required a majority of a board's directors to meet independence criteria demonstrating that they are not the CEO's stooges but can exercise unbiased judgment. For example, today, board members cannot be considered independent if they have previous or current business relationships with the company they serve as a board member.[9] These criteria are still far too weak to make directors truly independent, but Safeway's board was so badly compromised that it would have run afoul of even the all-too-flexible rules in place today.[10]

George Roberts, James Greene Jr., and Hector Ley Lopez, all A-list business tycoons, were three of these Burd friends. Roberts was one of the founders (along with his cousin, Henry Kravis) of the aforementioned KKR, the notorious buyout firm that owned Safeway before it went public. Burd first worked with Roberts as a management consultant for Safeway when KKR owned it, and Roberts eventually helped install Burd as president and CEO of Safeway after KKR took it public. Roberts still owned close to 8.7 million shares, or nearly 2 percent of Safeway's stock. Greene was another member of KKR and a Burd colleague. Finally, Hector Ley Lopez was the general director of Casa Ley, S. A. de C.V, a Mexican supermarket company of which Safeway owned 49 percent, rendering it unthinkable that Ley Lopez could pose a serious check on Burd's judgment or authority. All three of these men knew Burd personally before being selected for the board.

Burd himself commented, "We've known Hector and the Ley family for more than 18 years, and have an enormous respect for their abilities as merchants," upon Ley Lopez's appointment.[11] All three would today have run afoul of the NYSE independence requirements. And after the unexpected shareholder "attack by sea," all three would lose their Safeway board seats.

Not yet fully grasping his own vulnerability, Burd had every reason to confront the strikers with confidence. He had secured himself and his management team financially, developed corporate allies to share a war chest through the coming months, and seeded his board of directors with loyal allies and friends. Indeed, he had good reason to believe that he could emerge from the strike with his reputation enhanced for being a hard-nosed, superstar CEO who could make what Wall Street liked to call "the tough choices."

Burd could look to contemporaneous examples of CEOs who fought their own workers and emerged both wealthier and with higher status, even if the companies themselves fared poorly. For example, Albert "Chainsaw Al" Dunlap fired 11,200 workers— more than one-third of the workforce—at Scott Paper during just twenty months as CEO in the mid-1990s, pocketing over $100 million before moving on to Sunbeam Corp., where he tried to break his own record, announcing 12,000 layoffs—50 percent of Sunbeam's workforce—four months into his tenure. Other CEOs, like "Neutron" Jack Welch and Don Graber, similarly laid off workers: in Welch's case, more than 100,000 at General Electric. These examples may have made Burd overconfident. He did not and probably could not foresee the ambush he was about to face—a labor-led shareholder campaign to oust him and his allies from control of Safeway. This campaign would leave Burd barely hanging on to his role as CEO and result in his friends and allies—the business grandees Roberts, Greene, and Ley Lopez—being removed from the board and replaced by independent directors sent to babysit Burd before he could do more damage. These blows and the unflattering press coverage that would accompany them are interesting and surprising in their own right. But what matters for this book is not the blows themselves but who delivered them.[12]

It was not the strikers, though they laid the groundwork for what followed. It was a group of Safeway's labor and labor-affiliated shareholders and their allies who hit Burd hard after the strike. It was the California Public Employees' Retirement System (CalPERS), the New York City Employees' Retirement System (NYCERS), the New York State Common Retirement Fund (NY Common), the Illinois State Board of Investment (ISBI), the Massachusetts Pension Reserves Investment Trust (MassPRIT), the Connecticut Retirement Plans and Trust Fund (CRTF), the Oregon Public Employees Retirement System, and the Washington State Investment Board (WSIB) who revolted against Burd and his board after the strike ended.[13] Almost all of Burd's preparations against the strikers weakened his position vis-à-vis these shareholders.

Interestingly, a small number of powerful private investment managers quietly joined these labor and labor-affiliated shareholders, not because the investment professionals agreed with labor's politics but because they managed the shareholders' money. This last point, which I develop in later chapters, is crucial. Private investment managers like Blackstone and even KKR, whose politics and business practices might ordinarily place them in opposition to labor interests, may find themselves backing labor interests because they want to manage the trillions of dollars held in public pension funds—labor's capital.[14] The political implications of this are underappreciated and underexploited by labor.[15]

CalPERS, NYCERS, and the remaining painfully acronymed pension funds are not your typical investors. They invest the retirement savings of 30 million working and retired public servants like school teachers, police officers, firefighters, nurses, emergency medical technicians, sanitation workers, and more. Their much smaller union fund cousins invest the retirement savings of unionized private sector workers like carpenters, electricians, and construction and hotel workers. Their annual median salaries range from a low of $32,000 for construction workers to a high of $61,000 for police officers.[16] These are the people I'm referring to when I use the term "working-class shareholders." I recognize that there is a vast literature on the question of who counts as working class versus middle class, one that encompasses a broad array of concerns including income, level of education, race, gender, family networks, and so forth. Some of these workers may be classified as middle class just because they have pensions, though it's important to note that, on account of these pensions, millions of public sector workers—40 percent of them—are not entitled to participate in Social Security.[17] For almost all of these workers, loss of their jobs and pensions would leave them on the knife's edge of poverty, if not impoverished. All share straightforward interests in maintaining their jobs and securing their retirements, interests that overlap with those of millions of other working people. And in their contests with corporate boards and managers, with hedge funds, and with private equity funds, the class distinction between them and their antagonists could not be clearer, however one characterizes it.

The workers who contribute to these pensions often elect peer workers to represent them on the funds' boards of trustees. Public pension fund boards also have members who are state or local elected officials, including governors, state treasurers, state attorneys general, and mayors. In the smaller private sector labor union funds, corporate managers sit alongside worker representatives on fund boards. As individuals, the people who contribute their retirement funds to these institutions are not wealthy; they have modest salaries and modest pensions that, individually, add up to little economic clout. But combined, their pension funds add up to more than $5.6 trillion.[18] That's a sum of money that can intimidate even Chainsaw Al and make servants of Wall Street's masters of the universe. That may sound like hyperbole, but it's not. If there's one general take-away from this book, it's that the long-predicted power of labor's capital is becoming real, that it is already transformative, that it has only begun to realize its enormous potential, and that its friends are much less aware of that potential than its enemies.

Sean Harrigan was a union leader who occupied a unique niche at the time of the Safeway strike. He was the international vice president of the UFCW, the union that represented Safeway's workers and called the strike. He was in charge of the UFCW's West Coast operations and a former Safeway employee. He knew the company and its workers personally before moving onto a job in charge of organizing for the UFCW.[19] But uniquely for a union leader heading into a strike, Harrigan held a commanding position in the world of labor's capital—in fact, he had reached the pinnacle of that world. He was the president of CalPERS, which at the time had 1.3 million members and $166 billion in assets.[20]

CalPERS is the largest pension fund in the United States, and one of the largest funds of any kind in the world. That was true in 2003–4, and it remains true today.[21] Its power may be difficult to appreciate for those who are unfamiliar with it. Its influence is evidenced repeatedly throughout this book, but for now, it suffices to note that its massive size ($323 billion in assets today) makes it an investor that companies are loath to cross. It sits on a huge pool of capital that can make or break investments. Once invested, it has the power to challenge management actions through shareholder voting, litigation, and influence over other investors. There are only a small handful of funds in the world that are larger than CalPERS, and probably none that is as publicly aggressive. Then as today, to ascend to the presidency of CalPERS was to become one of the most powerful investment voices in the world. To reach that perch, Harrigan had to outmaneuver some of the savviest politicians in California. He defeated San Francisco mayor Willie Brown in a head-to-head battle for the presidency, outpolling him in an eight-to-four vote by their fellow board members. Brown's candidacy had been backed by then–California governor Gray Davis, to no avail.[22]

At the outset, I should note one startling fact about Harrigan's involvement with this Safeway episode. While he openly participated in the strike, he denied involvement in the shareholder campaign that followed. I don't believe that denial, and I don't think he wanted it to be believed. At the time, Harrigan himself dropped several coy hints that he was more deeply involved than he could let on, and much of the evidence points in that direction. The union leader had strong legal reasons to disavow being a protagonist in the shareholder campaign that followed the strike, or at least in coordinating that campaign with the strike, for reasons I explain below. Perhaps more importantly, Harrigan's participation would have violated a deeply held American taboo that worker pension funds are only supposed to care about their shareholder interests, to the complete exclusion of worker interests, interests that are often inseparable. In the Safeway fight, Harrigan appeared to violate that taboo.

Ultimately, the precise contours of Harrigan's participation matter less than examining the Safeway fight to contrast two mechanisms by which workers can pursue their interests: a strike and a shareholder campaign. No other single historical episode offers a more direct way to compare the two. Still, because of the aggressive and transformative role Harrigan would play in these events, he, too, would lose his job, just like Roberts, Greene, and Ley Lopez. Harrigan was no saint. He was highly confrontational and abrasive, with a tendency to overplay his hand. I don't write about him to hold him up as a paragon. I write about him because I believe that he, CalPERS, and their pension allies punched their way to a new set of tactics that must be refined and widely adopted if labor is going to reassert itself in the twenty-first century.

Two Early Harrigan Campaigns

To give a sense of the threat Harrigan and CalPERS posed to Burd, I want to briefly describe two other shareholder campaigns Harrigan led shortly before taking on Safeway. First, in fall 2003, barely six months into Harrigan's tenure at CalPERS and just two months before the Safeway strike, the New York Stock Exchange revealed that it had granted its CEO and chairman, Richard Grasso, $187 million in compensation, most of it payable immediately. The NYSE was then a nonprofit organization, and the pay package probably made Grasso the highest paid head of a nonprofit organization in the country.[23] The NYSE board of directors and compensation committee that granted Grasso his pay package was composed of people he was supposed to regulate in his role as NYSE chair and CEO. The public rightly perceived his inflated compensation as a conflict of interest, arguably a payoff from the regulated to their regulator. The pay package was announced in the aftermath of the Enron and WorldCom debacles and in the midst of ongoing equity analyst scandals on Wall Street, in which then–New York attorney general Eliot Spitzer caught Wall Street analysts falsifying their research recommendations to please important clients. Grasso's compensation provoked widespread criticism. For weeks, he fought hard to keep both his job and the money, appealing to the public's patriotism by reminding them that he had reopened the stock exchange just a few days after 9 / 11.[24] It appeared that he would succeed.

Then Harrigan, joined by the head of the nation's second largest pension fund, the California State Teachers' Retirement System (CalSTRS), and the California state treasurer, publicly called for Grasso to resign and to forfeit his pay package. As Harrigan told *The Guardian,* "It was outrageous. . . . Here you have the largest stock exchange in the world that should set the absolute right example. Then you've got a guy like Dick Grasso who's got this $188m package. I said it as clearly as I could: it was an example of the pig being in the trough and our job was to get him out of the trough." Grasso resigned the next day.[25]

Similarly, less than three months after becoming the head of CalPERS, Harrigan called for the ouster of one of the nation's most high-profile and charismatic "imperial CEOs," Michael Eisner, CEO and chairman of the board of Disney. Under Harrigan's leadership, CalPERS spearheaded a shareholder revolt against Eisner, who had spent twenty years at the company. At the time, Disney had incurred a series of setbacks, including a stock price that had fallen 23 percent in five years, an SEC investigation over failure to adequately disclose board conflicts, and an infamous shareholder lawsuit against the company because Eisner paid his friend Michael Ovitz $138 million to serve as Disney's president for less than two years. Eisner's self-regarding mismanagement of the company incurred the ire of Roy Disney, a former board member and nephew of Walt, the company's founder; the two main proxy advisory services, Institutional Shareholder Services and Glass Lewis; and, first among prominent shareholders, CalPERS.[26] CalPERS's backing was the decisive turn. The fund, which owned 9.9 million shares, worth $260 million, announced that it would withhold votes from Eisner's reelection to the board in the 2004 annual shareholder vote.[27]

CalPERS's decision to oppose Eisner came with a typically Harriganesque flourish: "We have lost complete confidence in Mr. Eisner's strategic vision and leadership in creating shareholder value in the company. . . . Shareholders should send the message loudly and strongly that it is time for Disney to get a more focused strategy."[28] Pension funds in New York, Massachusetts, and elsewhere quickly signed on to the withhold vote campaign against Eisner. Although not the first of its kind, prior withhold campaigns had often resulted in modest tallies that still led to the ouster of the board chair. For example, Time Warner boss Steve Case was forced to resign as chairman of the board after a 22 percent withhold vote the year before—meaning 22 percent of the shareholder electorate refused to vote for him. The Disney shareholder revolt resulted in an unprecedented 43 percent withhold vote for Eisner, demonstrating CalPERS's ability to bring other shareholders along with it.[29] As a technical matter of corporate law, Eisner therefore still won reelection, because at least some shareholders voted for him in an uncontested election. But Disney's surviving board members were not stupid. They registered the enormous shareholder disaffection with Eisner, deciding to retain him as CEO but stripping him of the chairmanship (while still leaving him on the board) and replacing him with fellow board member George Mitchell, the former Democratic U.S. senator from Maine.[30]

For Harrigan and CalPERS, leaving Michael Eisner in place as CEO while denying him the chairmanship was not good enough. After the withhold vote, they called for Eisner to resign all of his positions—CEO included—and permanently sever his connection to the company. Six months later, Eisner announced that he would retire as CEO when his contract expired. Harrigan was still not assuaged. He demanded that Eisner resign from the board too, because "[Eisner's] continued presence on the board would prevent the company from the clean break that is needed to restore investor confidence." Eisner eventually resigned from the board as well.[31]

One cannot minimize the stunning nature of these two conquests by Harrigan. Shareholder revolts against sitting CEOs are extremely rare, and successful ones rarer still. For one person and one fund to lead the charge in taking down the CEO / chairs of the New York Stock Exchange and Disney—two of corporate America's most iconic companies—within months of each other was an achievement of lasting historical significance, one that has been too quickly forgotten.[32] These successes make it easy to imagine what Harrigan might have been thinking when Safeway's Steven Burd announced his plan to cut pay for Safeway's workers.

The Safeway Strike

From the beginning, for both Harrigan and Burd, their fight was about more than just the particulars of the new contract at Safeway. As Harrigan himself described it, "If they break our backs here, they will view this as an opportunity to pillage UFCW members and their union contracts throughout the country. This is a real watershed."[33] Some might dismiss such claims as the hyperbole of conflict. But why wouldn't UFCW employers try to do what Harrigan feared, for the same reason Burd did it: to increase profits by reducing labor costs? Harrigan and the UFCW needed more from this strike than just a fair contract for their workers. They needed to deter others in Burd's position from attempting the same. To achieve that, they needed to change the math.

Once the strike began, with workers walking off the job at Safeway and other supermarkets across California, the UFCW took its case straight to the court of public opinion. The union took out newspaper ads in Washington, D.C., Baltimore, Denver, Seattle, and Northern California. Targeting workers and consumers, ads like these began appearing on the radio:

First, Safeway's CEO Steve Burd sold about $20 million worth of company stock. Then, he forced me and seventy-thousand [sic] other workers onto the streets to save our families' health benefits. We're out of work—shoppers have been inconvenienced—and Safeway stock prices have taken a nose dive—but—Steve Burd is looking out for himself. It's time to turn the tables—I'm Kathy Shafer, a twenty-eight-year Safeway-Vons employee. Send Steve Burd a message—please don't shop Safeway when you see our picket lines. A *message from the working men and women of the UFCW—we're holding the line for healthcare for all working families.*[34]

The UFCW also began targeting an unusual audience in its public relations campaign against the company, one not typically sympathetic to unions and their strikes. In an advertisement in the *Wall Street Journal,* the UFCW attacked Burd's poor management of Safeway: "Which is the most effective way to improve Safeway's bottom line?" the ad asked. "A: Stop CEO Steve Burd's mismanagement. B: Cut Health Care Benefits for Workers." Quoting a *Los Angeles Times* editorial, the advertisement stated, "It would take [the healthcare costs of] the company's local unionized workforce the better part of three decades to do as much damage to Safeway's bottom line as Burd did with a single merger deal in 1998." The text emphasized Burd's incompetence ("He miscalculated again . . ."), arguing that Burd had alienated both workers and customers "in one of the richest markets in the country." Finally, it concluded, "Stop Steve Burd before he loses even more money for the company."[35]

The *Wall Street Journal* ad is bereft of individual human voices, devoid of personal faces of the Safeway strike. Instead, it was designed to affect the opinions of people Burd actually cared about: investors and retail-sector analysts. It aimed to convince *Wall Street Journal* readers generally that Burd was incompetent, and to lead investors to question whether Burd should remain in his position.[36]

The effectiveness of either of these ads is anyone's guess, but they demonstrate a broader range of options available to labor than is typically deployed. Some audiences are more likely to respond to moral claims favoring workers, others to arguments about the bottom line for shareholders. There is little reason to confine appeals to one or the other, although some progressives find it distasteful to frame these issues in the language of shareholder interests rather than worker interests. People who take the position that corporations and shareholders are inherently exploitative are deeply uncomfortable with the idea of working-class share-holders. After all, what does it mean when workers own shares in companies run by other workers? What does it mean when worker-shareholders "exploit" other workers? When the exploited exploit the exploited? Are working-class shareholders a kind of "human shield" protecting the 1 percent, who are the real share-holders in our society?

These are complex philosophical and political questions that re-veal some of the inherent contradictions of labor's capital, and I will attempt to address them as they arise.[37] But for the most part, I view these concerns as highly theoretical and mostly imprac-tical, not least because labor's capital exists. Nearly thirty million people directly depend on the $3–6 trillion in assets invested in these funds; tens of millions more indirectly depend on them.[38] There is no going back to a world in which labor and capital are mutually exclusive, lined up across a barren cavern of confronta-tion—at least not in developed economies.

My view is that working-class shareholder power is a vehicle for reintroducing the voices of middle- and working-class people into the corridors of power from which they have otherwise been exiled. And the increased exercise of this shareholder power can produce two basic changes: first, many more people could retain more of the economic surpluses that they themselves have created, restoring wealth to the parties that generated it; and second, mar-kets, which are inherently structured to respond to shareholders, will respond to these middle- and working-class shareholders in ways that, by extension, will make them more responsive to middle- and working-class people more generally.[39]

The case for expanding the power of worker shareholders within a market context treats the fact of working-class shareholders not as an inconvenient truth but as an important tool for rebalancing economic outcomes. Skillful use of such power is already transpiring and offers a promising way forward not just for labor but for middle- and working-class people more generally. Labor and progressives should double down on it, not walk away from it, and not let it be destroyed by the Kochs, the Arnolds, and others. Put differently, nothing is more likely to stop workers from storming the barricades than the rallying cry: "Workers of the World Unite! You have nothing to lose but your pensions." These workers have skin in the game—not nearly as much as they should, but enough to enable them to fight for more. The rational goal for them to pursue is to identify and exploit genuine sources of real-world power to bend the current system toward their own needs, including allying, when it makes sense, with other shareholders, students, activists, endowments, environmentalists, impact investors, and mutual funds. The divergent fates of the Safeway strike and the Safeway shareholder campaign that followed illustrate the point.

A hint of that surprising shareholder campaign appeared early in the strike. In December 2003, the UFCW approached CalPERS, seeking its help with Safeway. This was akin to Harrigan appealing to himself for aid. CalPERS responded to the UFCW by writing a public letter to Safeway stating that the company's "blatant disregard for quality of life issues for your long-term employees is having a significant impact on our investment in your corporation." The UFCW embraced the CalPERS letter, publicly declaring its hope that it would encourage other investors to follow CalPERS's lead.[40] Burd and Safeway brushed aside whatever threat the letter implied.

As the strike lingered on, a group of religious leaders tried to enter the fray. In late January 2004, three and a half months into the strike, these leaders, accompanied by workers and their children, traveled from Southern to Northern California to "personally deliver a message to Safeway Inc. Chief Executive Steven Burd." Clergy and Laity United for Economic Justice, or CLUE, a group of four hundred religious leaders from Los Angeles, began their pilgrimage north with a rally at a Pavilions Supermarket in Sherman Oaks, California, where blessings were offered by Christian, Jewish, and Muslim leaders. The *Los Angeles Times* quoted Rev. Jim Conn, urban strategist for the United Methodist Church of Southern California, saying, "We are praying for this man, Burd, who has been so recalcitrant, so cold to his workers. He needs to know about the lives he is affecting." The workers rode buses north to the accompaniment of Spanish songs by Fidel Sanchez of the Pico Union Shalom Ministry. They spent the night on the floor of a high-school gymnasium and arose early the next morning to go to Burd's house in fittingly named Alamo, where they planned to deliver thousands of handwritten cards and letters asking him to relent on his negotiating positions.[41]

Cynthia Hernandez, a checker and stocker who was having difficulty providing for her family during the strike, said, "I want [Burd] to see our faces. I want him to know that we exist." Burd didn't feel the same way. He wasn't home. And even if he had been, it would not have mattered, because the protesters were stopped a mile away from his house by the town's sheriffs. Six clergy were allowed to approach the home, where they encountered private security and Burd's personal representative. Together, they held hands and prayed. The workers left, and Safeway conceded nothing. The strike went on and on and on, with negotiations and mediations. Along the way, Safeway, Kroger, and Albertsons suffered a combined $1.5 billion in lost sales. Workers were also hurt, making just $25 a day paid by the unions. Toward the end, they were joined on the picket lines by Senator John Kerry of Massachusetts, the future secretary of state and shortly to be the Democrats' presidential nominee for the 2004 election.[42] Neither Kerry nor the company's losses from the strike were sufficient to deter Burd from pursuing his cost-cutting course.

The strike finally ended after almost five months of struggle, making it the longest supermarket strike in U.S. history. As always after strikes of this magnitude, both sides declared victory. But the weight of the evidence suggests that the press, the workers, and even the unions themselves viewed Safeway as a defeat, at least internally. According to the *Los Angeles Times,* whose reporters closely followed the walkout, "The contract the negotiators crafted has been widely viewed as a victory for the supermarkets, especially because it includes a two-tier system under which stores will pay new hires much less in wages and benefits than veteran workers." Similarly, the *New York Times* reported that "many union members complained Friday that the settlement gave no raises and meant a lower wage tier and skimpier health plan for new hires."[43] There can be no dispute: Safeway supermarket workers were worse off than they had been before the strike. Thus, union leaders were forced to define victory not in terms of prestrike worker wages and benefits but in terms of how much worse off workers could have been in the absence of the strike. This arguably was a victory of sorts, but it didn't feel like one, and no amount of spin could make workers feel otherwise.

Companies have always had greater economic resources than unions during strikes, but in recent decades, that gap has expanded dramatically. In the 1960s, one-third of American workers were unionized. Those workers paid dues, and those dues funded comparatively powerful union organizations. Today, barely more than 10 percent of the U.S. workforce is unionized, and most of those workers are in the public sector, working for state and local governments (and contributing to the pension funds that have become the source of working-class shareholder power and that would pounce on Burd shortly after the strike ended). A smaller workforce means fewer dues-paying members. Fewer dues means fewer resources to bring to a strike, the number of which has plummeted in recent years.[44] Fewer resources also means you cannot bargain as effectively. Ineffective bargaining means fewer union jobs at lower and lower wages, which means even fewer dues, and so on and so forth. The decline of unions has a ripple effect far beyond union members themselves, correlating with lower wages and greater economic inequality everywhere. Pick the metaphor of decline that most appeals to you. For me, it summons images of global warming and melting glaciers, in which massive and seemingly eternal structures that once scarred the earth find themselves in quiet but merciless retreat, only occasionally dramatized by an ice shelf collapsing into the ocean and creating a splash, but with most of the real damage done in the ceaseless, minute-by-minute cracking and grinding and melting that moves absolutely and only in the wrong direction. Were it not for the shareholder part of this story, the Safeway strike would have been just one more shelf collapsing unremembered into the sea of history.

Here are some more data points of interest, documenting a different, positive trend: As of June 30, 2015, CalPERS had $315 billion in assets, or $117 billion more than it had in 2004 at the time of the Safeway strike. It also had 400,000 more members than it did in 2004, for a total of 1.8 million members. The same is true for all of the other labor's capital funds that would rally to the cause against Safeway. NYCERS's assets have increased from $42.7 billion in 2004 to $63.6 billion in 2015, the NY Common from $136.4 billion to $197.9 billion, the Illinois State Board of Investments from $10.4 billion to $15.8 billion, MassPRIT from $34 billion to $65 billion, Connecticut Retirement from $31 billion to $40.4 billion, Oregon's system from $51.7 billion to $68.8 billion, and the Washington State Investment Board from $57.2 billion to $85.1 billion.[45] The simultaneous decline of labor and the rise of labor's capital suggests what the future of labor power must look like if there is to be a future for labor power at all. Like much twenty-first-century power generally, it will draw on shareholder power as a source.

The Pension Funds Mobilize a Shareholder Campaign

The end of the strike at Safeway was not the end of the struggle. On the contrary, at some point during the negotiations, Sean Harrigan, or the UFCW, or both, threatened Burd with a shareholder campaign in connection with Safeway's upcoming shareholder meeting in May 2004. As evidence emerged that this threat would become real, the public reaction was one of great skepticism. Initial reports indicated that any shareholder campaign against Burd would be viewed as a long shot.[46]

The *Chicago Tribune* first broke the story on March 25, 2004. It reported that the Illinois State Board of Investment, which oversees the pension funds of the state of Illinois, was coordinating with several other large investment funds to oppose the reelection of Steven Burd and two other directors at the May 20, 2004, Safeway shareholder meeting. According to the *Tribune,* the ISBI took the "unusual step" at a March 5 meeting of its executive board, which voted to team up with other pension funds in an effort to thwart Burd's reelection as CEO and chair of Safeway. "Safeway's share price movement has been disastrous," said Bill Atwood, the Illinois board's executive director, introducing the theme. "It's been one of the worst performers over the past five years."[47]

With this subtle but entirely persuasive shift in how to frame what went wrong at Safeway—what was wrong with Burd—the struggle took on a new dimension. The *Tribune* further noted that several funds were scheduled to appear at a press conference to announce the campaign later that week. In turn, Safeway accused CalPERS of being behind the press conference and the shareholder campaign, publicly hammering the point that Harrigan, CalPERS's president, was also the executive director of the UFCW, which had just finished striking against the company. CalPERS, the *Tribune* article observed, had led the recent proxy fight against Eisner at Disney.[48]

Beyond gaming the shareholder vote, Safeway had tactical reasons to publicly call out Harrigan for leading the strike and the shareholder campaign. The company wanted to intimidate Harrigan at the outset by putting him on notice that he was in legal jeopardy. As head of CalPERS, Harrigan had fiduciary duties to put the interests of CalPERS's beneficiaries ahead of his own interests and those of any other organization.[49] Safeway was indirectly proposing to the media that Harrigan was using CalPERS's power for the benefit of the UFCW and Safeway's workers and therefore arguably breaching his fiduciary duties to CalPERS. Pay no attention to Burd's abysmal performance, said Safeway, this is about Harrigan taking CalPERS on a joyride for the benefit of the UFCW. Of course, the reality is that Harrigan's actions could be both—that CalPERS and the other funds were acting in solidarity with Safeway workers and in their own interests as shareholders in a troubled company.

This is an excellent example of how the game is played. The companies insist that the activists are only interested in labor issues, and the activists insist that they are only interested in shareholder issues, as if these two concerns were always mutually exclusive. Here, Safeway was following this playbook. It was using rules designed to protect workers to protect itself instead. It is hard to believe that Safeway suggested that Harrigan might have a legal problem because the company was worried about *CalPERS's beneficiaries*. It wasn't. It was worried about protecting Burd. But just because the company used this legal threat to protect itself doesn't mean it was wrong on the law. Trustees like Harrigan *are* responsible for paying out pension benefits to workers over a thirty-year time horizon or more, and we do not want to let them stray too far from that mission. That leads to a constant debate over where to draw the line for such trustees— what they should and should not be able to do.

The threat from Safeway was enough to induce Harrigan to remain publicly silent for most of the shareholder campaign, though he did not formally recuse himself from it. Contemporaneous press reports indicate that he was involved behind the scenes. "Just because you carry a union card," he said at the time, "doesn't mean you have to recuse yourself."[50]

The shareholder assault that followed the strike emphasized two themes: Steven Burd incompetently engineered numerous failed acquisitions, destroying $20 billion in shareholder value and causing a 63 percent decline in the company's stock price over five years; and because four out of nine board members were affiliated with KKR, and because eight out of nine board members had profited from separate business deals with Safeway, the board faced conflicts of interest that inhibited its ability to independently oversee Burd. Therefore, (1) Burd should be fired from the CEO position; (2) to prevent future abuses, the role of CEO and chairman of the board should be split rather than held by the same person; and (3) shareholders should oppose Burd's reelection to the board and that of the two other directors whose terms had expired.[51]

Having identified the campaign messages and targets, the final task was to win the election. There were actually two campaigns: the public, formal campaign, and the private, informal one. By the public campaign, I mean the effort to rally the shareholder electorate to vote against Burd and the two other candidates up for reelection, William Tauscher and Robert I. MacDonnell. As is often the case in shareholder campaigns, its most important single target was an entity that actually had no right to vote at all: Institutional Shareholder Services, or ISS.[52]

ISS is a powerful organization in the corporate world. To understand its importance to shareholder campaigns, consider the following hypothetical. Imagine if the endorsement of one newspaper in a U.S. presidential election could determine how one out of four voters cast their ballots. Such an endorsement would be the decisive factor in most elections. That is the role ISS played at the peak of its power in shareholder elections, and it is a role it largely continues to play today. Because large, diversified institutional investors (like pension funds) may hold thousands of investments in their portfolios, they are required to vote in thousands of elections every year. If they devoted sufficient resources to studying the issues and candidates in all of those elections, they would have time for nothing else. Therefore, they outsource most of the research to proxy monitoring services (the proxy is the shareholder ballot) like ISS or a smaller competitor, Glass Lewis. ISS makes recommendations on almost every election and proxy proposal, and many diversified institutional shareholders vote those recommendations. Empirical studies have shown that ISS alone can swing as much as 25 percent of the shareholder electorate with its advice.[53] With a yea or nay from ISS, either side in a shareholder fight is almost halfway toward its goal: an electoral majority.

Both the pension funds and Safeway management lobbied ISS for its recommendation. Hammering away at Burd's poor performance and at the conflicted board of directors, the shareholder campaigners pushed ISS to back its efforts to unseat the three directors up for reelection. The tactic partially worked: ISS recommended a withhold vote for Steven Burd, that is, ISS recommended that shareholders oppose Burd's reelection to the board of directors. But it offered no opinion as to whether Burd should remain as CEO, leaving that to the new board, and it did not recommend against the two other directors who were up for reelection. The other proxy advisory firm, Glass Lewis, recommended that the company split the roles of CEO and chair.[54] It was not a grand-slam home run for the shareholder campaigners, but with recommendations against Burd's reelection to the board and in favor of splitting the role of CEO and chair, the shareholder threat to Burd went from a long shot to a significant challenge.

These recommendations ignited an all-out war between the campaigners and the company. Safeway was determined to protect its CEO. And the campaigners were unwilling to stop pursuing the other directors just because ISS recommended against doing so. This takes us to the private shareholder campaign that ran alongside the public one, a campaign that may have been just as effective if not more so. This one targeted board members who were not up for reelection, specifically George Roberts and James Greene, KKR founder and partner, respectively.

Ed Smith described for me what happened. At the time, Smith was international vice president of the Laborers International Union of America. He was also the chair of the ISBI and the Central Laborers' Pension Fund, where he had served as a pension trustee for over twenty years. As part of the campaign, Smith and other pension fund leaders demanded a meeting with Roberts.[55] The meeting stood in sharp contrast to the non-meeting between Burd and the Safeway workers at Burd's house in Alamo. The pension funds were not greeted by Roberts's private security detail and a personal representative who offered to pray with them, but by Roberts himself in his office. The meeting was brief, to the point, and resulted in an immediate and tangible outcome.

The shareholders told Roberts that his personal relationship with Burd was interfering with his ability to oversee the CEO and serve as a check on his authority; that the depth of the relationship between Safeway and KKR was a problem; and that it was time for Roberts to, as Smith put it, "get off the board."[56] KKR managed billions of dollars in pension money, including Illinois pension money under Smith's authority. Roberts's failure to comply with the pension funds' demands could jeopardize hundreds of millions, if not billions of dollars in pension fund assets under management for KKR.

This was an easy call for Roberts. He agreed to resign from the Safeway board and to take Greene with him. No shareholder vote on the subject was even necessary, because the shareholders that mattered—the laundry list of pension funds, several of whom were significant KKR clients—had already decided. Roberts and Greene were gone. Two out of three board members were finished before the fight began.

The shareholders' successful private targeting of Roberts and Greene vacated two board seats that could be filled with people more independent from Burd than they were. But it also allowed Safeway to spin their departures as the company's own idea. In turn, Safeway sought to undermine one of the key appeals made by the campaigners: that Burd and the board were not listening to shareholders and that therefore the company needed new board members who would reflect shareholder views. But we *are* listening, Safeway could reply: we have dismissed three board members. (In addition to Roberts and Greene, the company announced it would dismiss Ley Lopez.) The company also appointed one of its existing directors, Paul Hazen, the former CEO of Wells Fargo, as a new lead independent director.[57] The position of lead director is often proposed by management as a second-best solution to shareholders seeking to strip the chair role from the CEO. It leaves the CEO as head of the board but purportedly empowers another director to set the agenda for board meetings and act independently. These were significant concessions on the part of the company. But no sophisticated observer would conclude that it had taken these steps on its own, in the absence of the shareholder campaign.

Of the other two directors who were formally up for reelection, Tauscher and MacDonnell, Tauscher in particular drew the campaigners' attention. Connecticut state treasurer Denise Nappier, who oversaw the Connecticut retirement plans and trust funds, had previously written a letter to the Safeway board pointing out that Tauscher, a purportedly independent director, "engaged in approximately $3.5 million in related-party transactions involving Safeway." That meant he benefited from side deals with Safeway, undermining his independence as a board member. Given that Tauscher was the chairman of the firm's executive compensation committee, and therefore set Burd's pay, the fact that he was allowed—presumably with Burd's approval—to profit from his dealings with Safeway could compromise his ability to fairly negotiate Burd's compensation on behalf of Safeway, to say the least. The other board member up for reelection, MacDonnell, was yet another KKR man. These facts make it astonishing that ISS still backed the reelection of Tauscher and MacDonnell, but it did, helping them win reelection. Still, because Tauscher's business relationships with Safeway created a conflict of interest in setting Burd's pay, he was forced off the executive compensation committee. And MacDonnell was forced off the audit committee, ending some of the most blatant conflicts. Thus, the campaigners' actions led to the removal of three close Burd allies from the board, the appointment of an independent lead director, and the removal of Tauscher and MacDonnell from sensitive committee positions. But the campaign did not result in the removal of Burd himself, who won reelection, largely on the argument that the board-level shakeup was due to his own renewed attention to shareholders.[58]

With that, the Safeway fight ended, though its repercussions continued to reverberate.

Assessing the Significance of the Safeway Fight

In assessing what happened at Safeway and comparing the relative effectiveness of the strike and shareholder campaign, several noteworthy differences between the two become apparent. The strike was an extended episode in trench warfare, requiring the mobilization of tens of thousands of workers with scarce economic resources to support them, and resulting in significant disruption to the workers themselves, their families, and Safeway's customers. The shareholder campaign that followed it was closer to a drone strike. It happened very quickly, it required the mobilization of comparatively few people and limited resources, and it was aimed directly at the top of the opposing organization. The parallels to other forms of twenty-first-century combat are striking—and suggest a need for labor to evolve its tactics to suit the times. That evolution is already taking place, though not quickly enough. These results do not suggest wholesale abandonment of strategies that were successful in an earlier time, just as the success of drone technology does not suggest the abandonment of conventional armies. But labor must expand its range of options to attain its ends.

The significance of the Safeway fight is twofold: first, it demonstrated the possibility of new tactics for deterring corporate misconduct by directly targeting the corporate officers that make destructive decisions; and second, it offered the opportunity to examine, in one coherent episode, the *relative* decline of the strike as an effective means of struggle, and the simultaneous emergence of a new, twenty-first-century approach, the shareholder campaign. In considering the effectiveness of the latter, I want to add one more point about the Safeway fight. I want to discuss not just what happened but what else could have happened. Specifically, I want to discuss the role of an offstage villain in this tale, Wal-Mart.

Although Wal-Mart was not a party to this dispute, its presence could be detected in all aspects of the fight. While Safeway's economic harms were primarily the result of Burd's misbegotten empire building and failed supermarket acquisitions, the imminent entry of Wal-Mart Supercenters into the California market motivated Burd to take a hardline position with Safeway workers—or, at least, it served as a convenient pretext for that hardline. (In fact, it took years for Wal-Mart Supercenters to enter the California market, but that didn't stop Burd and Safeway from using the threat to extract concessions that enhanced profits at the expense of worker compensation.)[59]

Wal-Mart's ability to pay lower wages to its nonunion workers threatened not only Safeway but the UFCW too, which had an ongoing interest in Safeway's success as a unionized workplace.[60] This is an important point to keep in mind for conservative critics of labor's capital, who want to claim that it's all about maximizing labor's interests to the detriment of the company and other stakeholders. In fact, labor's capital has an interest in investing in thriving companies that pay workers their fair share. Burd could and did argue that Wal-Mart's lower wages would be passed on to its consumers in the form of lower prices, which would undermine

Safeway's ability to compete. The message to Safeway's workers was, you can work for me for less than you make now, or you can work for Wal-Mart, or perhaps not work at all.

Given the Wal-Mart threat, one might think that fighting Burd was futile. Safeway workers would either have to be paid less, or not be paid at all, because the company would eventually be destroyed by the seemingly unstoppable Voldemort, Wal-Mart. But the shareholder campaigners had leverage over Wal-Mart for the same reason they had leverage over Safeway—because they, too, were Wal-Mart shareholders: CalPERS, NYCERS, all of them. For example, CalPERS's comprehensive annual financial report for 2003 provides a snapshot of the holdings of its largest investment fund, the Public Employees' Retirement Fund (PERF), as of June 30, 2003. (CalPERS manages fourteen separate funds but PERF is the largest.) According to this certified annual financial report, at the time of the Safeway strike, PERF owned 16,855,600 shares of Wal-Mart, which at $53.67 a share had a total market value of $904,640,000. PERF's Wal-Mart stake was one of its top ten holdings.[61]

This introduces a dilemma. These funds, and the workers whose retirement proceeds they invested, profited from the same company that was undermining the economic well-being of other workers, including UFCW workers. One might ask, why were they invested in Wal-Mart at all? The automatic response is that Wal-Mart was a good investment, and pension funds are responsible for funding the retirements of their beneficiaries, not playing politics. That's true. These funds must prioritize their obligation to fund the retirements of the folks who contribute to them. But that means prioritizing the economic well-being of their contributors, which does not always mean chasing the highest returns to the funds regardless of the disastrous economic consequences of those investments for those who contribute to them. One could view the pension funds' investments in Wal-Mart as potentially "corrupting," in the sense that such an investment can be a tool for allying labor with the very forces that most actively seek to undermine it. This is a serious concern, and one that drives some progressive skepticism toward labor's capital.

I would argue that this concern, though real, is overblown and is a species of the problem faced by labor any time it gains actual economic and political power. The situation of labor's capital in the United States is comparable to successful labor-funded and -influenced political parties in Europe and elsewhere, with the Democratic Party occasionally playing that role in the United States. Any worker-friendly entity that manages to become part of the power structure risks being tainted by it. In my judgment, this problem is far less troubling than facing no conflicts of interest because you have no power at all. Labor unions should be so lucky to once again face this dilemma in the United States, as they did in the 1940s, 1950s, and 1960s when they were the dominant force in the Democratic Party.

So why didn't these shareholder activists challenge Wal-Mart directly? As it happens, there is some mixed evidence suggesting they did, if behind the scenes. CalPERS's comprehensive annual financial reports suggest that it sold a huge number of Wal-Mart shares during the Safeway strike, at least briefly, perhaps as a kind of warning shot. I already noted CalPERS / PERF's large stake in Wal-Mart as of June 30, 2003, four months before the Safeway strike. In fact, Wal-Mart was CalPERS's fifth largest holding. In CalPERS / PERF's next comprehensive filing, dated June 30, 2004, Wal-Mart was no longer on the fund's top ten list.[62] In fact, it is not listed anywhere in the report at all. To drop off the list, the CalPERS / PERF's stake in the company would have had to fall from $904,640,000 to—at a minimum—somewhere below $725,759,000, which was the size of its tenth-largest holding. (I cannot see how large the drop actually was. I can only tell that it fell below $725 million.) The drop is not explained by a fall-off in Wal-Mart's stock price. The stock closed at $53.67 on June 30, 2003, and at $52.50 on June 30, 2004, nowhere near a large enough decline to explain the change in CalPERS's Wal-Mart stake. If CalPERS sold zero Wal-Mart shares, the value of its holdings would have dropped from $904,640,000 to $884,919,000, which should still have placed Wal-Mart seventh on the list, ahead of Bank of America and behind American Insurance Group.[63] That means CalPERS / PERF would have had to sell, at a minimum, around $140 million in Wal-Mart stock in the period that coincided with both the UFCW strike and the shareholder activist campaign that followed, assuming that this document is correct. The size of this selloff—if it took place—may have played some role in the decline in Wal-Mart's stock price during that time, something that the company's managers would have noticed. (I say "if" because there are other publicly filed documents that seem to contradict the comprehensive annual financial report, though I note that the report was audited by Deloitte and Touche, a leading accounting firm.)[64]

If the selloff did take place, it could have been just a portfolio rebalancing for diversification purposes. But it also could have been a tactical divestment either in an effort to punish Wal-Mart for its labor practices or at least to dissociate CalPERS from Wal-Mart at a time of high-profile labor conflict.[65] And if the divestment did not take place, then we are left with the original question about how worker funds should deal with investments that undermine workers. Divestment typically has three goals: to hurt the targeted company by putting downward pressure on the stock price, to harm the target through bad publicity generated by a high-profile divestment, and / or to protest some action taken by the company or otherwise dissociate the fund from that company.

The Safeway strike, the shareholder campaign, and the prospect of a Wal-Mart divestment—whether it occurred or not—suggest an array of legal and policy questions. Does there always have to be a pure business rationale for taking investment action, or can such action be taken for other reasons? And if a pure business rationale is always required, how can it be distinguished from, say, a labor rationale? In the American context, it is often taken as a given that a business case and only a business case for investment action is appropriate, though I argue that the law suggests otherwise. In contrast, European pension funds have a track record of divesting from companies that violate the funds' labor standards, including Wal-Mart, never mind whether there was a pure business case for such divestments.[66] Most recently, seven such funds, including retirement funds in Denmark and Sweden, divested from budget airline Ryanair because of labor issues.[67] They said they did so for labor reasons, and did not offer an accompanying investment rationale. They do not share the American taboo against combining the two. In contrast, when the California State Teachers Retirement System divested from gun companies after the Newtown, Connecticut, massacre in which a gunman killed six teachers and twenty first graders, it was forced to take the extra step of arguing that there was a strong investment reason to do so, citing the future risk of greater regulation of gun companies in America because of massacres like these. That argument ignores the fact that U.S. gun sales often spike after massacres and that there appears to be little

prospect for significant regulation in the near term that would reduce gun-company profits in America. I applaud CalSTRS's divestment but question the investment rationale for it. The most
likely reason for the selloff—moral outrage at profiting from the
weapon used in the slaughter—is the reason that dare not speak
its name.[68]

Should U.S. pensions follow their European counterparts and
divest over labor issues, as the Danish and Swedish funds did at
Ryanair, or as many funds divested from South African companies over apartheid in the 1980s and 1990s? Should they ignore
these concerns entirely, opting to maximize returns first, foremost,
and forever? Is the answer somewhere in between, giving funds
flexibility to consider labor issues alongside business ones in making
investment decisions? What does the law require here? And law
aside, what is the right strategy—to divest, or to remain engaged as
an investor with the power to change investee behavior through
shareholder campaigns or litigation?

For the sake of transparency, I'll state outright that I do not think
that federal or state law requires, or should require, funds to ignore the overall economic impact of a fund's investments on
workers in the name of maximizing returns. Obviously, returns
are crucially important to the health of any pension fund and to
worker retirement security. But consider the perverse situation of
public employee pension funds maximizing returns—or at least
trying to—by investing in companies that privatize their own
workers' jobs. It is literally the case that the pension funds of some
firefighters, police officers, prison guards, teachers, public engineers, and custodians are directly funding private firefighting companies, private security firms, private ambulance corps, private
prisons, and other companies that privatize public services, directly

undercutting these public workers' own wages and benefits. Arguably, the whole purpose of such firms is to undercut the wages and benefits of public workers. These investments may even undermine the fund itself, because job losses result in fewer fund contributors.[69] This point should be emphasized: maximizing returns in this context not only harms your own beneficiaries but can damage the fund through loss of contributors.

Despite these troubling facts, one prevalent view of fiduciary duty suggests that taking into account anything other than investment returns, even your own contributors' jobs, is an extraneous consideration and even a breach of the fiduciary duty of loyalty.[70] I disagree and argue for a broader view of fiduciary duty that would require at least some assessment of how an investment could affect the jobs of your fund participants, and consequently, contributions they make to the fund (or that are made on their behalf by employers). The flip side of this same argument embraces proactive investments that create worker jobs, and therefore fund contributors, even if returns on those investments may be lower than competing investment prospects. I argue that it is entirely appropriate for trustees to consider workers' *economic interests* beyond just maximizing returns to the fund, a view that has been at least implicitly blessed by two courts.[71] And I further argue that when these interests conflict—that is, when worker retirement fund interests conflict with worker interests—they should not automatically choose one over the other. Instead, fund managers should assess whether siding with their shareholder interests or workers interests would be more economically beneficial to the fund's participants, and act accordingly.

There is one very important caveat here: pension funds are, and should be, required to remain diversified, and nothing about my "worker first" view should permit a departure from diversification. That legal obligation exists both by statute and under the fiduciary duty of prudence.[72] Any other approach would be not just illegal but insane. Combining diversification requirements with a worker-first view puts funds where I think they should be: broadly and conservatively invested in the market while still positioned to use shareholder influence to improve labor's economic prospects.

At the opposite extreme from the narrow maximize-returns view, and stretching beyond the jobs-focused view I advocate, is one permitting investment decisions on almost any basis, including purely social or political considerations. For the left, it might be divesting from energy or tobacco companies. For the right, it might be divesting from companies that manufacture abortion pills or engage in stem-cell research. How far away from direct economic considerations should pension trustees be allowed to stray? These decisions affect the soundness of these funds, the retirement security of workers, and the potential cost to taxpayers in the (low probability) event of a bailout. Most of us reject the idea of letting trustees play pure politics with pensions, but where to draw this line is obviously not easy.

We return to these considerations throughout the book. But I summarize my framework for analysis here. We can imagine two basic ways of assessing how pensions—or, for that matter, any investors—make investment decisions. The first is economic analysis; the second is political, social, or moral analysis. By economic analysis, I mean analyzing the economic costs and benefits of an investment to the investor. By political / social / moral analysis, I mean analyzing how particular investments align or clash with the investors' other values. The extent to which jobs and labor issues should be considered by pension funds can fit into either category, as a question of economic interest or as a question of moral and political values. Which category they fall under has significant legal and policy implications.

Most of my focus is on economic criteria. My argument is that fund trustees should broaden their economic perspective beyond blindly maximizing returns that can undermine their own workers' jobs and the fund itself, to a more holistic view of workers' economic interests in their investments. Ironically, departing from the narrow maximize-returns view does not necessarily entail accepting reduced returns. There is a substantial body of evidence—contested evidence, but evidence all the same—suggesting that environmental, social, and governance sensitive investment portfolios actually obtain higher returns than maximize-returns portfolios do. (Social and governance criteria often take labor concerns into account anyway.) Regardless, the "worker-centric" view includes considering workers' interests in their jobs and benefits in making investment decisions, within the overarching framework of remaining diversified. Ultimately, in the extreme case, that means allowing funds to trade off investment returns for other economic benefits like jobs and increased contributions to the fund, insofar as the reduced investment returns are offset by these other economic benefits.

The most important reason why I favor this approach as a matter of law and policy is that it would allow pensions not just to manage the challenge of privatization but to use their pension power to create jobs and contributors. There is no greater opportunity to do so than the prospect of massive infrastructure spending in America. Although it has not yet come to pass, both President Donald Trump and Senate Democrats have embraced a proposed trillion-dollar infrastructure investment program.[73] Even if this remains nothing more than political talk in the near term, some significant spending on infrastructure seems almost inevitable in the United States, given its current decrepit state. Talk in the political sphere has already prompted significant capital-raising efforts in the private sector focused on infrastructure. Worker-first would empower pensions to shape such investment by giving them additional legal cover to pursue the hiring of union labor or "prevailing wage" compensation for workers on any infrastructure project in which they invest. Such union workers would in turn contribute to these pension funds, creating a virtuous circle and potentially delivering an adrenaline shot to the ailing labor movement.

This worker-centric view stands in contrast to efforts to destroy these pensions entirely, converting them into individually managed 401(k)s. Much of the contemporary debate over pensions is shaped by the widespread perception that these funds are underfunded and that they are imminently at risk of requiring a taxpayer-funded bailout. It is unquestionably true that a small number of local pension funds are in bad shape. But the view that most public pension funds face an imminent catastrophe of underfunding is a perversion of the truth. It treats the worst-case scenario as inevitable and ignores evidence that most of these funds stand on a firm financial footing. It relies on a kernel of truth for some pension funds to paint a broad picture of public pension funds in crisis. It puts the most pessimistic spin on the future uncertainty of pensions. It insists that real but manageable problems with modest solutions are actually huge problems requiring radical reform. It ignores the primary cause of pension underfunding, which is the decades-long refusal of employers to pay their obligations to workers. And it is a view that has received far more traction than its competitors because it has been widely promoted by Charles and David Koch's Americans for Prosperity, and John Arnold's Laura and John Arnold Foundation, among others. Most damning of all, this view has been used to justify turning public pension funds and labor union funds into individually managed 401(k) funds or the equivalent, even though there is strong evidence that 401(k)s leave workers with insufficient retirement assets.[74] The drive to replace pensions with 401(k)s or individual retirement accounts (IRAs) would not only jeopardize the retirement security of millions of Americans. It would destroy the very activism described in this book. That's not a bug of pension reform but a feature.

Safeway's Aftermath

Burd remained Safeway CEO for nearly a decade after the strike, finally retiring in 2013. He left the company fourteen months before it was acquired by supermarket rival Albertsons (which in the interim had been bought by Cerberus) for $9.2 billion.[75] Burd received $7.5 million in stock for that deal and made in excess of $100 million during his time as Safeway CEO.[76] In contrast to Burd, Harrigan lost his CalPERS job by the end of 2004. Leading fights against Richard Grasso, Michael Eisner, and finally Steve Burd earned Harrigan a long list of powerful enemies. When Republican Arnold Schwarzenegger defeated Democratic incumbent Gray Davis in a California gubernatorial recall election in 2004, those enemies saw an opportunity to take down Harrigan. Widespread media reports suggested that Governor Schwarzenegger pressured the California Personnel Board to cause Harrigan's "unceremonious firing," as the *New York Times* described it, though Schwarzenegger denied involvement. Still, as the *Times* reported, "tempestuous as his short reign may have been, Harrigan did well by CalPERS shareholders, raising the fund's assets to $177 billion from $116 billion in less than two years." Harrigan, as you might have guessed, did not go quietly. He published an op-ed in the *Los Angeles Times,* "The Corporations Couldn't Tolerate My Activist Voice," touting his and CalPERS's accomplishments, accusing Schwarzenegger and the U.S. Chamber of Commerce of ousting him, and proclaiming the rise of the corporate governance movement—the shareholder movement to reform corporations from within.[77]

Although Harrigan's career did not end after he lost the CalPERS presidency, he never regained the prominence he had attained in his twenty-two months leading the fund. He subsequently served as president of the Los Angeles Fire and Police Pensions Board, a significant fund with over $10 billion in assets, but still far less prominent and influential than its statewide counterpart. Harrigan ultimately resigned from that board along with another board member—a billionaire former finance chair for the Republican National Committee named Elliott Broidy—after an SEC investigation over pay-to-play allegations. A mania of such charges occurred in 2009–10, but the allegations were never substantiated against either man. Harrigan has since disappeared from public view.[78]

In the decade following the Safeway fight, working-class shareholder power would expand massively. Many of the barriers confronted by the Safeway shareholder campaigners would collapse in the face of pressure brought by the generation of shareholder activists that followed Sean Harrigan, Ed Smith, and Denise Nappier. These fighters would strip Burd's peers of many of the tools he manipulated to entrench himself, vastly increasing business leaders' accountability to shareholders like CalPERS. Among these activist achievements, but by no means the only one, was the successful advance of "proxy access" (the subject of the next chapter) through a torturous, dozen-year fight that continues to this day. These new activists would also successfully fight for the CEO-worker pay rule, which requires companies to disclose how much their CEOs are paid relative to the median company worker—a rule that initially appeared to be vulnerable under the Trump administration but that now appears safe, at least in the very near term.[79] Shareholder activists would decisively win the fights to destagger corporate boards and institute majority voting in director elections. They would successfully lobby for the most important provisions of the Dodd–Frank Act. They would deploy new tactics to force hedge funds and private equity funds to prioritize the needs of working-class shareholders or face harsh economic consequences. And perhaps most importantly, they would learn to use their shareholder power to help create more jobs for workers.

In so doing, these activists would learn to advance the interests of workers by doing what any politically mature movement does. At times, they would advance worker interests directly. That is particularly true in their long-overdue conflicts with hedge funds and private equity funds, where they would push back against funds trying to undermine pensions, kill worker jobs, and charge excessive fees (though this last fight would come much later than it should have). At other times, the activists would advance their own interests by simultaneously advancing the interests of others. That is true of the leadership role these activists would come to play in the corporate governance movement, the movement to make corporate managers more accountable to long-term share-holders, mostly entities that are looking to pay out retirement benefits over a thirty- to forty-year time horizon. As leaders of the corporate governance reform movement, working-class shareholders have represented the interests of all long-term, diversified shareholders, including themselves but also mutual funds, foundations, and others. In so doing, these funds have not only enhanced the value and power of their own retirement funds but have made themselves indispensable to almost everyone else in the market. Those alliances will hopefully reap rewards as labor's capital faces increasing legal and political challenges in the near term.

2

The New Suffragists

The Fight for Meaningful
Corporate Elections

There are many reasons why banks and corporations are
not particularly afraid of either the Securities and Exchange Commission (SEC) or Congress, even during rare phases when they
become muscularly pro-regulation. One reason why is because,
for a time, industry captured the U.S. Court of Appeals for the
District of Columbia Circuit, a federal appeals court, and used
it to undermine congressional and regulatory interventions against
business interests. The "D.C. Circuit," as it is known, is the most
powerful of the thirteen federal appeals courts because it hears appeals related to agencies of the federal government based in the
capital. True, the U.S. Supreme Court is the ultimate legal authority in the land. But the Supreme Court hears about eighty
cases per year. The D.C. Circuit hears around 1,100.[1] As a practical matter, the D.C. Circuit has the final say on far more cases of
import than does the Supreme Court. The most well-funded and
well-connected inside-the-beltway lobbyists understand the power
of the D.C. Circuit and concentrate their legal and lobbying efforts accordingly.

From 2008 to 2010, Democrats controlled the White House and both houses of Congress, triumphing in the aftermath of the worst financial crisis since the Great Depression.[2] Corporate lobbies and temporarily disenfranchised Republicans opposed to the sweeping financial reforms adopted in that period quickly devised a legal strategy designed to use the courts to undo them. That strategy focused successfully on the D.C. Circuit. And in the case of *Business Roundtable v. SEC* in 2011, these efforts inflicted a deep blow against working-class shareholder activists.[3] But, ironically, this same case, and its aftermath, became one of the best examples of how these same activists—like New York City comptroller Scott Stringer—ultimately outmaneuvered Republican judicial opposition to succeed where Congress and the SEC failed.

"Proxy access" is, in Sean Harrigan's words, "the mother lode of meaningful corporate reform."[4] Imagine if a president of the United States seeking reelection could require that his name be the only one appearing in voting booths. Someone could still run against him, but the challenger would have to incur the enormous cost of paying to circulate ballots with her name to voters, while the incumbent's name would automatically appear on ballots at taxpayer expense. The challenger would have to individually mail entirely separate ballots to voters, who would have to bring those ballots with them to use on Election Day. If the challenger failed to mail her ballots, or if she mailed them but voters did not bring them to the polls, then the only available ballot in the voting booth would be the one with the incumbent's name on it. Voters could still abstain, or they could vote for the incumbent, but they could not vote for the challenger.

If this took place in actual U.S. presidential elections, it would be flatly unconstitutional. But this is how corporate elections work.

Corporate boards nominate themselves for election or reelection and put only their own names on the "proxy," or corporate ballot, that is sent to shareholders at company expense before any shareholder meeting. Others can choose to run against these board members if they want to. But to do so, they have to pay to create their own separate proxies, track down all of the company's investors, mail them to those investors, and then exhort them to use the new ballots in the election. That costs many millions of dollars. Only the most affluent and concentrated investors—hedge funds—can afford to challenge corporate boards by printing and mailing their own proxies to run competing candidates in what is called a "proxy fight."[5]

Even hedge funds only run a proxy fight in the most exceptional circumstances, because the cost is so high. For everyone else, such a fight is insane. That's exactly how the two most powerful business lobbies, the Business Roundtable and the U.S. Chamber of Commerce, like it. They like a world in which shareholders who want to challenge directors like Safeway's Steven Burd, William Tauscher, and Robert MacDonnell—or, for that matter, Disney's Michael Eisner—have no practical choice but to run a "just vote no" campaign, rather than run a competing candidate. Historically, the best an opponent could hope for in a "just vote no" campaign, or a "withhold vote," is that the reelection total was so low that it shamed the board into removing a board member who was technically reelected but with an embarrassing vote total. That's what happened to Eisner. But overall, the fact that it is almost impossible to get a competing candidate on the ballot is one of many reasons why corporate elections have always been a joke, an oxymoron. It's why people who understand corporate elections scoffed when Justice Anthony Kennedy wrote in his 2010 *Citizens*

United opinion that, if shareholders were unhappy with a company's political expenditures, they could take action against management "through the procedures of corporate democracy."[6]

The Proxy Access Rule

Proxy access would help fix the enormous imbalance favoring incumbents over challengers in corporate elections. It would not mean that anyone could nominate themselves to be included on the corporate ballot. But it would give certain shareholders direct access to the proxy. It would allow a limited number of long-term, diversified shareholders (like pension funds and mutual funds, not short-term-trading hedge funds) to directly place their own competing nominees on the same proxy as the board's nominees, at no cost.[7] In my hypothetical presidential election above, it would mean nothing more than letting the challenger's name be printed on the same ballot as the incumbent's. Not any challenger, but an established challenger. Access means nothing more than adding a few lines of text to a piece of paper that must be printed and mailed regardless. And yet, the Business Roundtable and the U.S. Chamber of Commerce have fiercely opposed this simple reform by every means available.

Efforts to adopt proxy access in the United States go back as far as the 1940s, but the contemporary story has its origins in the early 2000s. In 2001, the American Federation of State, County, and Municipal Employees (AFSCME), a prominent public employees union, began drafting proxy access shareholder proposals and submitting them to a handful of companies.[8] The effort was led by two activists: Rich Ferlauto, a former young Republican who became one of the leading architects of labor's shareholder power, and Beth Young, an attorney who runs a solo law practice out of her apartment in Flatbush, Brooklyn, and whose behind-the-scenes strategic and legal influence on labor's shareholder activism has played a pervasive and under-acknowledged role in many wins of the last decade. Both Ferlauto and Young embody qualities shared by many of the shareholder activists I have met or interviewed—they combine a shrewd tactical sense with a romantic, idealistic view of their jobs. (Young told me that a line from *Hamilton: An American Musical* keeps popping into her head while she's working: "How does a ragtag volunteer army in need of a shower somehow defeat a global superpower?")[9]

AFSCME's initial proxy access proposals were a direct response to the Enron and WorldCom accounting scandals, in which two Fortune 100 U.S. companies collapsed within a year of each other—causing a combined $85 billion in losses—because they were engaged in massive accounting frauds. Suddenly, questions of corporate governance, of corporate accountability, were injected into the public debate. Although AFSCME had a team of research analysts, none of them focused exclusively on issues of corporate governance. That had been Ferlauto's specialty when he worked at Institutional Shareholder Services (ISS)—the proxy advisory firm mentioned in Chapter 1—shortly before joining the union's shareholder activism team. AFSCME's leader at the time, Gerald McEntee, wanted to expand the union's corporate governance activism precisely because the retirement funds of its many members were invested in the largest public pension funds, which faced enormous risks from fraud in the marketplace. The best way to generate corporate accountability, reasoned Ferlauto and Young, was to make shareholder voting a meaningful exercise through tools like proxy access.[10]

Initially, AFSCME hoped that proxy access might be included in the Sarbanes-Oxley legislation of 2002, which imposed new governance and accounting requirements on public companies in the aftermath of Enron and WorldCom. But when it became clear that would not happen, Ferlauto and Young filed shareholder proposals seeking proxy access at half a dozen companies. (Shareholders have the right to submit their own proposals to be included in the proxy and voted on at the annual meeting, though they must meet certain legal requirements and are almost always opposed by the board.) All of Ferlauto's and Young's shareholder proposals were opposed by their respective boards, and the SEC sided with the corporate boards every time, permitting exclusion of the proposals. In other words, the SEC—the commission that is supposed to protect investors—allowed companies to ignore these proposals and not submit them to their shareholders for consideration at their annual meetings. In 2003, when the SEC let yet another company, AIG—the same AIG that, four years later, would lead the country and the world into the financial abyss—ignore yet another AFSCME proxy access proposal, the union finally got fed up and sued, winning a surprising reversal at the Second Circuit Court of Appeals in New York.[11]

At this point, the SEC announced it would review the court's legal opinion and consider instituting a proxy access rule of its own.[12] But the SEC never followed through. This death-by-delay approach was consistent with the SEC's phlegmatic pace of regulation and enforcement in the George W. Bush era, particularly under the leadership of Bush's first and third commissioners, Harvey Pitt and Christopher Cox.

Then came the financial crisis of 2008, and the strong desire of Senator Chris Dodd of Connecticut and Congressman Barney

Frank of Massachusetts to leave a legacy of financial reform before retiring from Capitol Hill. The Dodd-Frank Wall Street Reform and Consumer Protection Act of 2010 finally gave shareholder activists the opportunity—and the SEC the political and legal cover—to draft a proxy access rule, or so they thought. Falling under the subtitle "Strengthening Corporate Governance," a section of the act entitled "Proxy Access" authorized the SEC to make a rule requiring the corporate ballot to include "a nominee submitted by a shareholder to serve on the board of directors."[13] In other words, shareholders—rather than just the board itself—could nominate board candidates and have those nominees listed on the ballot. Fearing a legal challenge, Congress sent a strong signal to the courts that it expected deference to the proxy access rule, which it left the SEC to implement. The legislative history of the act explicitly states that the SEC should be given "wide latitude in setting the terms of such proxy access."[14]

Perhaps the drafters of this language hoped to test the principles of conservative judges who had long attacked liberal "judicial activism." Conservatives have repeatedly decried purportedly unaccountable activist federal judges who were too quick to overrule legislation adopted by Congress or to apply new meanings to constitutional provisions. That's why Chief Justice John Roberts, in his Supreme Court confirmation hearing, famously described the role of a justice as a passive umpire: "It's my job to call balls and strikes and not to pitch or bat."[15] The legislature clearly indicated that it expected the SEC to be given wide range on proxy access, a signal to the judiciary to abide by its role of interpreting laws passed by Congress, not legislating on its own.

The rule that the SEC actually proposed was comfortably among the more conservative versions of what Congress itself had considered. It limited the use of proxy access to long-term shareholders only, barring its use by shareholders—most likely hedge funds—who were looking to move into the stock, engineer a quick price increase, and then sell. In other words, the rule flipped the status quo so that hedge funds would still have to pay to circulate their own ballots but long-term, diversified shareholders could nominate candidates whose names would appear on the proxy. Rather than empowering any shareholder to use proxy access, the rule also required that the shareholder own 3 percent of the company, or join a small group of investors that reached the 3 percent threshold combined. That number may sound small, but it's not. Even the very largest pension funds own less than 1 percent of the companies they invest in. As a practical matter, the 3 percent threshold would almost always require a group of large investors to work together to reach it and nominate a candidate, eliminating outlier or gadfly candidates. (As it happens, 3 percent was the same threshold Ferlauto and Young had fought for several years earlier in their AFSCME shareholder proposals. That's not altogether surprising, given that Ferlauto was then working at the SEC on the proxy access rule itself.)[16]

The rule also required that only shareholders who owned a stake in the company for a minimum of three years be allowed to use proxy access. By limiting its use to long-term shareholders who owned a substantial stake in the company, and forcing those shareholders to team up with others who likewise had significant holdings, Congress and the SEC empowered primarily retirement funds like state and local public pension funds, labor union funds, and mutual funds. These funds are "universal owners," that is, they are diversified investors who own most of what's for sale in the stock market and invest over a thirty- to fifty-year time horizon.

Presumably, these are the same investors whose interests are best aligned with long-term economic growth, precisely the shareholders we would want to empower in a proxy access rule. Finally, the rule allowed proxy access to be used for no more than a quarter of the total outstanding board seats.[17] So, if a corporate board had twelve seats, proxy access could be used to contest no more than three of them per election. The other nine directors could still run effectively unopposed. It was hardly the French Revolution, but it was a start.

There's no doubt that Congress fully understood that proxy access would empower state and local public pension funds and labor union funds, that is, working-class shareholders. First, any action that empowers long-term, diversified investors empowers working-class shareholders, period. That's not just because working-class shareholders are themselves long-term, diversified investors striving to pay out benefits to workers who contribute to them, decade after decade. It is also because other types of long-term, diversified shareholders, like mutual funds, which primarily invest the retirement savings of white-collar workers, engage in comparatively little activism since they face conflicts of interest. Activism tends to antagonize its corporate targets, like CalPERS's challenges to Disney and Safeway. Unlike public pension and labor union funds, mutual funds (like Vanguard and Fidelity) profit from having their 401(k) plans on the platforms of large public corporations, again like Disney or Safeway or, for that matter, Wal-Mart. These funds do not want to antagonize corporate managers who can punish them by removing their 401(k) plans from the list of those offered to a company's employees. For example, according to a recent study by the 50/50 Climate Project, Vanguard voted against management at energy companies 22 percent of the time, but it supported zero challenges to companies where Vanguard serviced retirement plans.[18]

Mutual funds also compete with each other, unlike pension funds and labor union funds. You can't take your pension away from CalPERS and give it to New York State's retirement fund—your pension is directly tied to your job. But you can take your 401(k) from Fidelity and give it to Vanguard; investors often "roll over" their 401(k)s and other investments from one mutual fund to another. To the extent that mutual funds were to expend resources on activism that would benefit all shareholders, they would be benefiting their competitors too. Using your own resources to help your competitors is not what good capitalists do. It's called the free-rider problem. Why should I bear the cost of an activist play that will work to the advantage of my competitors?

Mutual funds also remain passive because mutual fund analysts prize their ability to obtain information about company performance from CEOs or CFOs, who are much less likely to return their phone calls or respond to their requests if their funds are simultaneously challenging the corporate leaders. Also, mutual fund managers populate the same class as corporate managers: they travel in the same social networks, attend the same business schools, join the same clubs, send their kids to the same schools—unlike the trustees of public pension funds, who are teachers, firefighters, and other public employees. Consequently, mutual funds have remained largely inactive. It is true that some mutual funds have recently begun to dip their toes in activist waters, most notably State Street's 2017 sponsorship of the *Fearless Girl* sculpture opposite the Wall Street bull in lower Manhattan, coinciding with its announcement of a new shareholder voting policy favoring women board members. Similarly, Vanguard and BlackRock in 2017 supported environmental proposals—made by other investors—at a couple of energy companies. But overall, mutual funds are far less likely to make use of proxy access than public pensions. For this reason, almost any reform that empowers long-term, diversified shareholders primarily empowers the subset of those investors who are willing to use that power: working-class shareholders like public pension funds and labor union funds. Of course, in order for these shareholders' candidates to actually win, they would need the support of other shareholders.[19]

Moving beyond the logic of the marketplace, Congress had an excellent way of knowing that public pension and labor union funds would be empowered by proxy access: they were the ones lobbying for it. The Council of Institutional Investors (CII), a coalition of public pension funds, labor union funds, and a limited number of corporate pension funds, lobbied intensely for proxy access and against an earlier version that would have set a higher threshold of 5 percent stock ownership available only to single shareholders. "A 5 percent ownership requirement would effectively shut out those large, long-term, responsible investors—largely public and union pension funds—most willing to engage companies and hold them accountable," CII told Congress.[20] In other words, a 5 percent threshold would hardly have been proxy access at all. So Congress abandoned that idea.

Congress could also have gone in the opposite direction, by establishing effectively no shareholding threshold, so that anyone who owned even one share for a short period of time could access the proxy. But there is little point in accessing the proxy if you have no reasonable chance of nominating a candidate who can win. Working-class shareholders have the clout to nominate serious challengers, and to the extent that individual, small-stakes shareholders ever make proposals, those proposals have zero chance of passing without public pension and labor union support. Congress clearly grasped this. It is crucial to understand this point if we are to understand what was so wrong about the D.C. Circuit's decision in this case. Congress knew perfectly well who it was empowering when it adopted proxy access: public pension funds and labor union funds.

There were two basic reasons for Congress to empower these shareholders. First, the Democratic Congress liked these shareholders' left-leaning politics; they were natural allies. Additionally, Congress believed that empowering these shareholders, even with their "special interest" concerns about workers and jobs, would benefit *all* shareholders by holding corporate managers accountable. Congress had made precisely the same policy decision fifteen years earlier, under Republican control. In 1995, Congress passed the Private Securities Litigation Reform Act, which placed institutional investors like public pension funds in control of class-action lawsuits brought on behalf of defrauded investors, such as those against Enron and WorldCom for accounting fraud. The Republican Congress did so out of concern that plaintiff-side class-action lawyers—who not coincidentally contribute heavily to Democrats—were reaping too much of the benefit of shareholder lawsuits for themselves, settling cases too quickly and too cheaply, and charging high attorneys' fees. Institutional investors with large losses could help monitor lawyer behavior, assuring better outcomes for shareholders. Regardless of its political motivations, this reform worked. The evidence is clear that when public pension funds take control of these suits as lead plaintiffs, defrauded shareholders recover higher damages and pay lower attorneys' fees.[21] That doesn't mean these funds never have special interests. It means that their activism can benefit everyone with a stake in making sure that companies are well-governed.

Ultimately, whatever motivated Congress to empower working-class shareholders matters little to the legal analysis, because Congress has the power to adopt proxy access. Conservatives were perfectly entitled to disagree with proxy access on policy grounds. But when they lost that fight, they did what members of both parties do: tried to find something "illegal" about a policy choice they disagreed with.

Dodd-Frank, including proxy access, was signed into law on July 21, 2010. Barely a month later, on August 25, 2010, the SEC adopted its proxy access rule. Five days after that, the *Wall Street Journal* ran an overwrought op-ed, "Alinsky Wins at the SEC": "Sold in the name of 'shareholder democracy,'" the *Journal* opined, "this new rule will mainly be used not by mom and pop investors, but by union funds and other politically motivated organizations seeking to force mom and pop to support causes they otherwise would not."[22]

The *Wall Street Journal*'s argument that protecting corporate board members from having to run against actual competitors was for the benefit of "mom and pop," not the boards themselves, is perverse. (The paper advocated instead for rules making hostile takeovers easier.) The op-ed further credited the new rule as a victory for Saul Alinksy, the famed activist and author of *Rules for Radicals*. In his 1971 book, Alinsky identified shareholder activism as an important tool for advancing progressive interests.[23] Important as Alinsky's contribution was, two other books written just a few years later came closer to predicting working-class shareholder activism in its current form: Peter Drucker's strange and somewhat paranoid *The Unseen Revolution: How Pension Fund Socialism*

Came to America (1976), and a better book, Samuel Rifkin and Randy Barber's *The North Will Rise Again* (1978). There have also been numerous subsequent academic treatments of the topic.[24] Still, Alinsky remains a *bête noir* for the American right, and his name is often trotted out purportedly to discredit anything associated with it. It was also no coincidence that the *Journal* op-ed said "Alinsky Wins at the SEC," not "Alinsky Wins in Congress," which is in fact where he won. By blaming the SEC instead of Congress, the *Wall Street Journal* mapped out the legal and public relations attack that would follow: don't blame the democratically elected Congress for proxy access; instead, blame a purportedly rogue federal commission, the SEC.

On September 28, 2010, just two months after Congress included proxy access in Dodd-Frank, barely more than a month after the SEC adopted the rule, and just weeks after the *Journal* screamed about it, the Business Roundtable and the U.S. Chamber of Commerce sued the SEC—not on behalf of corporate boards and managers, but on behalf of mom and pop.[25]

Suing the SEC over Proxy Access

No one was surprised when the Roundtable and the Chamber chose Eugene Scalia as their lawyer. Scalia was the son of then-sitting conservative Supreme Court justice Antonin Scalia and the primary legal mastermind of the Republican strategy to dismantle Dodd-Frank, at least until the Trump administration took office in 2017, when a legislative strategy became feasible. (As of this writing, legislation passed in the House of Representatives has not been taken up in the Senate). To date, Scalia has filed at least six lawsuits aimed at undermining Dodd-Frank, all in the D.C.

Circuit.[26] More dismaying to proxy access advocates was the randomly selected panel of D.C. Circuit judges who would hear the Roundtable's case: Judge Douglas Ginsburg (no relation to Justice Ruth Bader Ginsburg), Judge Janice Rogers Brown, and Judge David Sentelle, all three Republican appointees.[27] These judges would decide whether to uphold a rule adopted by a Democratic SEC empowered by a statute named for two Democratic legislators, signed by a Democratic president, and passed in Congress with zero House Republican support and just two Senate Republican votes.[28] Judge Ginsburg and Judge Brown were particularly concerning. Brown had previously described the New Deal and minimum wage laws as "the triumph of our socialist revolution" and proclaimed that "private property, already an endangered species in California, is now entirely extinct in San Francisco."[29]

The presence of Ginsburg on the panel caused even greater concern. His legal smarts and conservative credentials were sterling enough to earn him President Ronald Reagan's nomination for a seat on the Supreme Court of the United States. Had the fact that he smoked marijuana as a law professor remained secret, he would be sitting on the Supreme Court today. After his drug use was exposed, his candidacy collapsed. Justice Anthony Kennedy was appointed to the seat that would have been Ginsburg's.[30]

There was nothing subtle about the support Ginsburg and the other D.C. Circuit judges showed for the agenda of Scalia and his fellow travelers. In an article published in the *University of Chicago Law Review* (years after the *Business Roundtable* case), Cass Sunstein and Adrian Vermeule criticized the D.C. Circuit for "moving in libertarian directions without sufficient warrant in existing sources of law, including the decisions of the Supreme Court itself." Sunstein and Vermeule further accused Judge Ginsburg, in particular, of having an "identifiable ideological valence."[31] In a vigorous reply to Sunstein and Vermeule, Ginsburg did not deny the charge but justified the valence, arguing that it is the role of the court to stand up to the administrative state, that is, to serve as a check on the SEC (and the Environmental Protection Agency, the Internal Revenue Service, the Department of Education, etc.). President Donald Trump's Supreme Court appointee, Neil Gorsuch, has expressed similar views in even more strident terms.[32]

Even granting the point that judicial deference to federal agencies is different from judicial deference to Congress itself, in the case of proxy access, Ginsburg was not standing up to just the administrative state but to Congress. He criticized what he characterized as "doctrines of extreme deference [to administrative agencies] by which the Supreme Court has relieved the judiciary in all but the most egregious cases of its responsibility to provide meaningful review." In *Business Roundtable v. SEC,* Ginsburg gave insight into what he meant by "meaningful review." During oral argument, he honed in on the fact that the proxy access rule empowered working-class shareholders, emphasizing Scalia's point that these union and pension shareholders have different interests than other shareholders. Therefore, the rule facilitated challenges by entities that did not have broader shareholder interests at heart. The SEC's lawyer, Randall Quinn, responded that the commission considered the special interest of pension funds and union funds but concluded that, even with these special interests, these funds could still take actions beneficial to all shareholders: "There's a potential benefit here of a board being responsive to those narrow shareholders [like union and public pension funds] who . . . might have ideas that would benefit the company as a whole."[33]

Several key points emerge from this exchange. First, the SEC adopted this rule knowing that it would empower working-class shareholders, because these shareholders are the only ones willing to speak up and challenge corporate management, even if they do have special interests. More importantly, this rule is what *Congress* wanted when it put it in Dodd-Frank, and Congress has the power to do so if it chooses. Congress does not have to justify this choice to the D.C. Circuit, and cleverly, Ginsburg and the other judges never discuss the fact that *Congress* included a proxy access provision in Dodd-Frank. They also never mention that Congress stated that the SEC be given "wide latitude in setting the terms of such proxy access." (In fairness to the court, the SEC's lawyer, Quinn, never mentioned this either, and should have.) Congress and Dodd-Frank were not mentioned at all during oral argument.[34] Instead, Ginsburg and the other judges acted as if the proxy access rule had been made up by the SEC entirely on its own initiative. By ignoring Congress and pinning everything on the SEC, Ginsburg made it sound as if the D.C. Circuit were out to stop a rogue federal agency from imposing some poorly thought out rule of its own making, when in fact, all the SEC was doing was implementing the direct will of the people's elected representatives in Congress, as it was ordered to do.

Ginsburg, Brown, and Sentelle unanimously voted to strike down the proxy access rule, directly defying the will of Congress and the expertise of the SEC. That meant it left the old rule in place, in which there was no way to run against the board unless you were willing to print up your own ballots to circulate to shareholders. A defender of this decision might argue that Congress said to create proxy access but also passed a separate law telling the SEC to conduct cost-benefit analyses of new rules. Therefore, the court just emphasized one congressional command over another. But courts, lacking independent economic expertise, have historically deferred to entities with such expertise, like the SEC, unless their action is so unreasonable as to be "arbitrary and capricious."[35] That's what Ginsburg, the non-economist with only law clerks working for him, declared about the SEC's cost-benefit analysis conducted by its staff economists—that their analysis and the rule it produced was arbitrary and capricious.[36]

Multiple subsequent studies have shown that the market viewed the SEC's proxy access rule—exactly as written—as increasing shareholder value.[37] For example, one Harvard Business School study showed that the market reacted negatively when the SEC stayed implementation of its proxy access rule because of the *Business Roundtable* lawsuit, and again responded negatively when the D.C. Circuit stuck the rule down, two findings that are "consistent with the view that financial markets placed a positive value on shareholder access, as implemented in the SEC's 2010 Rule."[38] Thus, Ginsburg placed himself in the role of guardian of the markets from public pension funds and labor union funds when the markets themselves valued the rule empowering these same funds against corporate boards.

The SEC decided not to appeal Ginsburg's decision. The ideological opposition to proxy access in the Supreme Court at that time, including from Scalia's father, would not have been very different from what the SEC encountered before the D.C. Circuit. (Nor would it be that different today, given that Gorsuch replaced Scalia.) Proxy access, discussed as far back as the 1940s, proposed and litigated by AFSCME in the early to mid-2000s, stifled inside the SEC by lobbying from the Chamber of Commerce, resurrected after the financial crisis and adopted in Dodd-Frank, once again seemed finished. For Scalia, the Roundtable, and the Chamber, the victory was resounding because of the muscular precedent it set for the D.C. Circuit in striking down other aspects of Dodd-Frank and financial regulations more generally.

What Ginsburg's decision also triggered was a shareholder activist response that, as of this writing, seems destined to win the proxy access fight anyway.

The Resurrection of Proxy Access

Scott Stringer grew up in the Washington Heights neighborhood of Manhattan, recently gentrified like much of the city, but not an affluent neighborhood in his childhood. He attended public school and graduated from the John Jay College of Criminal Justice. Starting at the bottom of the political ladder, Stringer steadily climbed rung by rung, first working as a legislative assistant to assemblyman Jerry Nadler, then, after Nadler won a seat in Congress in 1992, winning Nadler's seat in the New York State Assembly to represent the Upper West Side of Manhattan. Stringer spent the next thirteen years in that office. He lost a race for New York City public advocate in 2001 before winning the Manhattan Borough presidency in 2005. Eager to advance, Stringer repeatedly found himself thwarted by more affluent and better-connected politicians. Mayor Michael Bloomberg even suggested eliminating the office of Manhattan Borough president while Stringer occupied it.[39]

In 2009, Stringer considered a primary challenge to incumbent senator Kirsten Gillibrand, a fellow Democrat, but backed down at the behest of the Obama administration. He ran for New York

City comptroller in 2013. The comptroller is the chief financial officer of the city, "responsible for providing an independent voice to safeguard the fiscal health of the City, root out waste, fraud and abuse in City government and ensure the effective performance of City agencies." One of the comptroller's most important functions is overseeing New York City's five pension funds, including the massive New York City Employees' Retirement System (NYCERS). In total, these funds invest $160 billion in city employee pensions.[40]

The New York City (NYC) funds, combined, are among the largest in the United States. Historically, they have been activist and influential. For instance, consider the reaction of NYCERS to a 1991 decision by the Cracker Barrel Company to fire its gay employees. The company's press release stated that "Cracker Barrel is founded upon a concept of traditional American values, quality in all we do, and a philosophy of 100% guest satisfaction. It is inconsistent with our concept and values, and is perceived to be inconsistent with those of the customer base, to continue to employ individuals whose sexual preferences fail to demonstrate normal heterosexual values which have been the foundation of families in our society." NYCERS responded by filing a shareholder proposal that would require the company to implement a policy prohibiting discrimination on the basis of sexual orientation. NYCERS was blocked from proceeding with that proposal by the SEC for seven years in a row—just like the SEC would later block AFSCME's proxy access proposals in the 2000s—before the commission finally relented in the face of ceaseless pressure by the fund. Likewise, in the 1980s, NYCERS submitted dozens of successful shareholder proposals opposing South African apartheid.[41]

Through NYCERS and the other NYC funds, the New York City comptroller wields enormous clout in the investment world, much as Harrigan did through CalPERS. Not surprisingly, the comptroller job attracted stiff competition. Stringer's formidable foe in the 2013 campaign was disgraced former New York governor and attorney general Eliot Spitzer. Spitzer wanted the job to launch his comeback, stating, "There's substantial authority here that I think can be used in exciting ways." Stringer outpolled Spitzer 52 percent to 48 percent for the Democratic nomination, saying afterward, "Sometimes the guy without the resources but with a lot of heart can win the election." Stringer did so with unanimous support from the city's unions.[42] After winning the general election that November, he quickly became one of the most creative and influential shareholder activists in the country, prioritizing proxy access.

Stringer's approach to the proxy access problem in the aftermath of the D.C. Circuit's decision reminds me of a standard plot twist in war films ranging from *Lawrence of Arabia* to the *Lord of the Rings*. In such films, the ambitious protagonists learn early that a particular path to success is forbidden to them. They can't go through the desert, or the woods, or the mountains because some overwhelming menace lurks within. It's inevitable that toward the end of the film the protagonists realize that the only option left is to go across that desert, those woods, those mountains, to accomplish their goal. They enter the forbidden space, defeat the bad guys, roll credits, collect Oscar, etc., etc.

Through the years of struggle over proxy access, there has always been a "desert" option, the path not taken. That option is to fight for access one company at a time. AFSCME dabbled with that strategy at a half-dozen companies in the 2000s, mostly in the hope of triggering an SEC response. There are reasons why such an approach is viewed as a desert. There are roughly five thousand public companies in the United States.[43] Fighting for access company by company would seem to be an overwhelming task, even more so than getting Congress or the SEC to adopt a rule granting access to all of those companies at once. Imagine litigating a civil rights issue, like gay marriage, in five thousand states, not fifty. That's why access advocates initially targeted their hopes at Washington (ultimately in vain), and it explains why the D.C. Circuit decision seemed to be such a devastating setback. But again, like in the movies, because the desert option seemed impossible, the bad guys didn't bother to defend against it. The Chamber, the Roundtable, and their allies have never bothered lobbying or pushing for a legal defense that would bar the path to a company-by-company campaign.

A year after winning the comptroller election, Stringer initiated the Boardroom Accountability Project (BAP), designed to take the fight for proxy access directly to the companies in which the NYC funds were invested. In Stringer's view, pension funds across the country were all working on different pet issues leading to change that was "too incremental." He wanted to unite pensions under the banner of a single issue that could advance the interests of the NYC funds "while also moving the needle on issues like diversity, climate change, and executive compensation." This point is key. It demonstrates how labor's capital has attained success by building broader political alliances. Michael Garland played a key role in the NYC funds' proxy access effort. He is the assistant comptroller for corporate governance and responsible investment, a position he had assumed under Stringer's predecessor, John

Liu. Garland had started out in the AFL-CIO's Office of Investment. He filed a proxy access proposal for the AFL-CIO as early
as 2003. Garland subsequently moved to Change to Win, another
labor organization where he had pursued shareholder activism before joining the comptroller's office. Under Liu, the comptroller's
office had pursued the occasional shareholder proposal on human
rights or majority voting. In the aftermath of *Business Roundtable v.
SEC,* Garland suggested that that the NYC funds consider filing
proxy access shareholder proposals at ten companies, picking up
where AFSCME had left off a decade earlier. Stringer's response:
"Ten proposals? Why not eighty?" The Boardroom Accountability
Project was born.[44]

In its own words, BAP is "a national campaign to give shareowners a true voice in how corporate boards are elected at every
U.S. company. If we want systemic change to ensure that companies are truly managed for the long-term, we need more diverse,
independent and accountable directors. The ability to nominate
directors is a fundamental shareowner right and the starting point
for this transformation."[45]

Stringer, Garland, and their team devised a plausible way to
structure and win such a campaign, involving a combination of
targeting large, high-profile companies and directly campaigning
for proxy access at those companies, building shareholder allies,
and a related campaign of public shaming. From the beginning,
the ambitious hope was that if the project were successful in its
earliest, most high-profile fights, other companies would implement proxy access on their own rather than wait to endure the
humiliation of having it imposed upon them by their shareholders.
It quickly became a "put all our eggs in one basket" strategy, said
Garland, in that his office of eight people would devote the entire

proxy season to this one issue, risking a season of futility if the proposals failed.[46]

The NYC funds filed seventy-five proposals in the first year of BAP, fifty targeted at S&P 500 companies, a figure that increased the following year. True, while the S&P 500 represents just one-tenth of all U.S. public companies, it covers 80 percent of total market capitalization, meaning that those five hundred companies comprise 80 percent of the value of the entire U.S. market. Stringer and Garland hoped to target as many as half of all S&P 500 companies in the early years of BAP. The logic of this approach speaks for itself, but it is noteworthy that BAP targeted smaller companies too, since the NYC funds own around 3,500 stocks. Likewise, while the NYC funds filed all the proposals, they did not work alone. They aligned with other large pensions like CalPERS, CalSTRS, and Norges Bank (the Norwegian Central Bank, which oversees the Government Pension Fund of Norway, the largest fund of any kind in the world). These funds provided support to the campaign ranging from joining solicitations to sending staff to shareholder meetings to advocate for the proposals.[47]

How that initial target list was selected is of interest. Stringer and Garland targeted carbon-intensive industries, homogeneous boards, and companies with executive pay problems, including "33 carbon-intensive coal, oil and gas, and utility companies; 24 companies with few or no women directors, and little or no apparent racial or ethnic diversity; and 25 companies that received significant opposition to their 2014 advisory vote on executive compensation, or 'say-on-pay,'" meaning places where shareholders were unhappy with how much the CEO was making.[48] In short, BAP utilized what critics of labor's shareholder activism call "political criteria" to select the targets for its investment-related goal of obtaining proxy access.

The NYC funds' target selection illustrates a split in the shareholder activist community. It echoes a set of choices faced by the Safeway campaigners, one that shareholder activists always face. When it comes to investments in carbon-intensive industries, there are "divesters" and "engagers," namely those who favor dropping carbon companies from investment portfolios and those who advocate remaining invested, engaging management, and working for change from within. The Boardroom Accountability Project and Stringer come down on the side of engagement, pushing for proxy access to maximize shareholder voice within the company, rather than exit the investment. Similarly, diversity issues in general, and board diversity issues in particular, are frequently coded as "political" rather than "investment" issues. Regardless, public pension funds generally, and the NYC funds in particular, are disproportionately composed of female beneficiaries (for instance, the vast majority of public school teachers in New York City and elsewhere are women) and minorities (from 20–33% of public employees are African American, compared to 12% of the U.S. population). Given at least mixed evidence that improved board diversity affects returns—evidence cited by State Street in adopting its pro-women board members voting policy and sponsoring the political art *Fearless Girl* on Wall Street—the question of whether investment funds like the NYC funds may pursue such objectives seems self-evidently in the interests of plan participants and consistent with fiduciary duty.[49]

Stringer and BAP filed shareholder proposals at targeted corporations that mimicked, word for word, the rule that Congress and the SEC implemented before Ginsburg struck it down. They proposed that companies adopt a three-year / 3 percent ownership / 25 percent of the board threshold for proxy access, to be voted on a company-by-company basis.[50] It is difficult to overstate how well this strategy worked. In 2014, the first year of the campaign, 1 percent (5) of S&P 500 companies had proxy access. One year later, 117 companies had adopted proxy access, including 21 percent of the S&P 500 and several non–S&P 500 companies. By the beginning of the 2015 proxy season, that number had nearly doubled to 35 percent. The pace of change stunned corporate watchers, with a reform sought for nearly seventy years ripping through company after company with hardly a fight.[51]

By the end of the 2015 season, for the NYC funds alone, forty-three of their sixty-six shareholder resolutions calling for proxy access that actually went to a vote were passed by a majority of shareholders. Things improved further in the 2016 season. The NYC funds submitted seventy-two proxy access proposals. Fifty-two companies surrendered without a fight, avoiding a shareholder vote by adopting the NYC funds' proposed rule. Eighteen companies decided to take it to a shareholder vote: of those, the proposal prevailed at thirteen. And over the two-year period from 2014 to 2016, seventeen companies targeted by NYC funds for lack of boardroom diversity added either a woman or minority to their board.[52]

NYC funds also picked up allies along the way. TIAA-CREF, the mutual fund that invests the retirement savings of college teachers, wrote a hundred letters to investees requesting that they adopt proxy access along lines similar to those initially proposed by the SEC. By early 2016, thirty-nine of those companies had adopted it, and eventually seventy-three companies agreed. These were not formal shareholder proposals, and therefore required no actual shareholder vote, but a letter from such a large shareholder contributed to companies' adopting proxy access, as did the NYC funds' proposal work at other corporations. What explains many of these adoptions is the straightforward realization that the momentum was entirely on the side of the activists, and that there was little point in waiting for one to come calling. One company, 3M, preempted the NYC funds' challenge when its board adopted proxy access the same day that the funds proposed it.[53]

These swift victories, in which substantial shareholder majorities voted in favor of proxy access, demonstrate how badly the *Wall Street Journal* op-ed page and the D.C. Circuit misunderstood the story. It's not just that Alinsky won in Congress or at the SEC. He also won with shareholders generally, many of whom were fed up with the insulation of corporate boards and were willing to vote for proxy access alongside working-class shareholders, even though it would empower working-class shareholders, and even though working-class shareholders like the NYC funds were the ones proposing the rule. The SEC lawyer Randall Quinn was correct at oral argument in *Business Roundtable v. SEC:* "special interest" pension funds and union funds could act to improve outcomes for everyone.[54] That doesn't mean that these pension and union funds can't use the rule to their own advantage in certain circumstances. They can. It means that, even accounting for the potential of serving narrow interests with proxy access, the market concluded that having some credible threat to otherwise insulated boards of directors outweighed that risk.

Although the SEC did not appeal the D.C. Circuit ruling, its economists followed up with a study about the ruling's effect, and about the impact of the NYC funds' proxy access campaign.

Among other things, the study found that the surprise announcement of the Boardroom Accountability Project in November 2014 led to an immediate bump in price for targeted companies, supporting the claim that proxy access improved the value of those companies. The same study also made the point that, in some respects, companies might have been even better off had the D.C. Circuit left the rule in place.[55]

This study strongly supports proxy access and the Board Accountability Project. For one thing, the positive market reaction to BAP indicates that critics who decried proxy access as exclusively political are wrong, because the market bid up the price of companies targeted for access. There is no better vindication of investment purpose than that. Anyone trying to argue that Stringer and the NYC funds' board members breached their fiduciary duties by targeting companies for proxy access based on "political" criteria like diversity and the environment is going to lose that argument very quickly, in part because of results such as these. Other studies confirm that proxy access benefits shareholders, although there are studies to the contrary, and critical voices linger. After *Business Roundtable v. SEC,* the CFA Institute, a prominent association of investment management professionals, conducted a comprehensive review of the existing empirical studies on proxy access and concluded, "By and large, the results of these studies show that proxy access was received more positively than negatively by financial markets."[56]

Still, not everyone is persuaded, and in the field of corporate governance, people tend not to overreact to empirical studies. Clearly, it is important to consult empirical research on corporate governance reforms. But that research has well-known limitations.

For one thing, it must navigate a standard challenge faced in many social sciences. It is not possible to create two identical companies, one with proxy access, one without, and then observe which fares better in the market. There are no double-blind placebo-controlled studies in corporate governance. Stock prices can move for all sorts of reasons, and it can be difficult to isolate the effect of one reform from everything else going on at the company, in the market, and in the world, all of which affect prices.

There are still other reasons to approach the governance literature with caution. The literature is entirely focused on outcomes like stock price or firm value. Whether these measures alone are the only outcomes of interest is contested within corporate law. Furthermore, shareholders often describe proxy access and other corporate governance issues as "fundamental rights." BAP describes proxy access that way. Some investors opposed to the Financial Choice Act, the legislation designed to gut Dodd-Frank that has been passed in the House of Representatives but that has not yet been taken up in the Senate, and which would greatly restrict shareholders' ability to file shareholder proposals like the ones that led to proxy access, described their statement against it as the "Joint Statement on Defending Fundamental Shareholder Rights."[57] Many shareholders take the position that, as investors, they ought to have input into the companies they own. From their perspective, this is an issue of both efficiency and fairness. Shareholders do not want to be told by their corporate investees that they cannot add two lines to a pre-printed corporate ballot listing their board candidates' names. They do not want to be told that they must spend millions of dollars to separately print their own ballots if they want to exercise their right to run a competing board candidate. Some shareholders view this as an insult, and an empirical study claiming that they are better off not having a proxy access right is unlikely to persuade them to go without it.

There is one final, ironic point to be made about the D.C. Circuit's striking down proxy access and the shareholder activist campaign that followed. Had the court allowed the proxy access rule to stand, it would likely be much more vulnerable now, under a Trump-administration SEC. The SEC can reverse itself. It's a cumbersome process, but it is feasible. A Republican-controlled SEC could have rolled back proxy access rights. Instead, those rights are now largely beyond SEC control, having been settled by shareholder vote in the marketplace. In many respects, the D.C. Circuit's overreaching opinion had the perverse effect of strengthening proxy access rights.[58]

These developments followed two others that, combined with access, have dramatically transformed the landscape of shareholder voting. The first was the move to majority voting for directors, and the second was the destaggering of corporate boards.

First, majority voting. Until very recently, U.S. corporate elections applied a plurality voting rule, that is, if you received a plurality of the vote, you won. Everyone understands what it means to win a plurality vote—it's whoever has the most votes wins, even if the vote total is less than 50 percent. Plurality voting is an entirely sensible rule in races where there are more than two candidates. President Bill Clinton won the election in 1992 with a plurality of the popular vote, winning 43 percent compared to 37.4 percent for the incumbent President George H. W. Bush and 18.9 percent for Independent Ross Perot.[59] But a plurality voting rule is pathetic in elections in which you are running unopposed. Most of these elections result in vote totals for the sole candidate in excess of 90 percent of the shareholder electorate. Should you still be able to win election with a 10 percent vote total when you run unopposed? You do under a plurality voting rule. It's like winning gold for placing first in a solitaire competition.

Majority voting does nothing more than require that a candidate obtain over 50 percent in favor of her candidacy before she can take her board seat, even when running unopposed. The effect of this shift is obvious. In the dominant situation in which board members run unopposed—even in a world where proxy access is widely available—majority voting empowers shareholders to prevent the election of a board member they dislike by running a "withhold vote" or a "just vote no" campaign. The board member will not be reseated if he fails to reach the 50 percent threshold. That makes board candidates and board members more accountable to shareholders. The empirical evidence is mixed but, in my view, generally supportive of the connection between majority voting and firm value. Majority voting is another realm where investors view the question as one of fundamental rights, rather than just an instrument for improving value.[60]

As with proxy access, almost all of the shareholder proposals favoring majority voting have been brought by working-class shareholders. The United Brotherhood of Carpenters Fund, a labor union fund, has played a particularly important role in this fight. It alone filed 717 majority voting proposals between 2004 and 2014, including at American Express, Capital One, CVS Caremark, Exxon Mobil, General Electric, Halliburton, IBM, UnitedHealth Group, and Verizon. By 2010, 73 percent of S&P 500 companies adopted majority voting, numbers that rose to 79 percent in 2011, 83 percent in 2012, 87 percent by 2013, and 90 percent by 2014.[61]

The second major development to precede proxy access was the destaggering of corporate boards, so that the entire board is up for election every cycle, rather than just one-third of the board standing at any election. With staggered boards, it takes at least two election cycles to flip board control, which reduces responsiveness to shareholders. Substantial credit for this development belongs to Harvard Law School's Shareholder Rights Project (SRP), a now-defunct student clinic that once operated under the auspices of Professor Lucian Bebchuk and Scott Hirst. Not surprisingly, the clients of the SRP clinic were working-class shareholder institutions including the Florida State Board of Administration, the Illinois State Board of Investment, the Los Angeles County Employees Retirement Association, the Massachusetts Pension Reserves Investment Management Board, the North Carolina Department of State Treasurer, the Ohio Public Employees Retirement System, and the School Employees Retirement System of Ohio. (The Illinois and Massachusetts funds were both veterans of the Safeway fight.) These pension funds were also joined by the Nathan Cummings Foundation, a foundation that primarily focuses on economic inequality and climate change, and that uses the 96 percent of its portfolio that it does not give away every year to advance its agenda through shareholder activism.[62] The Nathan Cummings Foundation's involvement with the SRP is a small example of how working-class shareholders ally with other institutions, like foundations, to advance mutually beneficial agendas.

Over a three-year period from 2011 to 2014, the clinic filed dozens of shareholder proposals calling for destaggered boards at S&P 500 and Fortune 500 companies. It also negotiated agreements with companies not to file such proposals in exchange for the companies agreeing either to destagger their boards themselves or to put the issue to a shareholder vote. The clinic's work resulted in the destaggering of over one hundred S&P 500 and Fortune 500 corporate boards. Currently, more than 80 percent of the S&P 500 has a destaggered board. The empirical research on whether such boards improve firm value is hotly contested.[63]

Will proxy access, majority voting, and destaggered boards result in an immediate, overnight transformation of shareholder elections, and of the way corporations are run? Maybe. In the short term, barring a recession, almost all shareholder elections will remain uncontested, and boards will continue to be reelected most of the time with 90 percent or more of the shareholder vote. Viewed superficially, this seems like very little change. But accountability rarely manifests itself in public rebukes of people in power. Rather than risk a rebuke, the powerful instead alter their conduct to avoid it. This is most likely where the effects of voting reform will be found: in the thousands of subtle choices the powerful make when they know they have to explain themselves to others. But I do believe that with the next recession, whenever it comes, we will see a notable increase in challenges to incumbent directors. That would conform to a historical pattern in which shareholders are more receptive to change when markets are down, much in the way that voters are more open to change in election years taking place during economic downturns.

The long term is always difficult to predict, but it is not impossible to imagine a world in which the leaders of our largest and most prominent corporations regularly face contested elections, perhaps every few years. Even if contested elections do not become the norm, the occasional successful fight waged by shareholders could be enough to send a signal to the rest of the market, and to other directors standing for election. Regardless, for the first time in the roughly 150-year history of U.S. public corporations, their leaders are now generally susceptible to being challenged and unseated by shareholders. We have attained, for the first time, meaningful shareholder voting rights. This achievement is almost entirely attributable to working-class shareholders, and it is one of the best examples yet of their power.

It is hardly surprising that those who are opposed to this transformation will do everything they can to roll it back. That reaction is already gathering pace. As of this writing, the House of Representatives has adopted the Financial Choice Act, which includes a provision that would effectively eliminate shareholder proposals by raising the required ownership threshold even above what the NYC funds could meet on their own. That would not undo all of the work that BAP and others accomplished, but it would make it much harder to continue that work going forward. Had that rule already been in place, it would likely have shut down all of the shareholder voting campaigns described in this chapter. There are good reasons to believe this act will not make it through the Senate. If it does, it would be a sharp blow to shareholder activism, but it would not eliminate the gains already made. In short, while there is more work to be done, when it comes to shareholder voting, labor picked the right battles. It fought and won them early, in ways that will make these victories difficult to dislodge.

3

The Silence of the Lions

Reining in Hedge Funds and Private Equity

If you ever wanted proof of the myth of the sophisticated investor, look no further than the hedge fund industry. Hedge funds invest on behalf of purportedly sophisticated investors, meaning large institutions and "high net worth individuals."[1] Thus, working-class shareholders—"low net worth," "zero net worth," or perhaps "negative net worth" individuals—could never invest in hedge funds on their own.[2] But once aggregated into a large pension fund, worker retirement assets become legally eligible, finding their way into high-risk hedge fund investments all the same.[3] Massive sums of pension and union fund money have been invested in hedge funds. This has led to enormous strain between the two types of investors, with two basic flashpoints. First, some hedge fund managers have taken pension money and then turned around and publicly attacked and undermined pensions. Second, hedge fund underperformance has led some pensions to divest from them entirely, and to encourage others to do so.[4] Working-class shareholder activists have taken the lead in these fights.

Hedge fund performance is remarkably consistent: it has lagged behind overall market performance for more than a decade.[5] Since the early 2000s, hedge fund investors as a group would have been better off if they had instead purchased a low-fee, well-managed S&P 500 index fund. (In fact, according to one calculation, they would have been better off if they had invested in U.S. Treasury bills, which fund the operation of the U.S. federal government, widely considered the safest and most conservative investments in the world. For now.) S&P 500 index funds track the five hundred largest U.S. companies by market capitalization, which is one measure of company size (total shares outstanding x share price). Such funds are the benchmark for market performance. They profit not from making big bets on specific companies but from the overall long-term growth of the market. One of the best aspects of these index funds is that they are cheap to assemble and cheap for investors. It does not take much time and research; the manager more or less picks the top five hundred companies and invests in them automatically, keeping fees low. (I am oversimplifying here, but not by much.)[6]

Hedge funds are for investors who aspire to perform better than the S&P 500 index. They are also supposedly vehicles for protecting investors from market downturns because they are "hedged," that is, supposedly not correlated to overall market performance. Rather than just picking the top five hundred—rather than diversifying your investments—you pay high management fees to a super-investor who will pick specific companies to invest in, in the hopes of outperforming the index. (At least this is how value-oriented hedge funds work, as opposed to quantitative traders, momentum traders, algorithmic traders, etc.) It sounds like a compelling idea, but what usually happens is that investors pay high management fees and the hedge funds perform worse than the index. Under the usual pay structure, hedge fund managers immediately pocket 2 percent of whatever money their investors give them. So, on day one, you're down 2 percent. The managers then take 20 percent of the profits the fund makes with their investors' money.[7] So investors are already fighting with one arm behind their backs to make the equivalent of what cheaper index funds have to offer. Hedge funds are very often a bad investment for everyone except hedge fund managers.

The problem is best exemplified by Warren Buffett's bet with Protégé Partners. In 2008, Buffett bet Protégé, a hedge fund, one million dollars that an S&P 500 index fund would outperform it over ten years. Nine years in, the S&P 500 index is up 85 percent. Protégé is up 22 percent. The divergent performance between S&P 500 index funds and hedge funds is striking and leads to troubling questions as to why working-class shareholders have been pouring money into hedge funds for so long.[8]

Ironically, one answer is Warren Buffett himself, a high-profile example of a superinvestor who really has beaten the market in the long run. Buffett's distinguished record of investment performance is the foremost symbol and embodiment of a straightforward idea, albeit one exceedingly difficult to implement in practice: that a talented person can look closely at investments and make judgments that are superior to the market's judgments, beating the market, year in and year out. The main reason investors continue to opt for hedge funds is because some (very few) fund managers still do beat the market for short periods of time, with sometimes spectacular results. Knowing when one of these investors is going to get "hot" is more a matter of luck than skill, but that doesn't stop huge swaths of the market from giving it a try, at enormous cost to their investors. In a recent pronouncement on the subject, Buffett claimed that "investors wasted more than $100 billion on high-fee Wall Street money managers over the past 10 years."[9]

The basic problem with hedge funds is that it is extremely difficult to go on outsmarting the market for long. The risks in taking short positions (positions that bet on the decline of a stock, which can lead to massive losses if you're wrong), and the task of outperforming the market, year in and year out, is nearly impossible, particularly if you are charging the proverbial "2 and 20." This fact has been buttressed by an enormous body of research.[10] With millions of investors around the world trading, and with large institutional investors deploying sophisticated analysts constantly searching for new information about companies to trade on, markets move very quickly. Even if a trader figures something out first, it is exceedingly difficult to do that again and again. Consequently, most investors would be better off not paying those fees and just sticking with an index fund. But instead, many hedge fund investors simply can't let go of the idea that they can beat the index. They are forever "Chasing Eisman" or "Chasing Paulson."

Steve Eisman ran a hedge fund that was at the center of Michael Lewis's book *The Big Short*. Eisman famously made a fortune correctly predicting the housing market crash that led to the Great Recession of 2007. The book portrayed Eisman's smart, contrarian, often hilariously funny character, explaining why he was able to see what so many others were not. Admirable as that performance was, consider what happened to Eisman's funds after the crisis, that is, after the "Big Short" ended. He started a new fund, Emrys Partners. In plain language, it failed.[11] After Emrys collapsed, Eisman again did something totally unheard of in the hedge fund industry. Typically, when hedge fund managers fail, they do everything in their power to quickly restore their image as superguru investors. They admit they made a mistake, they grovel, they explain what went wrong, and why they are now better placed than ever to beat the market. After Larry Robbins of Glenview Capital Management lost 20 percent of his investors' money in 2015 (through October), he invited them to invest in a new Robbins fund, opining that "opportunity often feels like a punch in the face." Eisman was more candid. He told his investors: "Making investment decisions by looking solely at the fundamentals of individual companies is no longer a viable investment philosophy." He also publicly disclosed that he would cut his fees to a flat 1.25 percent management fee. Another fund manager who found huge success betting against the housing market, John Paulson, has lost $26 billion since. As of this writing, just $2 billion of Paulson's assets under management are from outside investors. Almost everything he invests now is his own money.[12]

Eisman's statement, like Buffett's criticisms, supported by decades of academic research, gives us some insight into an astonishing, even appalling trend in hedge funds: many have quietly become passive, that is, they do very little active management and may even be indexing their portfolios. At a minimum, they exhibit performance that is difficult to distinguish from indexing. That would be just fine, even welcome, if they gave back the fees. But to charge 2 and 20 on the theory that investors have hired a market-beating genius investment manager, only to turn around and have that manager index, is to sell a similar product as an index fund for ten times the cost, or more.[13]

Given that hedge funds are highly risky, that they overcharge and under-deliver, one might think that worker pension funds should be legally barred from investing in them. There was a time when that was the case. Before 1996, Congress allowed hedge funds to invest only on behalf of entities that had one hundred or fewer shareholders. This limit constrained the size of hedge funds. For example, the rule barred the vast majority of public pension funds and labor union funds from investing in hedge funds, because almost all of them have far more than a hundred shareholders or beneficiaries. But in 1994, the "Republican Revolution" swept through Congress as the GOP took control of the House of Representatives for the first time in forty years, as well as the Senate. The Republican Congress quickly passed the National Securities Markets Improvement Act of 1996, signed by President Bill Clinton, which revised the Investment Company Act of 1940 to exempt hedge funds that sold securities to so-called qualified purchasers, including institutions that managed more than $25 million in assets. In short, if a fund managed $25 million or more in assets—as almost all public pension and labor union funds do—it could invest in hedge funds. That opened the door for hedge fund managers to chase capital from public pension funds and labor union funds. In the five years following the 1996 reforms, institutional investor participation in hedge funds quintupled. While the Democrats have since recovered both houses of Congress from time to time, the 1996 reforms massively enriched the hedge fund industry in ways that have enabled it to purchase influence in both parties.[14]

That's because underperformance has not impoverished the hedge fund industry. Quite the opposite. Because of that 2 percent in asset management fees, and because they keep 20 percent of profits but don't give back 20 percent of losses, hedge fund managers have become enormously wealthy, less by outperforming the market than by convincing large numbers of investors to give them money to manage. Most hedge fund managers make money from their ability to *convince* investors that they will beat the market, not from actually beating the market. As Buffett put it, "There's been far, far, far more money made by people in Wall Street through salesmanship abilities than through investment abilities."[15] It is size more than performance that explains the wealth of many hedge fund managers. One might think that this is precisely why hedge funds ought to be regulated. Yet Congress, and regulators like the SEC, have largely failed to do so. The legal void is yet one more being filled by working-class shareholders.

Take, for example, Dan Pedrotty, formerly the director of pensions and capital strategies for the American Federation of Teachers (AFT), the shareholder activist arm of the powerful teachers' union.[16] After law school, Pedrotty found himself working at a law firm, representing the manufacturer of a bobblehead doll of NBA star Allen Iverson against another bobblehead doll manufacturer for alleged trademark infringement. Pedrotty thought to himself, "I've got to get out of here." He quickly jumped into political activism, working on the 2004 presidential campaign staff of Dick Gephardt, a Democrat and formerly the speaker of the House of Representatives. Pedrotty bore firsthand witness to what he described as the "murder-suicide" between Gephardt and Vermont governor Howard Dean in the 2004 Iowa caucuses that set the stage for John Kerry's win there and beyond. Later that same year, Pedrotty joined the Office of Investment for the AFL-CIO, which he ran for almost eight years before leaving to start the Capital Strategies program at the AFT. Pedrotty, one of labor's preeminent shareholder activists, has taken the lead in challenging the hedge fund industry.

Hedge funds were not Pedrotty's first fight. In 2007, while running the Office of Investment for the AFL-CIO, he participated in one of the most storied shareholder activist plays against a sitting CEO, one that would eventually be captured in a Harvard Business School case study. The campaign's target was Home Depot, a hardware and home repair company at the time being soundly outcompeted by archrival Lowe's. Home Depot had become embroiled in a stock options backdating scandal about which its board did virtually nothing, not least because it was riddled with the usual spate of conflicts and incestuous business relationships. At the time, Robert Nardelli served as Home Depot's CEO and chairman of the board. The company's lead director was Kenneth Langone, who had served on the board of directors of the New York Stock Exchange when it approved Richard Grasso's compensation, the same stratospheric compensation that triggered Harrigan's and CalPERS's ultimately successful effort to unseat Grasso. Langone recruited Grasso to serve on Home Depot's compensation committee, which negotiated Nardelli's pay package. This was *after* Grasso left the NYSE over his own excess compensation. Grasso was joined by the CEOs of several other companies, people who would be unlikely to set a precedent of reining in executive compensation. One of these CEOs was Lawrence Johnson of Albertson's—one of the supermarkets subjected to the UFCW strike described in Chapter 1, and more importantly, someone who, when he was negotiating his own pay package at Albertson's, had used the same lawyer that Nardelli hired to negotiate his Home Depot package. Thus, in representing Home Depot in its compensation negotiations with Nardelli, "Johnson was also facing off against his own attorney." Guess what Home Depot's compensation committee agreed to pay Nardelli, in exchange for declining market share and a stock options scandal? $300 million.[17]

Three labor activists decided to confront Home Depot over its failure to adequately cope with stock options backdating: Pedrotty, Damon Silvers (then associate general counsel of the AFL-CIO and today its policy director and one of the most well-known labor leaders in the country), and Rich Ferlauto of AFSCME, who I discussed in Chapter 2 for his early role in the proxy access fight. They wanted to make an example of Nardelli's outrageous pay package, which was guaranteed regardless of the company's performance. Although Nardelli took the extraordinary step of ordering his board not to show up for the company's annual shareholder meeting, where they would face the indignity of having to confront their own shareholders—the people who owned the company—he could not thwart the revolt. At the meeting, Pedrotty attended wearing a chicken suit to protest the board's cowardly absence. Shortly thereafter, the board fired Nardelli.[18]

A few years later, now working for the AFT, Pedrotty turned his attention to the hedge fund industry. In December 2012, Pedrotty was returning to Washington from a Chicago meeting of the Trustee Leadership Forum, a leadership organization of union and pension trustees. While waiting for his flight at O'Hare Airport, he reviewed a *New York Times* article, printed a few years earlier in the Fashion and Style section, titled "Scholarly Investments." The article was captioned by a photo of a hedge fund manager named Ravenel Boykin Curry IV, a white man smiling in his gray suit, crouching down and flanked by six smiling, uniformed, African American and Latina girls from the Girls Preparatory Charter School in the Bronx. Another photo showed John

Petry, a white male partner in the hedge fund Gotham Capital, smiling as he sat at a classroom table with a smiling African American boy, a book open before them. A third photo showed a smiling John Sabat, another white hedge fund manager, seated at a poker table at a charter school fundraiser, his hands covering two stacks of chips.[19]

The article, along with a piece published in *Institutional Investor* magazine, described how charter schools—broadly defined as government-funded schools that have a mandate to operate independently from the public school system—were the hot new charitable trend among "hedgies." These happy fund managers were raising money for New York City charter schools and organizations like Democrats for Education Reform. Curry was quoted describing the charter schools as "exactly the kind of investment people in our industry spend our days trying to stumble on . . . with incredible cash flow, even if in this case we don't ourselves get any of it." As to educational quality, the "Scholarly Investments" article cited two Stanford University studies on charter schools. One could not find performance differences between charters and public schools, and the other found that New York City schools outperformed charters.[20]

The debate over charter schools is highly complex and has been written about extensively elsewhere. To offer a very cursory outline of the controversy, charter school advocates argue that these schools provide an escape route for underprivileged students trapped in failing public school districts. Charter school critics argue that, in fact, such schools undermine public education by diverting resources from underfunded schools to charters that screen out the worst and most costly students, exacerbating the very problems they claim to solve.[21] More relevant for the purposes of this book is a subsidiary issue in the charter school debate, the question of teacher compensation, specifically teacher pensions.

Pedrotty's organization at the time, the AFT, has been critical of charter schools.[22] It has also taken the position that compensating teachers is good not just for teachers but for students too, since attracting and retaining talented educators is a crucial component of education. Among many other important issues, the AFT, the National Education Association, and others have continued advocating for teacher pensions even while embracing aspects of public-school reform. It is this position—advocating for teacher retirement funds—that has placed them squarely against many hedge funds, including some of those depicted in the "Scholarly Investments" article. These hedge fund managers, lacking any sense of irony, think public school teachers are overpaid and have been lobbying to undercut teachers' pension plans. These efforts have played out in an environment in which, according to recent data, the top twenty-five hedge fund managers made more money than all kindergarten teachers in the United States combined, while being taxed at lower rates than teachers.[23]

Some pro–charter school organizations like Democrats for Education Reform, StudentsFirst, and the Manhattan Institute have advocated eliminating or sharply curtailing teacher pensions. StudentsFirst, for example, grades teacher pensions on a scale of zero to four, giving states a zero for only offering defined benefit (or similar) plans, and a four if they offer defined contribution (or similar) plans.[24] Defined benefit plans are better for employees because they guarantee a fixed payment to the worker in retirement. They stand in contrast to defined contribution plans, like 401(k)s, in which employees contribute money to a retirement fund that they manage themselves, living on whatever is still left in the fund when they retire. Defined benefit plans place the risk of poor market performance on employers; defined contribution plans place those risks on workers. Unions have consistently fought to maintain defined benefit plans, wherever possible.[25]

As Pedrotty read this glorifying portrait of hedge fund managers who supported devastating cuts to teacher retirement funds, he wondered, "How much of our teacher retirement money is invested with these guys?"[26]

Quickly accessing the relevant information from Preqin, a hedge fund database, Pedrotty identified dozens of public pension funds—many of them teacher funds—that were invested in hedge funds run by managers who were simultaneously lobbying to cut teacher pensions through pro–charter school organizations. These managers included Paul Tudor Jones II, Paul Singer, and, fatefully, Dan Loeb of Third Point Capital LLC. Through these hedge fund investments, these teacher pension funds were quite directly funding their own demise. The findings were distressing. But Pedrotty also viewed them as an enormous, untapped organizing opportunity for the AFT. He drafted a memo to his boss, Randi Weingarten, the union's president, pointing out the connections among teacher funds, hedge funds, and efforts to undermine teacher pensions.[27]

Weingarten was intimately familiar with the struggles over public education in New York City. Prior to becoming president of the AFT, she had spent twelve years as president of the United Federation of Teachers, AFT Local 2, representing 200,000 New York City educators and other workers. A lawyer and former high school history teacher, she was a member of the Democratic National Committee and had repeatedly appeared on various "most powerful" and "most influential" lists. She faced off in contentious negotiations with mayors Rudy Giuliani and Michael Bloomberg over teacher contracts in the city, and had steered the AFT toward a policy not of opposing charter schools but of maintaining their consistency with aspects of public education, including adequate pensions for teachers and other educational workers.[28]

Weingarten authorized Pedrotty to begin work on a report outlining his findings. This ultimately became the AFT's "Ranking Asset Managers: A Retirement Security Report on Money Managers." The report, which Pedrotty coauthored with Brad Murray and Jessica Smith of the AFT, contained an "Investment Manager Watch List." Its first iteration, published in April 2013, listed thirty-three hedge funds that supported education reform movements that advocated gutting teacher pensions. According to Weingarten, the purpose of the "watch list" was to enable teacher pension trustees to make "informed decisions about the risks their plans face." The report stated that "[the AFT] is committed to shining a bright light on organizations that harm public sector workers, especially when those organizations are financed by individuals who earn their money from the deferred wages of our teachers."[29]

In the report, the AFT pointed out that "pension-fund managers have a duty of loyalty and prudence" to their participants and beneficiaries, working and retired teachers who had contributed to the fund. Conservatively framing those duties to meet the narrow standards of the prevalent "fund first" view, the report noted that the priority was to hire investment managers "that will provide competitive, risk-adjusted returns," and that "collateral factors were subordinate." Collateral factors included "a manager's position on collective bargaining, privatization or proposals to discontinue providing benefits through defined benefit plans." As long as collateral factors were subordinate to economic ones, and as long as consideration of collateral factors led to the hiring of qualified managers, trustees would not breach their fiduciary duties in considering them. The report then listed the hedge funds whose managers advocated eliminating defined benefit pension plans.[30]

The AFT "watch list" stunned the hedge fund community. Consider the reaction of one listed fund, Dimensional Fund Advisors. Dimensional was cofounded by Rex Sinquefield, who, after making a fortune investing on behalf of public pension funds and labor union funds, founded the Show-Me Institute in St. Louis, a conservative think tank. As the AFT report stated, "The Show-Me Institute has explicitly called for Missouri to shift to a defined contribution plan for state employees. . . . The Show-Me Institute is part of a larger network of conservative state-based organizations—the State Policy Network—that routinely advocates for pension privatization." At the time the report was issued, Dimensional invested on behalf of nineteen public pension funds and six union funds, all defined benefit funds, clients it could not afford to lose.[31]

Overnight, the fund "clarified" its views on defined-benefit plans. Dimensional chairman David Booth told *Pension and Investments* magazine that "[Sinquefield's] political aspirations and workings got us into the penalty box. That is not something he wanted to do." Pension plans are "how we make our living," Booth continued. "We are big fans of defined benefit plans." After landing Dimensional on the watch list, Sinquefield "quit" the fund's board. Desperate to get off the watch list, Dimensional then followed up with a letter to Weingarten from Stephen A. Clark, the fund's head of global institutional services. Clark mentioned Dimensional's long-term work on behalf of the defined benefit community. He wrote, "Dimensional is an ardent supporter of retirement security for all Americans and defined benefit plans represent one of the critical tools to achieve this important goal for participants." Similarly, after appearing on the list, Scott Kapnick, CEO of Highbridge Capital Management LLC, wrote to Weingarten, "I would like to assure you that Highbridge will not support StudentsFirstNY going forward. . . . Highbridge is proud to manage retirement assets on behalf of unions and public pension plans. . . . Highbridge is not opposed to defined benefit plans."[32]

After receipt of these letters, Weingarten and Pedrotty removed Dimensional and Highbridge from the watch list. Similarly, Aon, an investment consultant, had been participating in an organization called Illinois Is Broke for Bruce Rauner, Illinois's Republican governor. Governor Rauner had been a private equity fund manager who amassed a fortune investing public employee retirement money and then went to war to cut public employee benefits when he became governor.[33] Under pressure from the AFT, the California State Teachers' Retirement System, the New York State Teachers' Retirement System, and the United Auto Workers Voluntary Employee Beneficiary Association—Aon clients all—Aon not only dropped its involvement in Illinois Is Broke but joined the National Institute on Retirement Security, a labor-friendly retirement research and policy organization that has defended defined benefit pension funds for teachers and others. In March 2015, NYCERS voted against a $49 million investment in Gotham Capital, a hedge fund that appeared on the watch list and was depicted in the "Scholarly Investments" article. According to Pedrotty, since the issuance of the first report, twelve to fifteen hedge funds have stopped contributing to or left the boards of organizations that were attacking teacher pensions.[34]

Only one hedge fund manager openly fought with the AFT over the list: Third Point Capital's Dan Loeb. Shortly before the AFT released its first hedge fund list, Weingarten requested a meeting with Loeb, who was scheduled to address the semiannual Council of Institutional Investors (CII) conference, the organization composed mostly of labor union and public pension funds (including teacher funds), some of which invested with Loeb. Weingarten hoped to meet with Loeb at the CII meeting, where she hoped to persuade him not to oppose teacher pensions. Loeb dithered over the request, first agreeing to meet while denying that he advocated cutting teacher pensions, then canceling both his meeting and his CII appearance, all of which attracted considerable press attention. The title of Matt Taibbi's *Rolling Stone* magazine article could have applied to almost any of the hedge funds on the watch list: "Dan Loeb Simultaneously Solicits, Betrays Pension Funds."[35] Stung by the confrontation and the negative press coverage, Loeb retaliated by increasing his contribution to StudentsFirst by $1 million. His ego got the best of him. Shortly thereafter, Rhode Island's pensions dropped Loeb as a hedge fund manager, pulling $74.3 million from his fund, Third Point.[36]

Weingarten viewed her battle with Loeb as fundamentally about exposing hypocrisy. "Don't try to make a mint off teacher retirement funds and at the same time try to eliminate teacher retirement security," she said. It was Loeb, in her view, who tried to make their spat all about charter schools, when in fact it was about hypocrisy. "People were shocked . . . that a union that is disproportionately female would be engaged in capital strategies," she told me. The hedge fund world is almost totally male-dominated, with just 3 percent of senior investment roles at hedge funds occupied by women.[37] It is not a world that is used to women exercising authority over investment choices, Weingarten pointed out.

Almost identical fights have taken place with private equity funds. For example, after a senior adviser at Blackstone Group assailed defined benefit plans for public employees, NYCERS canceled a scheduled meeting with the fund. Shortly after the cancellation, Blackstone issued a statement: "Blackstone's view on public employee pensions is clear and unambiguous. We believe a pension is a promise. Working men and women should not have to worry about their retirement security after years of service to their communities. We oppose scapegoating public employees by blaming them for the structural budget deficits that cities and states face." As the *Wall Street Journal* reported, 37 percent of Blackstone's investment pool came from state and local pension plans. Similarly, to drive the point all the way home, after Kohlberg Kravis Roberts (KKR) wound up on the AFT watch list, it received a letter from the private equity firm's head of global public affairs, Kenneth Mehlman, a former chairman of the Republican National Committee. Mehlman wrote, "Over the past several years, we have worked, in partnership with legislators, policy makers and organized labor leaders, to advocate the importance of defined benefit plans as an option for public sector workers." The day after receiving the letter, AFT agreed to take KKR off the list. In fact, UNITE HERE, another labor union, has created a private equity fund watch list similar to the hedge fund list created by Pedrotty and Weingarten, one that categorizes such funds as "responsible" or "irresponsible," raising issues unique to the relationships between public pension funds and labor union funds, which I return to momentarily. These actions have even had spillover effects beyond the question of pensions and jobs. For example, Robert Mercer, the billionaire co-CEO of Renaissance Technologies and financial backer of right-wing causes, stepped aside as CEO and sold his stake in the fund after pressure brought by endowments and pension funds over his political activities, including from the Baltimore City Police and Fire Employees Retirement System, which pulled tens of millions of dollars from Renaissance in protest.[38]

The above examples illustrate how working-class shareholder institutions have been able to utilize their position as investors to push back on attacks against their workers. They provide further illustration of the power of working-class shareholders to challenge entities and individuals who are not used to getting pushed around, whether they be hedge funds, private equity funds, or the former chairman of the Republic National Committee. They also demonstrate how public pension and labor union funds can be used to undercut further assaults on the well-being of workers by some of the most powerful entities in society—hedge funds and private equity funds. Furthermore, these actions suggest mechanisms by which working-class shareholders can bend hedge funds to their will when it comes to other priorities like hiring union labor for a massive American infrastructure spending plan, should it ever manifest. In fact, in Pedrotty's new role as the head of capital strategies for the North America's Building Trades Union, where he went after leaving the AFT, the organizer played a key role in securing a once-unthinkable commitment from Blackstone. On September 5, 2017, the company announced its agreement with the union to adopt a responsible contractor policy to be applied to Blackstone's $100 billion infrastructure investment fund, which would "promote fair benefits, wages, working conditions, and training opportunities for construction workers on projects for Blackstone's dedicated infrastructure business."[39] I discuss this development further in the final chapter.

Here's one more example of labor's capital being used to advance causes with which workers sympathize. The Massachusetts Laborers Pension Fund, which invests on behalf of the state's Laborers International Union of North American (LIUNA) membership, used its power as an investor in a real-estate corporation, Brookfield Properties, to stop New York City mayor Michael Bloomberg from clearing Zuccotti Park after it had been taken over by Occupy Wall Street. Brookfield owned the park. As Barry McAnarney, the Massachusetts fund's executive director, wrote to Brookfield:

> Our pension fund investments represent the hard-earned retirement security of thousands of men and women who have dedicated their lives to building our country. . . . Many of our members suffered as a result of the reckless financial dealings of major firms on Wall Street. The protesters at Zuccotti Park are courageously standing up against these wrongdoings and in support of working-class people. To silence the voice of Occupy Wall Street would be an assault on each of our members and all they have worked to achieve.

These efforts delayed the city's emptying Zuccotti Park by more than a month, allowing Occupy Wall Street time to gain exposure and make its voice heard.[40]

The AFT's fight with hedge funds, the similar pushback against private equity funds, the responsible contractor policy deal with Blackstone, and the Massachusetts Laborers' intervention on behalf of Occupy Wall Street enable us to revisit some of the legal and policy questions introduced in Chapter 1. They show how working-class shareholders can wind up funding efforts inimical to their own interests, or, conversely, shaping events in workers' interests, depending on how that power is wielded. That brings us back to the discussion of the scope of pension trustee fiduciary duties.

First, there is one other legal rule worth mentioning here, "the investments of equal value rule." This rule reflects an interpretation of the fiduciary duties of pension trustees by the U.S. Department of Labor. It says that fund trustees may choose between two or more investments for any reason as long as they are of equal value, that is, as long as they have the same risk-return profile. That's the line Pedrotty was drawing in the report: that trustees could choose one investment manager over another for "collateral" reasons as long as the investment managers were equally qualified. How one calculates "equal value" is uncertain, and the setting of choosing investment X over investment Y is somewhat artificial, but at bottom, fiduciaries have free rein to select investment X over investment Y for any lawful reason as long as the investments are of equal value. The rule still roughly prioritizes returns, since it does not permit selection of an investment of lower value, but it gives trustees leverage in choosing investments on the basis of criteria that go beyond returns. That presents an opening for trustees to pull money from hedge funds that attack pensions.[41] It give trustees some leeway to choose a hedge fund with a similar strategy and fee structure whose management does not try to undermine pensions over one that does. Weingarten and Pedrotty were functioning within the confines of that rule in their ranking report. Thus, activists have found ways even to work within the confines of the fund-first view.

The problem with this rule—and one reason why I argue for a broader, "worker-centric" interpretation of fiduciary duty—is that the rule empowers trustees to deliberately choose a worker-hostile fund over a worker-friendly fund for the same reason. That can happen when labor-hostile politicians take control of pension fund boards. A worker-centric interpretation would make it more difficult for labor-hostile politicians or trustees to invest labor's capital in investment managers that will use this capital to undercut workers. Where the fund-only versus worker-centric distinction becomes particularly important—and where the investments of equal value rule provides insufficient protection—is in the context of public pension investments in companies that privatize their own workers' jobs.

The Massachusetts Laborers Pension Fund's letter to Brookfield Properties presents a slightly different issue. Did writing a letter in defense of Occupy Wall Street's continued presence in Zuccotti Park constitute an investment decision? Did it have to? There is no investment or divestment decision here, simply a request regarding the use of the park. Did this prioritize the interests of a third party, Occupy Wall Street, over the value of the fund's investment in Brookfield? On some level, one simply wants to be able to say that the fund took this step because it believed its members would support it, period, and that no investment rationale was required. Even considering investment effects, though, it is not at all clear there were any. What were the actual costs to Brookfield and, by extension, to its investors, including the fund, of delaying clearance of the park? Under a pure investment analysis, one would consider those potential costs before making this request. One would also consider the potential benefits. (Both were probably minuscule.) Someone searching deeply for an investment rationale might argue that Zuccotti Park's fame as the site of a historic episode would lead to an increase in tourism that would help Brookfield and its investors. More to the point, my assumption is that the costs and benefits were both too trivial to implicate fiduciary duties at all.

Ultimately, fiduciary duties are almost exclusively about process, rather than outcomes. Investment decisions can succeed wildly or can turn disastrously wrong. It is not a breach of fiduciary duty to make a bad investment. It is a breach to make an investment choice, or one affecting the value of an investment, without any reasonable assessment of its risks, rewards, costs, and benefits. This should extend beyond returns alone, to tangible economic benefits like jobs. The law requires an appropriate level of deliberation, one proportional to what is at stake.

A similar analysis applies to Pedrotty's call for pension trustees to consider hedge fund attacks on pensions in making investment decisions. First, under the investments of equal value rule, a fund could switch from one hedge fund manager to another, assuming these are investments of equal value. That switch can occur for any reason, including a hedge fund's attacks on pensions. Some might distinguish between the hedge fund itself and the founder, but this is an example where the distinction is often meaningless. (Most hedge funds are built around the mythical status of one great founding stock picker whose personality and business practices are scarcely distinguishable from the fund itself.) In addition, under the worker-first view, attacks on the very pensions that are making the investment in the first place, and the potential effects of such attacks on the retirement security of worker-contributors, could be appropriately considered too. That's not to say that such considerations automatically tilt the investment choice one way or the other. But they should be an appropriate part of the matrix of considerations.

One might ask, is it even necessary to take into account hedge fund attacks on pensions when the case against hedge funds is so strong on pure investment grounds alone, including outsized fees and poor performance? That poor performance squarely raises the question of why public and union pension funds would ever invest in hedge funds. Poor performance led Weingarten and Pedrotty to take on an even more ambitious task: outright divestment from hedge funds.[42] They already had a great template to work with, established by Dennak Murphy while working for the Capital Stewardship Program of the Service Employees International Union (SEIU).

Dennak Murphy and CalPERS's Divestment from Hedge Funds

Dennak Murphy began his career on the traditional side of the labor union movement, working in political and nonprofit organizations. Like some labor activists I spoke with, Murphy recited the work lineage of his mentors before discussing his own work. He wanted me to know that he worked for Fred Ross Jr., son of Fred Ross Sr. The elder Ross had been trained as an activist by Saul Alinsky, had met Cesar Chavez, and had participated in the lettuce and grape boycotts. He, in turn, trained many other activists, including his son, Fred Jr. Murphy met the younger Ross through an organization called Neighbor to Neighbor, a grassroots institution that provided (and still provides) a variety of support services and community advocacy. Ross Jr. eventually moved on from Neighbor to Neighbor to work at the SEIU, and he brought Murphy with him in 1999.[43]

Murphy signed on to be the first fulltime SEIU employee dedicated to shareholder activism. Today's SEIU Capital Stewardship Program has been described as the "gold standard" for working-class shareholder activism, but it was just getting started when Murphy joined. According to him, as with much of the rest of the labor movement, the SEIU somewhat belatedly realized that pension fund investments could affect labor as much as the disbursements the funds made to support the health and retirement benefits of unionized workers. Today, the SEIU has 95,000 members who contribute to CalPERS, an enormous investment. Where and how CalPERS, or any other fund, actually invested the SEIU's money had not traditionally been its focus. Murphy and others began to change that. Two organizing fights over janitors in Houston and security guards in Los Angeles led the SEIU to realize the importance of the investment side of pension funds.[44]

In the 1990s, pension funds like CalPERS made substantial investments in entities called real estate investment trusts (REITs), which, in turn, controlled more than one-third of the class A office space in Houston. These REITs resisted efforts at unionization and wage increases. Arguably, their investors, including the pensions, had an interest in maintaining low wages, and that's what the REITs wanted. But the SEIU took a different position. In its view, unsurprisingly, unionization and improved worker compensation benefited investors in the long run. Better-paid janitors would be better employees whose long-term employment and comparative job security would make them more efficient workers, less likely to, among other things, violate child labor laws by bringing their children with them to help mop floors, as occurred frequently with nonunionized workers who were paid too little to cover childcare expenses.[45]

Similarly, in Los Angeles, the SEIU represented security officers who worked in buildings owned by REITs in which pensions were investors. Security in most L.A. buildings at the time consisted of young men, even teenagers, who would work for a few months, then get fired and replaced by new workers, keeping wages low. The SEIU argued that hiring better-paid, unionized workers with deep experience working in security, giving them stable jobs that lasted years and came with a pension, would improve building security and save investors money in the long run. They argued that giving workers a vested, long-term interest in the building would help them build knowledge of who worked there and who didn't, and therefore improve security. This approach would also create new contributors to the pension system. In the SEIU's view, there was and is a strong business case for improving the working conditions of workers. The SEIU was beginning to realize that developing relationships with pension funds and making the economic case for improving worker compensation and working conditions was an important organizational goal. Worker issues aside, Murphy and others also realized that they could not sit back and just let the investment professionals handle the portfolio. They needed to pay attention to how their retirement funds were being invested.[46] Murphy would carry that insight with him years later, when he shifted his focus to CalPERS.

In 2001, CalPERS decided to make its first investments in hedge funds. CalPERS called it the "absolute return strategy," a phrase that would come to have a comically bitter meaning. Murphy recalls attending meetings about the absolute return strategy in which hedge funds "were presented as this amazing group of funds and firms that would make money no matter what "because: computers." Murphy recalls being skeptical, but when he and others raised concerns with hedge fund managers or CalPERS investment staff, the response was to describe hedge fund investment strategies as "scientific" and "objective." Over time, Murphy's initial skepticism about CalPERS's hedge fund investments would morph into opposition and then outright alarm. He became convinced that it was in the interests of CalPERS's beneficiaries and its SEIU members to dump hedge funds.[47]

How Murphy pursued that objective is almost as interesting as the objective itself. His style stands in contrast to how we usually imagine activism and activists. Activism is frequently thought of as aggressive, attention-seeking, and confrontational; it draws stark lines and looks for a fight. And that is often as it should be. But Murphy operated differently. He spoke not of aggressive fights but of cultivating relationships at CalPERS and then quietly and persistently asking questions. In his view, the key to cultivating relationships included "no surprises." He observed, "If we were going to raise an issue with the [CalPERS] board, we would give everyone notice in advance." That, in turn, created an atmosphere of trust among Murphy, board members, the investment staff, the governance staff, and other key players at CalPERS.[48]

As to persistently asking questions, those questions were simple and straightforward: How much were hedge funds charging CalPERS in fees? How were the hedge funds performing compared to the rest of the CalPERS portfolio? From the beginning, Murphy reports, he received two consistently alarming responses to these questions. First, no one could actually say how much

CalPERS was paying in fees because the fees were not disclosed separately, merely bundled into overall performance, a shocking industry practice that turned out to be widespread when it came to pension fund investment in both hedge funds and private equity funds. (Sadly, CalPERS seems not to have learned the lessons of Murphy's persistent questioning, having recently revealed that it could not be sure what it was paying private equity fund managers either.) Second, the hedge fund portfolio consistently underperformed expectations. But, according to Murphy, rather than allow this underperformance to call into question the absolute return strategy, CalPERS's outside investment consultants remained committed to keeping hedge funds in the portfolio, as were certain members of the investment staff. On two or three occasions, the program was reshuffled, with some investment personnel and hedge fund managers hired or fired. But performance did not improve.[49]

As the years of underperformance began to stack up, Murphy's persistent questions began to sound less like the pesky inquiries of some gadfly union leader without a background in finance and more like intuitive, commonsense concerns. Still not receiving any satisfying answers, Murphy made some back-of-the-envelope calculations of his own. He assumed that the hedge funds were charging the traditional 2 and 20. He ran basic calculations and reached the startling conclusion that hedge fund performance was about the same as overall portfolio performance, but that the fees were far higher.[50]

The financial crisis of 2008 might have led some observers to seriously question these hedge fund investments, as Murphy had done from the beginning. The whole purpose of a hedge fund was to provide downside protection for investors during a financial crisis or recession. Because hedge funds were supposedly not correlated with the rest of the market, they would outperform in a downturn. That turned out not to be the case. And yet, hedge funds survived the bloodletting. Ironically, because of the enormous losses generated in the financial crisis, pension funds had large liabilities and fewer assets with which to meet them. Therefore, the hedge funds argued, post-crisis investors needed them more than ever to outperform the market recovery and make up for lost ground.[51] Hedge funds stayed in the portfolio.

Still, Murphy persisted. Eventually, the hedge fund numbers became so grim they could no longer be justified or explained away. Not surprisingly, a combination of existing personnel who were skeptical about hedge funds and the arrival of new personnel helped shift the balance, eventually leading CalPERS to make a shocking divestment decision.

In 2003, Priya Mathur was elected to the board of CalPERS, after the launch of the hedge fund program. She was a financial analyst with an MBA from the Haas School of Business at the University of California Berkeley, who oversaw the $9 billion capital investment infrastructure program for the Bay Area Rapid Transit District. Convinced that CalPERS had an unduly short-term investment focus, she initiated a reorientation of its investment approach, culminating in an investment beliefs statement focusing CalPERS on long-term, sustainable investing.[52] Similarly, Janine Gilot, who joined CalPERS as the number two person in the investment office after having worked at Barclays, was skeptical of both hedge fund and private equity fees and performance. Murphy also credited Curtis Ishii, a longtime CalPERS employee who worked in fixed income, as being a hedge fund skeptic.[53] In 2014, when Ted Eliopolous took over as CalPERS's chief investment officer, he asked Ishii to review the absolute return strategy. Ishii's review was conclusive. He stopped all travel of hedge fund staff, stopped new hiring, and recommended that the program be shut down.[54]

Later that year, CalPERS stunned the hedge fund world by announcing that it was divesting entirely from hedge funds—a $4 billion divestment. In its final fiscal year prior to divestment, CalPERS had paid $135 million in management fees on its $4 billion hedge fund portfolio. The hedge funds returned 7.1 percent, while the rest of CalPERS's portfolio returned 18.4 percent. It was a perfect illustration of the main problem with hedge fund investing: the illusion of beating the market too often ends in underperformance at high cost. Numerous financial experts reacted to the news, pointing to its potentially dire consequences for hedge funds and the extraordinary nature of the divestment. As Miles Johnson stated in the *Financial Times,* "Those [hedge fund] managers that fail to heed the CalPERS warning do so at their peril." Stanford's Ashby Monk proclaimed, "As someone who spends his life watching public pension fund behavior, I can tell you unequivocally: This. Is. Big." Steven Davidoff Solomon of Berkeley's law school and the *New York Times* argued that "CalPERS made an entirely rational decision to exit. The fees would have been wholly justified if the returns were there. But they were not."[55] CalPERS's hedge fund divestment, it turned out, was just the beginning.

In 2014, Murphy attended a meeting in Chicago at the invitation of Randi Weingarten and the AFT. Weingarten and Pedrotty were already deeply concerned about hedge funds. They wanted to know what Murphy had done at CalPERS, and how it could be scaled up to a broader, nationwide effort.[56]

What emerged from that meeting was a study, commissioned by Weingarten and Pedrotty, of public pension fund investments in hedge funds. The results would ultimately lead its authors— Elizabeth Parisian of the AFT and Saqib Bhatti of the Roosevelt Institute—to title it "All That Glitters Is Not Gold: An Analysis of US Public Pension Investments in Hedge Funds." The authors utilized publicly available data to assess eleven public pension funds' investments with hedge funds. They compared the performance of the hedge fund allocations to the pension funds' overall performance and to the fixed-income portfolio allocation. The bottom line: the hedge fund investments led to $8 *billion* in lost revenues for the pension funds. Hedge fund investments lagged behind the overall pension portfolios in most years under study. Despite that fact, during this period, hedge fund managers earned an estimated $7.1 billion in fees from these pension funds alone, meaning that, on average, the pension funds paid roughly 57 cents in fees for every dollar earned during the time period under study.[57] In effect, the study confirmed Murphy's back-of-the-envelope calculations about CalPERS's absolute return strategy, and confirmed the same problem existed nationwide.

Important as the study and press coverage were, it was the connection to the shareholder activism of the AFT and others that enabled the research to be used as a blunt weapon against hedge funds. Armed with this study, pension funds began to turn the tide on hedge fund investments. By early 2016, pension funds' retreat from hedge funds moved into high gear. The Illinois State Board of Investment pulled $1 billion in investments from hedge funds, diverting them to private equity and lower cost stock funds. The last quarter of 2015 marked the first time in four years that there were net withdrawals from hedge funds, and investors—including pension funds but also endowments and insurance companies—pulled out another $19.75 billion in January 2016. Overall, public pension funds' hedge fund allocation dropped by around 40 percent from 2012 to 2015.[58] Public pension funds have not abandoned hedge funds entirely. A handful have even increased their hedge fund allocations.[59] But the overall reduction has been meaningful, and perhaps more importantly, pension fund attitudes toward hedge fund investing have become far more skeptical about fees and performance. Perhaps now, pension funds won't wait a decade on high-cost, losing investments before dropping hedge fund investments. Moreover, these divestments have had spillover effects, with university endowments also dumping hedge funds.[60]

The AFT followed up its "All That Glitters Is Not Gold" report with another published in 2017 targeted at hedge funds and private equity funds. This report, entitled "The Big Squeeze: How Money Managers' Fees Crush State Budgets and Workers' Retirement Hopes," found that one of the most important factors in the underfunding of public pension funds is the high fees charged by hedge funds and private equity funds. It further calculated how much these funds would have saved if they had paid 1 and 10 percent rather than 2 and 20.[61] Although it is too soon to tell what impact this report will have, it seems reasonable to conclude that it will put downward pressure on fees, if not lead to further divestments from hedge funds and perhaps private equity funds too.

Considering pension fund investments in hedge funds, the high fees, and the poor performance, one might rightly ask, where were the regulators? Why didn't they step in? They actually tried to, to an extent. In 2004, the SEC created a rule requiring hedge funds to register, only to see that rule struck down by the D.C. Circuit, the same court that struck down proxy access. As we will see, that rule was then revived in Dodd-Frank by working-class shareholder activists.[62] What the struggle against hedge funds by the AFT, SEIU, CalPERS, and others demonstrates is the ability of working-class shareholders to exercise their shareholder power to defend themselves when no one else can or will.

4

Checks and Imbalances

Saying No to the Imperial CEO

No single idea is more closely associated with the founders of the American republic than the concept of checks and balances. Because the framers believed that too much power vested in one person would inevitably lead to tyranny, they separated the powers of government into three distinct branches—executive, legislative, and judicial—to thwart the acquisition of excessive power by one person. That insight has since spread from debates over government to all kinds of institutions, including corporations. But many people deeply invested in American corporate law abhor the mere mention of checks and balances in the corporate context. They view the concept as an impostor, a Trojan horse smuggled into the holy city, where it threatens their own view that corporations should create centralized authority. For most of U.S. corporate history, this supposed Trojan horse has been kept outside the wall. But the investing public is increasingly resisting this view, just as it has been challenged abroad. Calls for greater shareholder democracy inside corporations are easy to find, and changing attitudes about corporations explain the sharp changes in shareholder voting rights described in Chapter 2 as least as much as the Board Accountability Project does. Increasingly, investors are asking why basic insights about voting rights, litigation rights, or institutional structures learned from our shared experience of other institutions might not also apply in the supposedly private sphere of the corporation.

Take, for example, the two most powerful positions inside the corporation: the board chair and the chief executive officer. The CEO leads the company day to day. The board chair leads the firm's board of directors, a committee with ultimate legal / fiduciary responsibility for the corporation. These board members are mostly self-nominated, their membership ratified by shareholders who rarely have any meaningful choice. Probably the board's most important responsibility, and especially the board chair's, is to hire, compensate, and supervise the company's management, particularly the CEO. Anyone operating with checks and balances in mind, anyone concerned about excessive aggregation of power in one individual—particularly if you are worried about misconduct— might sanely think that the board chair and the CEO should not be the same person. In most parts of the world, they're not. Not true in America, ironically, where the default is for the two positions to be held by one person. We call this the "imperial CEO," and a sharp critique of it has emerged in recent years.[1] Just like we might not want U.S. presidents to have final say on the constitutionality of their own actions, so we might not want CEOs to have final say over their own pay or performance assessments. The imperial CEO issue is just one of the concerns about the current state of American corporate leadership. Other prominent worries include the absolute level of CEO pay, the disconnect between CEO pay and firm performance, and the ratio of CEO-to-worker pay.

Working-class shareholders have taken the lead in challenging these pathologies.

The fact that American CEOs also serve as board chairs is not normal. In Australia, Canada, Finland, Germany, the Netherlands, New Zealand, Singapore, the United Kingdom, South Africa, and many more countries, the CEO-chair role must be split as a matter of law, norms, stock exchange rule, or governance codes.[2] The logic of separation is straightforward. To have a CEO who is also the board chair is analogous to having a president who is also chief justice of the Supreme Court. It is to have a CEO who is effectively accountable to no one, particularly if that board and CEO are insulated from shareholder accountability. In the United States, most large, publicly held companies have imperial CEOs.

The imperial CEO has its advocates. Some argue that such CEOs strengthen and centralize corporate decision making, assuring that the person who runs the company on a day-to-day basis, the CEO, is also the person actually in charge, the board chair.[3] According to research by Stanford professors David F. Larcker and Brian Tayan, over the past twenty years, opinions on the issue at U.S. companies have been inconsistent. Overall, the percentage of imperial CEOs of S&P 500 companies has dropped from 77 percent in 2000 to just over half today. That suggests a drift in the market against them, one in which working-class shareholders have played a key role. As with empirical evidence on other corporate governance issues, whether splitting the role of CEO and chair correlates with improved share price or firm value is a matter of dispute.[4] The important point is that shareholders, working class or not, may reasonably doubt the benefits of an imperial CEO. That brings us to the question of CEO compensation.

U.S. CEOs, imperial or otherwise, are paid far more than their international counterparts. The ratio of American CEO compensation to that of median company employees is far higher than in other markets, as is total CEO compensation.[5] A lack of corporate accountability is not the sole explanation for this disproportionate compensation, although one interesting study finds that American imperial CEOs are paid more than CEOs who face an independent board chair. (Interestingly, according to the study, the results are just the opposite in Europe.) Still, the evidence demonstrates that superior performance is absolutely *not* one of the reasons why U.S. CEOs are paid so much more than their international peers.[6]

As with shareholder voting (proxy access) and hedge and private equity fund abuses, working-class shareholder activists have taken on the issue of CEO pay and power. Activist efforts to rein in U.S. CEOs have taken three primary forms: (1) shareholder proposals to split the roles of CEO and chair, which have met with only moderate success; (2) "say on pay" votes that have become ubiquitous and mandate shareholder votes for or against executive compensation, which seem to have had a modest, salutary impact on CEO pay; and (3) the "CEO-worker pay ratio," which requires companies to disclose the ratio of their CEO's compensation to the compensation of the median company employee. The disclosure of CEO-worker pay ratios became law in the Dodd-Frank Act. Although there were indications that the newly Republican-controlled SEC under President Donald Trump would block implementation of the rule, as of this writing, it appears that it will go into effect starting in 2018. (It could still be blocked in future years by the SEC or by new legislation.) Such disclosures should enable shareholders to discern whether the compensation practices of firms are properly incentivizing the bulk of their employees, shifting the unhealthy and unjustified focus away from the pay of just one person. Undoubtedly, some activists hope that this CEO-worker pay rule will have the most impact on American conversations about economic inequality since Occupy Wall Street injected the phrase the "1%" and the "99%" into the lexicon.[7]

Splitting the Roles of CEO and Board Chair

For a time, Lisa Lindsley was one of the most feared, high-profile shareholder activists in the country. Smart, creative, and aggressive, she served as the director of capital strategies for the American Federation of State, County, and Municipal Employees (AFSCME). AFSCME is a public employees union with 1.6 million members who have over $1 trillion in retirement assets invested in public pension funds. Its size, both in terms of membership and assets, has enabled it to play an outsized role in the history of labor's shareholder activism. The Capital Strategies program founder, Rich Ferlauto, brought several early proxy access proposals and lawsuits, as discussed in Chapter 2. Lindsley succeeded Ferlauto in the role, directing the program from 2010 to 2013. In some respects, she was a brash and confrontational leader in the mold of Sean Harrigan. She once challenged Michael Dell at Dell's annual shareholder meeting to resign as CEO after the SEC fined him $4 million and forced the company to pay $100 million to settle securities law charges against it. Just months into her job running Capital Strategies, the *Wall Street Journal* editorial page attacked Lindsley personally. Her offense? Writing a letter to financial adviser Lazard Ltd. about the risks posed by its tax-avoidance strategies and pointing out that tax avoidance did not necessarily benefit AFSCME's members, who, after all, are public employees whose jobs are funded by tax dollars.[8] In its editorial, the *Journal* raised the same red herring arguments about breach of fiduciary obligations that Safeway had tried to use against Harrigan.

At the peak of her power, Lindsley came close to unseating one of the most prominent imperial CEOs in the world, JPMorgan Chase's Jamie Dimon. This ultimately failed effort yielded surprising advantages for AFSCME and demonstrates the potential for this activism to benefit labor beyond the well-being of its pensions.

Unlike many of the shareholder activists discussed so far, Lindsley did not grow up in the labor movement. Unusually, she came to activism from a prominent perch on Wall Street. From 1991 to 1995, Lindsley worked as a managing director at Bear Stearns. One of the world's great investment banks until it collapsed during the financial crisis of 2008, Bear Stearns was ultimately acquired by JPMorgan in 2008 for a humiliating $10 per share (its stock had once traded as high as $171.51 per share) in a deal brokered by the U.S. Federal Reserve. Long before that debacle, Lindsley had moved to Argentina to open Bear's Buenos Aires office, managing equity deals and initial public offerings (IPOs) across Latin America. Prior to joining the company, Lindsley had been a vice president at Bank of New York and earned her MBA at New York University's Stern School of Business.[9]

But after nearly a decade in banking, Lindsley started feeling restless with her work and decided to take her skills to the microfinance industry. In the late 1990s, she worked for Accion International, setting up the Gateway fund to invest in microfinance in Latin America. Feeling increasingly politicized by her work, which brought her face-to-face with issues of poverty and economic inequality, Lindsley eventually returned to the United States and joined the Howard Dean campaign for president in 2004. It was on that campaign that she first met labor union representatives. After a brief stint as the director of operations for Voices for Working Families, an organization dedicated to increasing political participation among communities of color and women, Lindsley joined the United Food and Commercial Workers Union—Harrigan's union—as the deputy director of its Capital Stewardship Program. A few years later she made the jump to AFSCME, eventually taking over the Capital Strategies program in the middle of the financial crisis, when Ferlauto left to join the SEC.[10]

From the beginning of her stewardship of the AFSCME program, one of Lindsley's priorities was restoring corporate checks and balances by filing shareholder proposals to split the roles of CEO and chair. In 2010, she and her team—including the able John Keenan, who runs AFSCME's program today—began filing such proposals. At the time, the widely held view within the activist community was that the financial crisis of 2007–8 was produced, in part, by governance failures at the nation's banks. The emerging evidence suggested that the packaging and repackaging of American home mortgages into mortgage-backed securities, which were then sold to investors, took place while bank personnel knew that mortgage lending standards had collapsed and mortgage default risks had soared. The banks further knew that the high ratings given these securities by ratings agencies were inaccurate and distorted by the banks' own financial models. Whatever else that could be deduced from the prevalence of American imperial CEOs, they were running the nation's banks that drove the U.S. economy off the cliff. Not surprisingly, some early, successful, post-crisis efforts to hold imperial CEOs accountable targeted bank heads. In 2009, shareholders successfully voted to split the roles at Bank of America. Within a year of that vote, Bank of America's CEO / chair Ken Lewis left the company. After shareholders voted against Citibank's Vikram Pandit's pay package in a "say on pay" vote, Pandit too left the company.[11]

JPMorgan's Jamie Dimon was the only leader of a major U.S. bank to emerge from the financial crisis with his reputation enhanced. In December 2010, the *New York Times Magazine* ran a cover story by Roger Lowenstein called "Jamie Dimon: America's Least Hated Banker." The *Times* credited Dimon with being a hands-on manager who directly reviewed trading data rather than relying on summaries prepared by staff, and for reining in mortgage lending comparatively early. JPMorgan did incur massive losses on bad loans during the crisis, including primarily mortgages, but, in sharp contrast to its competitors' performance, it still made profits every quarter. Because of the comparative strength of JPMorgan's balance sheet during the crisis, the Federal Reserve backed the company's acquisition of two failing banks, Bear Stearns and Washington Mutual. As a result, JPMorgan is far larger today. As I write this, the company has $2.4 trillion in assets and is the largest bank in the United States.[12]

JPMorgan's size raises profound concerns about it being "too big to fail." When a bank is too big to fail, it is more likely to make excessively risky investments. If those investments succeed, the bank and its shareholders reap the rewards; if they fail, the government will presumably step in with a bailout to prevent systemic harm to the economy.[13] For similar reasons, large banks like JPMorgan have been dubbed "too big to jail," that is, too big to be subjected to criminal prosecution for fear of negative systemic effects if their leaders are charged or convicted. And, likewise, they are "too big to manage," that is, too large and too complicated to be managed in the familiar corporate form, and certainly not by one, all-powerful imperial CEO. The theory of splitting the role of CEO / chair is rooted in the idea that an unchecked, unaccountable CEO will not be as vigilant a leader as one who must account for his or her decisions to an independent board chair.

For Lindsley and AFSCME, the strategic and tactical question became whether it made sense to file a proposal at JPMorgan against Jamie Dimon, or to target some other imperial CEO. The arguments against were straightforward enough: Dimon was "America's Least Hated Banker" and likely to be reasonably popular with shareholders. The arguments in favor seemed stronger to Lindsley. Dimon was still a banker, a deservedly unpopular trade in 2012. He was presiding over a financial institution that had grown massively during and after the crisis, raising all of the "too big to" arguments. Even if Dimon was personally popular, or at least not wildly unpopular, the principle of splitting the roles applied with equal if not greater force to whoever happened to be running JPMorgan Chase on account of its size, influence, and potential to pose systemic risks. Finally, numerous investigations by regulators of the company's foreclosure practices persuaded Lindsley and AFSCME that there were serious management lapses at JPMorgan—lapses that might deteriorate over time. (That intuition turned out to be prophetic.) So Lindsley and AFSCME went ahead and filed a shareholder proposal at JPMorgan calling for the company to split the roles of CEO and chair. Ultimately, they would do so three years in a row, between 2011 and 2013.[14]

Because the 2011 attempt attracted little notice and little support, I am focusing on the 2012 and 2013 filings, calling them "round one" and "round two."

Here is AFSCME's supporting statement for the 2012 proposal, drafted by Beth Young. ("That's the thing with Beth," Lindsley told me, "if she drafts your proposal, it's going to be good"):

SUPPORTING STATEMENT

JPMorgan's CEO James Dimon also serves as chairman of the Company's board of directors. We believe the combination of these two roles in a single person weakens a corporation's governance which can harm shareholder value. As Intel former chairman Andrew Grove stated, "The separation of the two key jobs goes to the heart of the conception of a corporation. Is a company a sandbox for the CEO, or is the CEO an employee? If he's an employee, he needs a boss, and that boss is the board. The chairman runs the board. How can the CEO be his own boss?"

In our view, shareholder value is enhanced by an independent board chair who can provide a balance of power between the CEO and the board, and support strong board leadership. The primary duty of a board of directors is to oversee the management of a company on behalf of its shareholders. But if a CEO also serves as chair, we believe this presents a conflict of interest that can result in excessive management influence on the board and weaken the board's oversight of management.

An independent board chair has been found in academic studies to improve the financial performance of public companies. A 2007 Booz & Co. study found that in 2007, all of the underperforming North American companies whose CEOs had long tenure lacked an independent board chair (*The Era of the Inclusive Leader,* Booz Allen Hamilton, Summer 2007). A more recent study found worldwide, companies are now routinely separating the jobs of chair and CEO. In 2009 less than 12 percent of incoming CEOs were also made chair, compared with 48 percent in 2002 (*CEO Succession 2000– 2009: A Decade of Convergence and Compression,* Booz & Co., Summer 2010).

We believe that independent board leadership would be particularly constructive at JPMorgan, where there have been numerous federal and state investigations into our company's mortgage foreclosure practices (JPMorgan 2010 Form 10 K, p. 9).

We urge shareholders to vote for this proposal.[15]

Although the cited academic research is dated and the evidentiary picture has grown more complex, this statement succinctly summarizes the case for splitting the role of CEO and chair, not just at JPMorgan but more generally.[16] The company, in turn, responded by saying that "the Firm's board leadership structure already provides the independent leadership and oversight of management sought by the proponent." The company's main argument was that, even though Dimon was the board chair, the company also had a "presiding director" who "presides at any meeting of the Board *in which the Chairman is not present* and at executive sessions of independent directors," who "*may* call meetings of independent directors . . . and *may* add agenda items [to an agenda set by the Chairman]." The company also pointed out that 90 percent of its board and its entire Audit, Governance, and Compensation

Committees were composed of independent directors. (Keep in mind, companies have tremendous leeway in deciding who counts as "independent.") Finally, the board endorsed Dimon specifically as CEO and board chair, arguing that "the Board has determined that the most effective leadership model for the Firm currently is that Mr. Dimon serves as both Chairman and Chief Executive Officer."[17] It urged shareholders to reject the proposal.

Not long after the board's endorsement of Dimon, the world learned about the "London whale." On May 11, 2012—four days before shareholders would vote on whether Dimon should be stripped of his position as board chair—Dimon stunned the market with the news that JPMorgan had lost $2 billion in just six weeks due to trading by Bruno Iksil, dubbed the "London whale" by the press because of the massive size of his trades. News of Iksil's trading activity first hit the market the previous month, when the *Wall Street Journal* reported that the volume of Iksil's trading was so massive that it moved the credit-default swap index in which he traded. The high volume of trading was news in itself; the fact that it caused a $2 billion loss was scandalous. Dimon himself described the trades as "flawed, complex, poorly reviewed, poorly executed and poorly monitored." He warned that the trades could ultimately cause as much as $3 billion in losses, which they did by the end of that week. Ultimately, Dimon's estimate was off by more than 100 percent. Total direct losses to the bank from the trades added up to $6.2 billion. And those are just the direct losses. In response to the news, JPMorgan lost $20 billion in market value. The loss also required the market to reassess its view of JPMorgan's management. Revelations in the press that followed disclosure—about the bank's ailing and frequently absent chief investment officer and about feuding leaders in the New York and

London offices—exposed a level of internal dysfunction previously unknown.[18]

These revelations gave force and momentum to Lindsley and AFSCME's critique of Dimon's hold on the CEO and chair roles. AFSCME president Gerald McEntee gave his full-throated support to the union's endeavor to force change:

> Wall Street greed and conflicts of interest drove our economy into a ditch. JPMorgan Chase shareholders need to act together and tell the board that we want meaningful controls over risk and real oversight of management. We need an independent chairman of the board. The stakes are too high to leave Jamie Dimon unsupervised. Dimon denied that the "London Whale" was making risky bets, and now that this has turned out to be a fish story, shareholders need to step in.[19]

Lindsley herself echoed the theme: "Jamie Dimon should not be both the chief executive officer and running the board of directors that's charged with monitoring executives," she told Fox Business. "I think he's good and he should remain as CEO, he just shouldn't be his own boss. He shouldn't be the chair of the board." The problem, as Lindsley saw it, was that "looking for an infallible CEO is a fool's errand." Her critique of the imperial CEO was structural, not personal.[20]

One might think that releasing the news about the London whale just four days before the vote would have doomed Dimon's chances of winning. If corporate elections worked like political elections that might have been the case. In most political elections, even with absentee voting, the majority of people vote on Election

Day, although that has admittedly been changing.[21] But in corporate voting, many shareholders vote days and weeks before the actual shareholder meeting.[22] It's not unusual for half of the shareholder vote to be cast five days or more before the shareholder meeting, thus, in this situation, prior to the disclosures about the London whale. Typically, Institutional Shareholder Services (ISS) and Glass Lewis release their recommendations two weeks before the meeting, setting institutional voting in motion.[23] Given the high level of shareholder support for AFSCME's proposal—40 percent of JPMorgan shareholders voted to split the roles—it is reasonable to assume that a significantly higher percentage of shareholders who voted *after* learning about the London whale voted against Dimon.[24] If JPMorgan had disclosed the London whale days or even a week earlier, Dimon might well have lost his job as chair.

CEOs and companies are not supposed to have free reign to disclose such important information. When they have made an incorrect disclosure, for instance, they have a duty to correct it as soon as they learn the truth.[25] Dimon and JPMorgan were therefore obligated under the securities laws to disclose the losses as soon as they learned about them, particularly because those losses potentially rendered earlier statements about the company's earnings and revenues false and misleading. In a securities fraud class action brought against Dimon and the company by investors following the London whale debacle, the complaint alleged, among other things, that Dimon and JPMorgan concealed the "severity and risk" of the trades because Dimon faced an impending shareholder vote on whether to strip him of the chairmanship as well as a "say-on-pay" vote on his compensation.[26] The suit settled for $150 million.[27]

Although Dimon won round one in the fight to remain imperial CEO, the margin of victory was unsettlingly close. Many of us are conditioned by political voting to think that a 59–41 win for Dimon was a blowout. But CEOs regularly obtain shareholder votes in the 90 percent range or higher. (The year before, Dimon won 88.1 percent on the same issue.) When 41 percent of your shareholders think you should be stripped of your role as chair, it is more than just embarrassing. First, you face the same electorate the next year, not four years later, as in a presidential election. Even before the next vote, that level of shareholder unrest can have negative consequences for the bank, for its performance and reputation, and, by extension, for the compensation of its executives. In addition, Dimon and JPMorgan likely saw the vote numbers pre- and post-disclosure. (The numbers are provided by Broadridge, the company that tallies shareholder votes).[28] If those numbers were running against Dimon—if more than a majority postdisclosure were voting to strip Dimon of the chair—then he would have to worry whether he could survive the same vote the following year, when all of the electorate would know about the London whale before voting.

Almost immediately, Lindsley announced that AFSCME would file another proposal. This time, both Lindsley's approach and the company's reaction were quite different. First, Lindsley obtained powerful cosponsors. New York City comptroller John Liu (Scott Stringer's predecessor) as overseer of the NYC funds and the Connecticut Retirement Plans and Trust Funds run by Connecticut treasurer Denise Nappier, a veteran of the Safeway fight, agreed to support the proposal. Both of these funds had far larger sums invested in JPMorgan than the AFSCME Employees Pension Plan represented by Lindsley.[29] These public funds were also joined by

Hermes Investment Management, a private investment manager owned by British Telecom created to manage its pension funds. It's no surprise that the only private fund to sign on was based in the United Kingdom, where a split CEO / chair is the norm. In the 2013 proposal, instead of calling specifically for Jamie Dimon's position to be split in two, the sponsors called for JPMorgan's bylaws to be revised to require the company to have a separate board chair.[30]

Because the proponents came so close to unseating Dimon in 2012; because the NYC funds, Connecticut, and Hermes were huge, powerful players; and because of the March 2013 release of a detailed report by Josh Rosner, an influential analyst, "JPMorgan Chase: Out of Control," the company's response differed markedly in 2013. This time, two of JPMorgan's board members, Johnson & Johnson CEO Bill Weldon and former Exxon CEO Lee Raymond, met directly with Lindsley and her co-proponents. Lindsley characterized their view of the proposal as, "Hey, I was a chair and CEO too! Why take it away from Jamie? He likes it!" As to the London whale, Weldon and Raymond assured Lindsley, Liu, and Nappier that it was under control. According to Lindsley, while the proponents were making a structural argument that the company would be better governed if the roles were split, Dimon was calling up investors personally and saying things like, "Don't do this to me," and "I don't know what I would tell my wife and kids if I lost the chairmanship." Among other tactics, he threatened to resign if he lost.[31]

He did not. He won by a greater margin than he did in 2012 (68–32), beating back the threat, which has not since been renewed. That JPMorgan's stock price had climbed 20 percent in the intervening year (along with the rest of the market) didn't hurt.

Neither did the fact that the board cut Dimon's pay in half after the London debacle.[32] Labor did not win this particular battle. Yet, there was an interesting postscript to the relationship between AFSCME and JPMorgan.

In June 2012, after round one, Lee Saunders took over as AFSCME president. Saunders had grown up in a union home; his father was a bus driver, and his mother was a community activist turned community college professor. He began his career at AFSCME in 1978 as a labor economist and rose through the ranks to become its first African American leader. Lindsley began her crusade against Dimon under McEntee's leadership, and, appropriately, Saunders continued to support it once he assumed control of the organization. "Even a Master of the Universe can be swallowed by a London Whale. We need a system of checks and balances to protect shareholders," he said during round two, the 2013 fight.[33]

The fight between Lindsley and Dimon also took place during a particularly fraught moment for labor. In 2011, Governor Scott Walker of Wisconsin pushed through legislation that stripped the state's public employee unions of the right to bargain collectively. The *Washington Post* observed that as a consequence, "once-thriving -public-sector unions were not just shrunken— they were crippled. . . . The state branch of the National Education Association, once 100,000 strong, has seen its membership drop by a third. The American Federation of Teachers, which organized in the college system, saw a 50 percent decline. The 70,000-person membership in the state employees union has fallen by 70 percent." Governor John Kasich of Ohio pushed through even more extreme legislation that was ultimately beaten back by a statewide referendum.[34] Because of stunning losses during the financial crisis, there was widespread concern that pension obligations were unsustainable at the state and county levels.[35] Forty-nine out of fifty states revised their pension plans to reduce prospective benefits, increase employee payments, and in some instances shift at least a portion of the pensions from defined-benefit to defined-contribution funds.[36] Given the intensely hostile climate, Lindsley told me that there was a feeling in the activist and labor communities, "Does it make sense to open up a new front against Jamie Dimon and JPMorgan?"[37]

After Lindsley came up short in 2013, the AFSCME / JPMorgan story would take a different turn. In a surprising development, according to some of the activists I interviewed, Dimon called Saunders and requested an in-person meeting.[38] (JPMorgan Chase did not respond to my request for confirmation of whether this meeting took place.) According to this account, the two met privately and have not disclosed what was discussed. But what followed was an unusual and high-profile effort by JPMorgan to protect the pensions of AFSCME workers whose retirement funds were in dire jeopardy in the harrowing Detroit bankruptcy. This raises the speculative question of whether Dimon and Saunders cut a deal to protect AFSCME's workers' pensions in Detroit.

The Detroit bankruptcy is itself worthy of its own book (one has been written), but here I offer some necessary details.[39] Detroit filed for Chapter 9 bankruptcy protection in federal court in 2013, making it by far the largest municipal bankruptcy filing in the history of the United States. Detroit claimed to have between $18–20 billion in debt that it could not repay. The fact that Detroit successfully filed for bankruptcy protection sent a chill down the spine of labor leaders across the country. That's because public employee pensions are supposed to be legally protected. These protections vary from state to state, but the reason for those protections is straightforward.[40]

Pensions are deferred wages that have been diverted into a retirement plan. The employees have already earned that income. Failing to protect those earnings would be a kind of wage theft. No sane union leader would accept a percentage of worker compensation as a pension unless the pension were guaranteed. When Detroit filed for bankruptcy protection, it was attempting to use federal bankruptcy law to renegotiate its debts with creditors, including city employees to whom it owed billions of dollars in unpaid pensions. If Detroit could succeed in obtaining federal bankruptcy protection, the effects could extend far beyond the city. It would mean that other cities around the country could potentially renege on those pension obligations—even if they were "guaranteed" under state law or state constitutions—by turning to federal bankruptcy law. Thus AFSCME, which represented tens of thousands of Detroit workers, vigorously opposed the bankruptcy filing. AFSCME lost. On December 3, 2013, federal bankruptcy judge Steven Rhodes approved Detroit's filing, ruling that the city could impair the pensions, even though article 9, § 24, of Michigan's constitution commanded that pensions "shall not be diminished or impaired."[41] It was a bad, alarming precedent.

What followed the court's ruling was months of negotiations and wrangling with creditors before things took an auspicious turn, at least for the pensioners. In a tentative deal struck in April 2014, Detroit workers would have to accept, on average, a 4.5 percent cut to their pensions, with a maximum cut cap of 20 percent. Detroit police and fire pensions were not cut at all, though future cost of living adjustments were reduced. That's in contrast to threatened cuts of as high as 34 percent, and in contrast to other creditors who were asked to accept fifteen cents on the dollar. The plan would also allow Detroit to exit bankruptcy with its debts under control while avoiding the threatened sale of the Detroit Institute of Arts' collection to pay those debts.[42] But to make the deal work, the parties needed $800 million in philanthropy and state aid. That's where JPMorgan stepped in. On May 14, 2014, Jamie Dimon announced that the bank was making a $100 million investment in Detroit, part of the "Grand Bargain" that saved the city. The purpose of this bargain was "to cushion pension cuts for Detroit retirees and avert the sale of the city's art collection." Dimon quite bluntly stated, "I personally think [the pensions] should be protected," expressing his sympathy for Detroit pensioners looking to survive on an average of $20,000 a year in retirement.[43]

The shared interests between Saunders / AFSCME and Dimon / JPMorgan in this grand bargain are not difficult to see. First, Saunders and AFSCME were eager to protect the pensions of their workers. Failing to do so could seriously undermine the union's claim to represent the interests of its members, not just in Detroit but nationwide. Dimon would have been eager to improve his standing with AFSCME. Of course, JPMorgan's aid took the form of both grants and investments, investments from which JPMorgan expected to profit, including troubling investments privatizing public services. Multiple shareholder activists whom I interviewed for this book believed that there was a connection between the Dimon-Saunders meeting, JPMorgan's investment in Detroit, and AFSCME's shareholder activism. It is possible but unlikely that AFSCME gave up on filing the CEO / chair shareholder proposal a fourth time in exchange for JPMorgan's help in Detroit. (There is absolutely zero reason to believe AFSCME initiated this campaign three years earlier seeking such a benefit.) It seems much more likely that the shareholder proposals to split the imperial CEO caught Dimon's attention, and that Dimon might have sought to defuse the confrontational stance between the two organizations. Deal or no deal, the probability was low that AFSCME would have attempted a fourth proposal, especially after Dimon had beaten it at the ballot box following the London whale ordeal. It is also possible that JPMorgan might have participated in the grand bargain anyway regardless of the shareholder proposals AFSCME filed against Dimon.[44]

Still, even the whiff of a suggestion that AFSCME might rationally back off of its shareholder activism to advance other organizational interests is precisely what led the D.C. Circuit to flout a congressional command in Dodd-Frank and strike down proxy access.[45] It is the notion that worker pension funds are special-interest shareholders that might obtain some other benefits from their activism. There is more evidence of this in the hedge fund or private equity fund context than the corporate one, where we have seen the pursuit of investment goals that simultaneously advanced more generally applicable political ones like environmental or diversity improvements. But it remains possible and, in my view, potentially desirable. The problem with the argument that worker funds might have special interests is not that it is wrong. There is some truth in it. All shareholders have special interests. Corporate management is a special-interest group too, with its own lobbyists like the Business Roundtable and the U.S. Chamber of Commerce. The problem with the "special interest" criticism is twofold: first, it is selectively applied only against pension and union funds, and it ignores the possibility that, even with their special interests, investors overall benefit from labor's shareholder activism.

It makes little sense, as a matter of fairness or efficiency, to legally discriminate against only one type of shareholder's special interests, that of pension funds. The proper answer to the special-interest concern is for investors to be aware of these interests when dealing with each other and to act accordingly. These interests can also be dealt with on the corporate side, that is, through the fiduciary duties imposed on corporate managers.

In addition, in the rare instance where a working-class shareholder fund directly pursued only its own interest in the corporate (as opposed to hedge fund or private equity fund) context, we might rationally view that pursuit as compensation from the rest of us for our ability to free ride off of these funds in ways that improve our own retirements. After all, the weight of the evidence suggests, for example, that the NYC funds' fight for proxy access improved all of our retirement funds but was only actually paid for by the NYC funds and their allies. I would have liked to see JPMorgan adopt a split CEO-chair model, just as I would like to have seen proxy access adopted at companies across the S&P 500. I did not and do not have the power to make that happen, and neither do you. Players like CalPERS, AFSCME, and the NYC funds do. If it turns out that, from time to time, these funds also derive some direct and special benefit from their activist efforts, I view that as just compensation for bearing the cost of fighting the fights that the rest of us have no chance to wage.

Structurally speaking, in order to win over other shareholders in favor of their proposals, union and pension shareholders must look for ways to advance their own interests and those of other shareholders simultaneously, as Harvard law professor Lucian Bebchuk has argued. To an extent, this constrains worker shareholders from using their power to pursue proposals that only affect their own interests at publicly held companies. In contrast, they have more flexibility to pursue their interests directly vis-à-vis hedge funds and private equity funds, without having to appeal to a broader shareholder electorate. At public companies, if everyone believes that the only reason a union or pension fund is filing a certain shareholder proposal is to advance its own interests, then the proposal will gain no support and the threat of it will go away.[46] Thus, unions and pension funds in this context must work to win support from other shareholders, either by picking proposals likely to win a large following or by trading other benefits to shareholders in exchange for their support. On the other hand, because public pension and labor union funds are just about the only funds willing to confront corporate management—or hedge funds or private equity funds—the general pattern would be to skew those shareholder initiatives in the direction of labor. That's what makes labor's shareholder activism a center-left force. At public companies, it often has to appeal to a broad shareholder base but still tilts in favor of issues that speak to and benefit labor.

Moreover, other shareholders have their own special interests. Mutual funds have direct business relationships with companies quite apart from being their shareholders, most notably, in managing the 401(k) plans of company employees.[47] It's not surprising that they might take those relationships into account when making voting decisions. As referenced earlier, at least one study shows that Vanguard seems less likely to vote against management at energy companies where it manages the 401(k)s of employees compared to companies where it has no such business interests. That too is a special interest. So what? The fact that the interests of union and pension shareholders do not always align perfectly with the interests of other shareholders does not disqualify them from the pursuit of shareholder activism. (In fairness to mutual funds and their reputation for passivity, they have been inching closer toward activism, often under pressure from public pension funds, labor union funds, and foundations. For example, as noted earlier, State Street announced a new voting policy favoring pushing for gender diversity on boards, a policy that coincided with its famous unveiling of Wall Street's *Fearless Girl* sculpture. And during the 2017 proxy season, large mutual funds like Vanguard and BlackRock shocked the investment community by backing shareholder proposals brought by, among others, the Nathan Cummings Foundation, the New York State Common Retirement Fund, and the Church of England Endowment Fund at two energy companies, Exxon and Occidental Petroleum, pushing them to make greater environmental disclosures.[48])

Sovereign wealth funds are investment funds created and operated by nation states. The Abu Dhabi Investment Authority, the China Investment Corporation, and the Government Pension Fund of Norway are all investment funds that might not always maximize returns; they might also pursue nationalist or other political interests.[49] Hedge funds often move in and out of particular stocks quite quickly, in comparison to pension funds, labor funds, mutual funds, and sovereign wealth funds, which are longer-term investors.[50] Hedge funds might have short-term interests—interests in seeing short-term spikes in share price, for instance, even at the expense of long-term company performance.[51] The shareholder electorate is no more uniform than the political electorate, and sometimes, shareholder activism undertaken by a part of that electorate is multifaceted, with myriad interests. That is no reason to short-circuit shareholder activism, any more than it would justify ending political activism of one kind or another. The diversity and sometimes divergence of interests is simply reason for shareholders to be attuned to those interests, to intelligently find overlapping interests to pursue, and to occasionally tolerate the pursuit of special interests. That's the way a mature marketplace functions. The alternative to tolerating some level of special interest in this context is to silence all shareholders and let CEOs and other corporate managers make all the decisions, immune from any accountability. That is precisely what those who harp on these interests aim to bring about.[52]

In short, I don't know for certain if AFSCME's shareholder activism played a role in persuading JPMorgan to help save the pensions of AFSCME's Detroit workers, but I see little reason to object—and much reason to applaud—if that is in fact what happened. What this episode illustrates, at a minimum, is shareholder activism's potential as a tool for advancing labor's interests, indirectly or directly, and how it can draw power from working to benefit interests other than its own. It is a powerful tool that trends center-left, toward greater participation in economic growth of middle- and working-class people.

As for Lisa Lindsley, in an echo of Harrigan's fate after the Safeway fight, she left AFSCME shortly after losing the vote again at JPMorgan. She began consulting for Sum of Us, a shareholder activist organization that focuses investors on social issues like human rights.[53] As I write this, she is running for office in her hometown.

There are a couple of noteworthy postscripts to the ultimately unsuccessful effort to split the CEO / chair role at JPMorgan. In the ensuing years, Dimon initially recast himself as a governance-friendly corporate leader, spearheading the creation of governance best practices. Many of these principles enshrined JPMorgan's current practices, as it did for other signatories. It may well have been motivated by a desire to put an end to the struggle over corporate governance issues. Nevertheless, even viewed in short-term historical perspective, it is striking that the leader of the nation's largest bank, along with Warren Buffet and a dozen other CEOs, would commit to principles that included majority voting for directors, nomination of directors recommended by long-term shareholders, empowering independent directors to decide whether the CEO / chair is unified, a lead independent director if there is an imperial CEO, clawback policies for both cash and equity, and more.[54] They would not have done this on their own without a strong push from labor's capital.

That said, Dimon changed tack shortly before the Trump administration entered office. In his new capacity as chairman of the Business Roundtable, he pushed for reforms that would effectively eliminate the ability of shareholders to bring proposals like the one that nearly cost him the chairmanship of JPMorgan.[55] As I write this, that reform is part of the proposed Financial Choice Act, which has been adopted in the House of Representatives but not yet voted on in the Senate. If adopted, and there is good reason to believe it won't be, even large funds like the NYC funds will be stripped of the power to bring shareholder proposals. That fight continues.

Say on Pay

In Chapter 2, we met Rich Ferlauto, the founder of AFSCME's Capital Strategies program. Ferlauto started the early fights over proxy access. While serving as deputy director at the SEC, he helped draft the proxy access rule that the D.C. Circuit ultimately struck down, leaving Stringer / Garland / NYC funds and TIAA-CREF to grab the baton. Ferlauto also helped found the Office of Investment for the AFL-CIO. He participated in the fight over Home Depot CEO Robert Nardelli's pay. He founded the 50 / 50 Climate Project, a nonprofit organization whose mission is "to engage the 50 largest carbon footprint public companies to create effective long-term climate change strategies."[56] Almost all of the activism described in this book was at least touched, if not directly shaped, by Ferlauto, perhaps the most consequential shareholder activist of his generation. He died on May 8, 2017, after a long illness. He was sixty years old.[57]

Back when he was still at AFSCME, Ferlauto, again working with Beth Young, also played a lead role in targeting CEO paychecks through shareholder "say-on-pay" votes. A say-on-pay vote is just what it sounds like: a vote by shareholders to approve the compensation of the CEO (Ferlauto coined the term).[58] Such votes are "precatory," meaning that they are advisory votes that boards of directors are legally entitled to ignore. But directors do so at their peril. Those who defy the results of a shareholder vote face significant risk of a "vote against" recommendation from ISS and other proxy advisory firms in the next election.[59]

Ferlauto first began experimenting with ways to rein in CEO compensation back in the early 2000s, around the same time he began working on proxy access. He started out "in the vineyards," as he described it, "tinkering around the edges of executive compensation." He would chase retention bonuses (bonuses paid to executives simply because they stayed at the company), then tax gross ups (companies paying the taxes executives owed on their bonuses or other compensation), then pursue holding requirements

(requirements that executives hold a certain number of shares so that their incentives remained aligned with company performance). It was a game of whack-a-mole: some new form of compensation would always pop up somewhere else. The question was whether one could develop a snapshot of overall executive compensation. Following a U.K. model from 2003 in which shareholders received the right to vote on total executive compensation, Ferlauto sought to make the same work in the United States.[60]

In cooperation with Beth Young as legal counsel, the two initially tried to figure out if a say-on-pay shareholder proposal would be legal in America. Ferlauto and Young confronted a prevailing attitude at the SEC and in the corporate world that "if it didn't already exist, it must be illegal."[61] But there was no SEC "no-action letter" on the topic—no SEC authority specifically saying such say-on-pay votes were unlawful—so they decided to proceed. One reason say-on-pay votes might have been illegal is because corporations are created by state law, and state corporate law generally requires ultimate fiduciary authority to reside in the board of directors. Deciding on executive compensation is a core board function—perhaps *the* core board function—and therefore a shareholder proposal on compensation could be seen as an unlawful invasion of board prerogatives. But there was a simple legal fix for this problem. Such proposals could be merely precatory or advisory, rather than binding. That way, boards still retain the final legal authority.

In the mid-2000s, Ferlauto and Young filed a half-dozen early say-on-pay votes at prominent companies like Countrywide, in coordination with NYCERS, which was filing similar proposals at Home Depot and elsewhere.[62] The proposals did quite well but did not pass, earning vote totals in the 40 percent range.[63] As with many activist issues in the mid-2000s, the roaring economy was not conducive to corporate change. And as with many activist issues in the late-2000s, the financial crisis of 2007–8 altered that decisively.

The first near-miss for say-on-pay was the proposed Shareholder Bill of Rights Act of 2009, introduced in the U.S. Senate by Senator Charles Schumer of New York and cosponsored by Senator Maria Cantwell of Washington, both Democrats.[64] Activists including Ferlauto were deeply involved in shaping the Shareholder Bill of Rights and pushing for its adoption. Its primary proponents included an all-star list of leading labor's capital institutions, including AFSCME, CalPERS, SEIU, CII, AFL-CIO, the New York State comptroller (and head of the New York State Employees' Retirement System) Thomas DiNapoli, as well as the Consumer Federation of America and Nell Minow, former president of ISS and noted shareholder rights advocate.[65]

Not surprisingly, the usual suspects opposed the bill, including corporate management law firms like Wachtell Lipton and Clifford Chance, the U.S. Chamber of Commerce, and the Business Roundtable. (The Business Roundtable, whose influence has already been noted throughout this book, describes itself as "an association of chief executive officers of leading U.S. companies working to promote a thriving economy and expanded opportunity for all Americans through sound public policy."[66] The Roundtable's view of a thriving U.S. economy includes barring shareholders from voting on the pay of Business Roundtable members.) The president and CEO of the U.S. Chamber of Commerce's Center for Capital Markets Competitiveness, David Hirschmann, called the bill a "guise" under which labor could "achieve at the board table what they cannot achieve at the negotiating table."

Big-business lobbies are deeply offended that labor would try to do what big-business lobbies do: use their power to win favorable legislation that labor argues would benefit just about everyone except overpaid CEOs. These repeated complaints by big-business lobbies about labor's shareholder activism remind me of a satirical article about the 2016 Democratic presidential primary from the Borowitz Report: "Clinton Campaign Accuses Sanders of Trying to Win Nomination."[67]

The Shareholder Bill of Rights called for an end to staggered boards, for proxy access, and for an annual shareholder vote "to approve the compensation of executives."[68] The last two would ultimately be adopted in slightly different form in Dodd-Frank, which required companies to hold say-on-pay votes at least every three years.[69] After Dodd-Frank was adopted, shareholders at company after company voted to hold such votes every year, even though the statute only required them every three years. Once again, as with proxy access, the overwhelming support for annual say-on-pay votes by shareholders shows that the Chamber of Commerce and the Business Roundtable are precisely what they accuse their opponents of being: special-interest groups that claim to represent shareholders or a "sound economy" but that actually represent a small group of overpaid CEOs and corporate managers. The way the Chamber and Roundtable constantly accuse their opponents of behaving how they themselves behave reads like a case study in psychological projection.

Say-on-pay has had a number of high-profile successes. In 2012, 55 percent of Citigroup shareholders rejected CEO Vikram Pandit's pay package. Pandit left the company within months. After shareholders rejected the pay package of Abercrombie & Fitch CEO / chair Michael Jeffries two years in a row, the board stripped

Jeffries of the chairmanship and both simplified and cut his pay. The most famously recalcitrant company and CEO / chair has been Oracle's Larry Ellison, whose pay was rejected four years in a row by shareholders. Given the fact that Ellison owned 25 percent of the company, that's a lot of unhappy shareholders. His significant stake in the company he founded made it more difficult for the board to cut his pay, but he stepped down as CEO in 2014. Every year, shareholders reject the pay packages of CEOs at dozens of companies. In 2012, fifty-seven pay packages received less than 50 percent support; in 2013, fifty-seven; sixty in 2014; sixty-one in 2015; thirty-six in 2016; and thirty-one as of September 13, 2017.[70]

Say-on-pay skeptics point out that these numbers are taken from companies listed on the Russell 3000 index, meaning only about 2 percent of those corporations have faced a negative say-on-pay vote in any given year. Therefore, they argue, say-on-pay has failed. I disagree. First, during this same four-year period, coinciding with President Barack Obama's second term and the first nine months of President Donald Trump's tenure, the stock market underwent one of its most dramatic periods of growth in U.S. history, with the Dow Jones Industrial Average recovering from a low of 6,626.94 on March 6, 2009, to 22,956.96 as of October 17, 2017, surpassing the highs it attained prior to the Great Recession.[71] Say-on-pay votes to date have taken place in an environment in which it is difficult to imagine how shareholders could be happier with stock market growth, a sentiment that is undoubtedly reflected in these votes. Second, high rates of approval do not mean that the system is failing to rein in executive pay. Say-on-pay votes in the United Kingdom, which began in 2003, have consistently passed by similarly high margins, margins that were known to Ferlauto and other activists right from the beginning.[72] So the U.S. results have not come as a shock. What matters is not the approval rate but what effect these votes have had on pay to date, and what effect they will have going forward. As to the first question, although the evidence is somewhat mixed, the weight of it suggests that say-on-pay votes have had a real, if modest, impact in reducing CEO pay relative to overall company performance, a conclusion that is matched by the sentiment of experts in the investor community.[73] Part of that may stem from negative say-on-pay votes, but more of it comes from the desire by companies to keep pay in line to avoid an embarrassing say-on-pay rejection.

To appreciate why this might be the case, it helps to understand how ISS advises its customers on the issue. ISS looks at the company's absolute performance over one-, three-, and five-year time horizons; it looks at the CEO's pay relative to the firm's performance over time; and it looks at the CEO's pay relative to other CEOs at comparable companies. Based on these metrics, it advises investors how to vote. The net effect is to punish outliers.[74] CEOs whose pay is out of sync with company performance, or is too high relative to peers, will most likely incur a negative vote recommendation. Therefore, over time, the ISS recommendations force outliers back into line. Reducing outliers at the top end of the spectrum undercuts arguments CEOs can make as to why their own pay should be higher, based on those outliers' compensation.

As noted, votes to date have taken place in a high-growth environment. I predict that in the next recession, when investor sentiment sours, we will see an increase in say-on-pay rejections, or a substantial reduction in CEO compensation designed to avoid rejections, or both. In some ways, this would echo the pace of political change, in which we see only modest changes in most election years, with occasionally sharp changes in government control when voter sentiment shifts noticeably. As with political voting, the comparatively low rejection rates may simply reveal a rational investor preference for incremental over rapid reductions in CEO pay that could cause new, unforeseen problems.

Unlike efforts to split the roles of CEO and chair, say-on-pay votes now take place annually and have become a core part of what shareholders feel entitled to opine on. That simply did not exist a decade ago and appears to be slowing the growth of out-of-control CEO pay. That said, the Financial Choice Act just passed in the House of Representatives shifts the say-on-pay vote from an annual to a triennial vote or one taking place if there is a material change in executive compensation. If ultimately adopted, that rule may dilute the reform's effect somewhat.[75]

There is one other reform to CEO compensation practices that has yet to take effect, which may prove to be more potent than either splitting the CEO / chair or say-on-pay. Most interestingly, the proposed change happened almost completely by accident.

The CEO-Worker Pay Ratio

Working-class shareholders have also come to play the role of enforcer. For example, labor's capital frequently litigates cases that the SEC or other shareholders won't bring. In this section, we see another example, with working-class shareholders pressuring the SEC to implement a rule Congress ordered it to implement.

Given how much time, money, and effort is required to effect the slightest change in financial regulation—given how well Wall Street funds its vigilant and dogged lobbyists—it is astonishing that major changes can occur without the knowledge of regular

Washington players. But that is exactly what happened with the mandated disclosure of the CEO-worker pay ratio. In a legislative fluke in which a law was written by senators and Capitol Hill staffers without lobbyist input, companies will now be required to calculate and report the ratio of their CEO's compensation to the compensation of the median company employee. Those numbers are set to be reported in 2018, and if that happens, they will be ugly.[76]

According to data assembled by the *Washington Post,* based on the best current information, American CEOs are paid 354 times what the average worker is paid at the companies they run. That's more than double the next two highest countries, Switzerland and Germany, at 148 and 147 times respectively. CEOs in Australia, the United Kingdom, and Japan are paid, respectively, 93, 84, and 67 times what the average worker is paid. U.S. CEOs weren't always so exorbitantly paid relative to their employees. According to the Economic Policy Institute, in 1965, CEOs of the largest U.S. firms were paid twenty times their workers. As the study authors report, "From 1978 to 2014, inflation-adjusted CEO compensation increased 997 percent, a rise almost double stock market growth and substantially greater than the painfully slow 10.9 percent growth in a typical worker's annual compensation over the same period."[77]

Historically, because of the complexity around CEO pay disclosure and because data on average or median employee pay is not widely available, such studies have been based on informed guesswork. That may be about to change. Company by company, these numbers will now officially be reported, owing mostly to provisions inserted into Dodd-Frank by Senator Daniel Menendez (D-N.J.) under the auspices of a staff member named Michael Passante.[78]

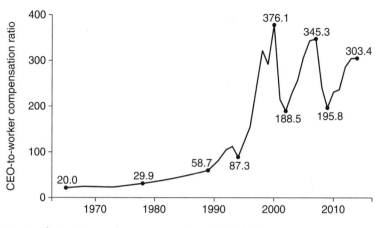

Ratio of CEO-to-worker compensation, 1965–2014

Note: CEO annual compensation is computed using the "options realized" compensation series, which includes salary, bonus, restricted stock grants, options exercised, and long-term incentive payouts for CEOs at the top 350 U.S. firms ranked by sales. Worker compensation includes wages and benefits for a full-time, full-year worker.

Source: Lawrence Mishel and Alyssa Davis, "Top CEOs Make 300 Times More Than Typical Workers," Economic Policy Institute, June 21, 2015, http://perma.cc/MP6M -KXSF, figure A.

In my effort to uncover how this provision ended up in the bill, I called Heather Slavkin Corzo, who runs the Office of Investment for the AFL-CIO, and asked her what she knew about it. I had assumed that some labor-side shareholder activists had lobbied for its inclusion, and that she might know who. Was she or anyone at AFL-CIO responsible for it being in the statute? "Nope," she replied. I got the same answer from every working-class shareholder activist I asked; none knew about it before it became law. And yet, were it not for Slavkin Corzo, the CEO-worker pay ratio would never have become a reality, notwithstanding Dodd-Frank.

Slavkin Corzo graduated from Boston University School of Law in 2005 and started her career working in the fund industry, but, "it just made my heart hurt." Her path into shareholder activism began in Democratic politics. She worked briefly as a field organizer for Moveon.org during the 2006 congressional election. Following that, she joined the Office of Investment for the AFL-CIO, where she spent seven years working as senior legal and policy adviser under Pedrotty. (The world of working-class shareholder activism is a small one. Too small.) Slavkin Corzo now holds Pedrotty's former position as the director of the Office of Investment for the AFL-CIO.[79] Like Pedrotty, she has made herself, and her office, one of the most important forces for shareholder activism in the country.

Dodd-Frank was adopted in 2010. Four years later, the SEC still had not created a rule implementing the CEO-worker pay disclosure. (In fairness to the SEC, Dodd-Frank commanded it to make eighty-six rules, and one of its very first—proxy access—was struck down. As of this writing, the SEC had promulgated sixty-seven of the rules required of it under Dodd-Frank.) In 2014, shortly after taking over as director, Slavkin Corzo began a media and lobbying campaign to keep the issue in the public eye and force the SEC to adopt a rule. She wrote several articles in support of it and appeared on CNBC multiple times to defend it. Representatives Raúl Grijalva of Arizona, Keith Ellison of Minnesota, and Maxine Waters of California, all Democrats, held a press conference urging adoption of the rule, arguing that

> the current culture of paying CEOs hundreds of times more than the typical employees hurts working families, is detrimental to employee morale, and goes against what research shows is best for business. Management expert Peter Drucker argued that a pay ratio not exceeding 20-to-1 or 25-to-1 is

ideal, and that higher pay ratios make it difficult to foster the kind of teamwork and trust that businesses need to succeed. Today's numbers dwarf that optimal ratio, contributing to stunning widening of economic inequality. 95 percent in income gains since the global financial crisis have gone to the top 1 percent while ordinary workers' pay has stagnated.[80]

In June 2015—almost five years after Dodd-Frank passed—the campaign received a turbo charge of support when Senator Elizabeth Warren, Democrat of Massachusetts, wrote a scathing letter to then-SEC chair Mary Jo White. Warren excoriated White and the SEC for failing to implement many of the rules required of it, and pointed out with some alarm that "the nation's largest financial institutions are mounting an aggressive effort to repeal, postpone, and dilute the laws Congress passed in the wake of the crisis." Number one on Warren's list of complaints was White's failure to implement the CEO-worker pay ratio rule.[81]

Seizing on the momentum generated by this letter, Slavkin Corzo organized a petition drive—ultimately signed by 165,000 people—encouraging the SEC to issue the rule. She also used an online tool to generate a thousand phone calls into the offices of the five SEC commissioners in support of it. Business lobbies may have missed the rule's inclusion in Dodd-Frank, but they mounted a vigorous campaign to delay implementation and to dilute the rule's effectiveness. The U.S. Chamber of Commerce claimed that being forced to disclose the ratio would cost companies $311,800 and 1,825 work-hours per year. Slavkin Corzo's response: "This is nonsense, plain and simple. Companies should already have this information on the books. Dodd-Frank asks companies to do some simple calculations. If more effort than this is required, it raises serious questions about how companies are fulfilling their financial reporting obligations."[82]

On August 5, 2015, the SEC issued the rule. As the SEC press release stated, the rule "provides companies with flexibility in calculating this pay ratio, and helps inform shareholders when voting on 'say on pay.'" The rule requires companies to disclose the ratio in a variety of legal documents, most notably in their annual reports to shareholders. The "flexibility" described in the press release is a concession to business lobbies, but one that activists I spoke to, including Slavkin Corzo, agree leaves the core of the rule intact. This flexibility allows companies to calculate median employee compensation "only once every three years and to choose a determination date within the last three months of a company's fiscal year. In addition, the rule allows companies to exclude non-U.S. employees from countries in which data privacy laws or regulations make companies unable to comply with the rule and provides a *de minimis* exemption for non-U.S. employees." It also permits companies to use statistical sampling in making the median employee calculation, a cost-cutting measure suggested by the AFL-CIO and ironically opposed by business lobbies, who did not want to reduce the rule's costs to make it more manageable but rather to kill the rule completely.[83]

Beginning in late 2017, public companies will now have to begin reporting their CEO's compensation relative to the compensation of their median workers. One benefit is to provide shareholders with the requisite information they need to properly vote on the say-on-pay question. Slavkin Corzo describes the benefits of this as being about "human capital management." "It's a noxious term," she told me, "but the basic idea is that, as the economy turns more towards service and away from manufacturing, investors need to understand how the workforce is trained, compensated, and retained. It's not good enough only to have that [compensation] information about the CEO. We need to understand it more deeply throughout the organization."[84] Investors should also know if the company pays its CEO hundreds of times more than its median workers and whether that CEO is in fact worth it. Although there is widespread skepticism about the investment rationale for the CEO-worker pay ratio, once again real investors seem more interested in it than anticipated. According to a recent survey by ISS, fully 75 percent of institutional investors intend to use these disclosures in their assessment of executive compensation issues. According to a memorandum circulated by Skadden, the corporate law firm, "The survey results contradict the commonly held view that investors will simply ignore the pay ratio disclosures."[85]

Finally, reporting the CEO-worker pay ratio is a way to reinject issues of economic inequality into the national and international conversation. It annualizes the disclosure so that companies report their ratios, which can then be debated during proxy season, roughly from March through June, when most companies hold their annual meetings. This information can have impact both within the corporate world and beyond it, influencing debates over tax policy, social welfare programs, and others. And the news stories write themselves. Who had the highest CEO-worker pay ratio in the country this year? Who had the highest in industry X? Why? How do the workers feel about their CEO's pay? How about investors? Who had the lowest ratio in the country? In industry X? Why? How have those numbers changed over time? How does unionization affect these numbers?

The enormous pressure brought by Senator Warren and Slavkin Corzo on the SEC and its chair, Mary Jo White, to finally issue the rule when it did may have saved it from extinction. Under the Congressional Review Act, Congress has an automatic right to revoke a new administrative rule, like the CEO-worker pay ratio rule, within one year of its being promulgated. Once that year has elapsed, the rule automatically takes effect. The only way for the SEC to reverse itself on that rule would be to conduct another formal study of its effects and then to open up any proposed repeal of the rule for public notice and comment. That is an extended, time-consuming process. In short, had the SEC been able to delay implementation of the rule for another six months, until January 2016 instead of August 2015, the Republican Congress could have eliminated it with a hand wave. Congress can still eliminate it but not without passing new financial legislation, with all of the complications that would entail.

That's not to say they won't try. Prior to the appointment of current SEC chair Jay Clayton, acting SEC chair Michael Piwowar, who fiercely opposed requiring companies to report the ratio, called for a review of the rule, citing unspecified "unanticipated compliance difficulties." (Piwowar initially opposed adoption of the rule, citing "Saul Alinskyan tactics by Big Labor and their political allies.")[86] He was clearly trying to delay implementation of the rule long enough for the Republican Congress to pass new legislation that would eliminate it. But that has not happened, and as a result, the SEC has indicated that companies should expect to proceed with reporting their CEO-worker pay ratios in 2018.[87] Even if it only lasts one year, and it may last many years beyond that, it will yield a treasure trove of information.

The CEO-worker pay ratio is not perfect. CEOs in industries with many low paid workers might fare worse than bankers, because even relatively low-level employees in the finance industry are paid far more than the low-level workers in manufacturing or food services. Fair enough. The ratio's most powerful effect may be to make within-industry comparisons, that is, the ratio for banks compared to other banks, consumer goods compared to other consumer goods, and so on. Overall, these disclosures should help arrest the trend shown in the figure above of runaway executive compensation. This disclosure takes the debate over the 99 percent versus the 1 percent and operationalizes it inside companies, creating yet another counterweight to the forces that continuously push executive pay upward. This data should also provide some insight into how companies compensate the rest of their employees. Reporting only on the CEO's pay tends to reinforce the "CEO as superhero" mythology, when in reality, properly incentivizing all employees is in the interests of shareholders too.

To sum up, working-class shareholders have led the fight against imperial CEOs on three fronts. They have fought with only moderate success to split the roles of CEO and chair in an effort to restore a functional system of checks and balances to the modern corporation, a system that exists in almost all comparable markets except our own. Activists have successfully instituted "say on pay," an annual shareholder vote on executive compensation. And they have fought for annual reporting of the CEO-worker pay ratio. In the next chapter, we see how working-class shareholders have fared in another extremely powerful market sector: private equity.

5

The People's Lobbyists versus Private Equity

Just over one hundred years ago, Louis Brandeis, lawyer and future Supreme Court justice, published *Other People's Money and How the Bankers Use It.* Among the book's many famous observations—which depressingly retains much of its century-old descriptive power—was the remark "sunlight is said to be the best of disinfectants; electric light the most efficient policeman."[1] Today, echoing Brandeis's argument, the principles of disclosure and transparency remain core to how we regulate finance. We rarely ban the sale of securities, though perhaps we should more frequently. Instead, we require full and complete disclosure about it, policed by antifraud provisions that govern the truthfulness and candor of that disclosure.[2] Failure to properly reveal required financial information, or disclosing false or misleading information, can result in extensive criminal and civil liability enforced by the Department of Justice, the SEC, state securities regulators, and shareholder lawsuits. We focus less on *what* financial products companies sell, more on *how* they sell them. It is perfectly acceptable for companies to offer highly risky securities to the public as long as those companies disclose all of the known risks.

There is a competing view to Brandeis's notion that regulation equals sunshine. That view says that regulation mandating disclosure costs more than it's worth, that it harms companies and shareholders, and that good companies have the right incentives to voluntarily disclose all of the relevant information investors need. Given these questions about the value of sunshine, of regulation, it's worth considering what kind of financial creatures prefer to live in the dark, and how we might expect them to behave. In the past ten years, private equity funds have been some of the main occupants there. Most of what we could find out about them is what they chose to tell us about themselves. But since Dodd-Frank, a light has been switched on, a dim light, but just enough to get a look at some of these creatures.[3] Working-class shareholders installed the light, the wiring, and the switch, and simply asked the SEC to turn it on. The SEC finally did.

The fight to install that lighting was led by Heather Slavkin Corzo, who pressured the SEC to issue the CEO-worker pay rule. Here, too, she played a key role, working in a coalition she helped create—Americans for Financial Reform (AFR)—to ensure that Dodd-Frank would empower the SEC to start shining its light on private equity. The way to do that was to require private equity funds for the first time to register and report on their holdings. That is no easy feat. As of 2015, private equity had $4.2 trillion in assets under management. Along with that comes massive lobbying power. Its leading lobbying arm in Washington used to call itself the Private Equity Council. It then changed its name to the Private Equity Capital Growth Council, and now it calls itself the

American Investment Council, for reasons that are too obvious to mention.[4]

The private equity business model has long been controversial. Some view it as essentially a financing mechanism, one that sharply favors those who control the fund over its investors, over taxpayers, and over the employees of the companies purchased by these funds. The private equity general partner—comprising the people who run and set up the private equity fund itself—relies on capital furnished by its investors, the limited partners, to purchase public companies and "take them private," just as both Kohlberg Kravis Roberts and Cerberus did with Safeway in Chapter 1. Private equity uses tax breaks, including the "carried-interest loophole," to obtain lower tax rates for its partners than that paid by most Americans.[5]

Victor Fleischer is a law professor at the University of San Diego, formerly the author of the "Standard Deduction" column for the *New York Times,* and recently served as co-chief tax counsel for Senate Finance Committee ranking member Ron Wyden (D-Ore.). In one of the most consequential, most cited, and most widely read works of legal scholarship of the past decade, Fleischer argued that the private equity industry's carried-interest loophole illegitimately enabled the industry to count profits made from their labor (which is taxed at the higher rate for income that most of us pay) into profits made from capital gains (which is taxed at a lower rate). This was "an untenable position as a matter of tax policy," according to Fleischer, who argued, among other things, that private equity profits should be taxed as ordinary income.[6] Fleischer's argument has been picked up nationwide, with as yet unsuccessful efforts to close the loophole in Washington, accompanied by local efforts by the Hedge Clippers, a labor-affiliated activist group that has pushed against this dodge in twelve states and the District of Columbia.[7]

Fleischer's appointment as Senator Wyden's tax council prompted a fraught reaction in some quarters: "Senator Ron Wyden Endangers Tax Reform with Hire of Radical Partisan Victor Fleischer," wrote *Forbes*. The article included the standard Alinsky reference: "[Fleischer's] appointment was praised by the Alinsky-esque 'Patriotic Millionaires' group he has worked with over the years."[8]

In addition to the controversial business model, the growing behind-the-scenes role of the private equity industry in virtually all aspects of American life has triggered widespread concern. The *New York Times'* "Bottom Line Nation" series on private equity captures much of the worry. The financial crisis of 2008 left states and cities in mostly temporary financial straits. Private equity stepped into that void, taking over public services including ambulance companies, railroads, highways, 911 call centers, water utilities, public golf courses, even courthouses. It used to be that if a state wanted to build a road, it could do so as long as it went through the regular process and allocated the requisite funds. Today, a state might need permission from a private equity fund to build that road, if the fund owns another road nearby from which it has the right to collect tolls. This ownership stake has given the industry an outsized voice in Washington and in state capitals. It has also led to the displacement of public worker jobs, an issue I discuss below.[9]

Slavkin Corzo worked fulltime on Dodd-Frank when it was being drafted. She was registered as a lobbyist on behalf of the AFL-CIO Office of Investment, the office she now runs. When the House of Representatives initially took up Dodd-Frank, it included a provision in the bill requiring the registration of private funds, including private equity funds. That meant subjecting these funds for the first time to the kind of disclosure regime described above. But when the bill got to the Senate, the registration requirement had mysteriously—or perhaps not mysteriously—disappeared. (Maybe it was just a coincidence, but Banking Committee chairman and patron of Dodd-Frank, Democratic senator Chris Dodd, represented Connecticut, home to a significant segment of the private equity industry.) Slavkin Corzo lobbied Senators Jack Reed (D-R.I.), Ron Johnson (R-Wis.), Carl Levin (D-Mich.), Sherrod Brown (D-Ohio), and Charles Grassley (R-Iowa) to reinsert the private fund registration provision into the bill. She particularly credited Senator Reed's efforts during the reconciliation process (reconciling separate bills passed in both the House and Senate) for restoring the registration requirement.[10]

This is but one small example of the obscure wrangling over obscure provisions buried deep inside a thousand-page piece of legislation that is the daily toil of the Washington lobbyist. The public can never hope to enter into this labyrinth; it can only hope it has sent in the right representatives. Private equity sent in hordes of extremely well-paid lobbyists. For the rest of us, there was Slavkin Corzo and AFR. This "national coalition of nearly 200 state and local organizations ranging from financial experts to community advocates" includes notable organizations like the Roosevelt Institute and the National Community Reinvestment Coalition. It was largely staffed by Slavkin Corzo and the AFL-CIO and set up to help institute the framework for financial reform that was laid out in the Special Report on Regulatory Reform, released on January 29, 2009, by the Congressional Oversight Panel. That panel was chaired by Elizabeth Warren, and her role in leading it is what made her a household name and laid the groundwork for her successful Senate run in Massachusetts. One of AFR's first priorities was to create the Consumer Financial Protection Bureau, a recommendation that came right out of the report and that was Warren's idea. When President Obama declined to appoint Warren to lead it, she returned north to run for Senate.[11]

Of course, critics will predictably argue that Slavkin Corzo and AFR were no different than the private equity lobbyists—there to represent their own interests, in this case, the interests of their union sponsors and others. And so they were. What were these interests? That pension funds were investing worker retirement savings in private equity funds they knew little about. That pension funds could hardly figure out what they were being charged by private equity funds. That pension funds were investing their workers' retirement savings in the surreptitious takeover of public schools, of firefighting companies, of police and ambulance services, of water treatment facilities, of toll roads, in short, in job losses for their own workers.[12] The experience of pensions directly contradicted the view that companies would automatically disclose all the information investors needed without mandated disclosure. Is this disclosure yet another special interest? Are fees, investment performance, and the private takeover of the public square only the concern of unions?

In my view, the interests of the people on whose behalf Slavkin Corzo and AFR advocated are far better aligned with the interests of most Americans than any other sector of finance. My confidence in the Slavkin Corzos of the world, in the activists portrayed in this book, is not that they selflessly martyr themselves on the altar of the public interest, though I do believe they are far more public-minded than any other financial actors. Instead, my confidence in them stems from the fact that the interests of their members coincide with the interests of a far greater percentage of the public than any other sector of finance. The tens of millions of Americans invested in these pension funds and union funds—and the many more who are dependent on them through family ties to fund participants and beneficiaries—are working- and middle-class people. They are increasingly marginalized in the halls of power. Their own elected representatives may show less interest in working for them than do the folks who run their pensions.[13]

Thanks to Slavkin Corzo, AFR, and others, Dodd-Frank included the requirement that private equity funds register and disclose their holdings, alongside many other financial reforms, including creation of the Consumer Financial Protection Bureau.[14] This was how Slavkin Corzo and others installed the lighting. The question then became whether the SEC would flick the switch and turn it on. It did so almost four years later, on May 6, 2014, and it offered some direct evidence relevant to the debate over the value of mandated disclosure.

Andrew J. Bowden was the director for the Office of Compliance and Inspections and Examinations for the SEC in 2014. On that day in May, he delivered a speech at the Private Equity International Private Fund Forum in New York. Titled, not coincidentally, "Spreading Sunshine in Private Equity," Bowden announced the results of the SEC's examinations of private equity funds based on the SEC's new power to conduct such reviews under the registration provision in Dodd-Frank. Bowden began with background about some of the conflicts inherent in the private equity industry. One is that private equity funds take over a company and then force that company to hire the private equity company as its adviser. He then described what the SEC found in its first 150 inspections since the registration requirement became effective:

> By far, the most common observation our examiners have made when examining private equity firms has to do with the adviser's collection of fees and allocation of expenses. *When we have examined how fees and expenses are handled by advisers to private equity funds, we have identified what we believe are violations of law or material weaknesses in controls over 50% of the time.*
>
> This is a remarkable statistic. Historically, the most frequently cited deficiencies in adviser exams involve inadequate policies and procedures or inadequate disclosure. . . . *So for private equity firms to be cited for deficiencies involving their treatment of fees and expenses more than half the time we look at the area is significant.*[15]

In short, when operating away from the sunshine, private equity funds were cheating on their fees and expense allocations "over 50% of the time."[16] We learned this lesson from Brandeis a hundred years ago. It's a shame to have to learn it all over again. It is impossible to imagine how these revelations might have taken place absent Slavkin Corzo, the AFL–CIO, AFR, and the other organizations that lobbied for private fund registration, particularly given the power of the private equity industry.

Since Bowden's speech, the SEC has pursued eleven enforcement actions against private equity funds for assorted securities law violations. One of these actions was brought against WL Ross LLC & Company, founded and run by Wilbur L. Ross, who today serves as secretary of commerce in the Trump administration. The

SEC found that his fund failed to disclose its fee allocations to certain other funds it advised, resulting in them "paying higher management fees between 2001 and 2011." In response, the company revised its billing practices, returned $11.8 million in fees, and paid a $2.3 million penalty.[17]

Important as such enforcement actions may be, and subject as they are to whoever sits in the White House and therefore controls the SEC, the highest value of this disclosure is to enable transparency about fees and to monitor private equity's investment activities more generally. To offer a simple example, Leonard Green Partners, one of the largest and most successful private equity funds, disclosed in its Form ADV (a required disclosure form) that the firm was charging portfolio companies—the companies (like Safeway) purchased by the private equity fund with money furnished by its investors, including its pension and labor fund investors—for the first-class, private, and business-class air travel of its executives. That prompted an investigation by one of its investors, UNITE HERE, into how the firm was billing its travel expenses.[18]

UNITE HERE, a union representing workers in the hotel industry, created a private equity watch list similar to the one Pedrotty and Weingarten built for hedge funds.[19] Since 2013, it has published this list, labeling eighteen private equity funds as "irresponsible" and thirteen "responsible." Irresponsible private equity funds are those that have, among other things, repeatedly refused requests to meet with the union and "had a longstanding, unresolved dispute at a hospitality-related property or portfolio company." UNITE HERE is able to apply its pressure as an investor to demand greater transparency and disclosure. But it also does so to advance the interests of its members, whose pension benefits are directly tied to their ability to work, and to their compensation, precisely the same issues the union may be negotiating "at a hospitality-related property or portfolio company." Such unions have also taken to negotiating side deals with private equity funds that require the funds to use union labor whenever possible.[20]

Unions have also turned to pension investors for aid when embarking on unionization efforts or negotiating wages and working conditions with private equity owners. For example, members of the Communications Workers of America successfully turned to the New York State Common Retirement Fund ($192 billion in assets), an investor in private equity fund Apollo Global Management LLC, for aid in beating back concessions sought by the company from workers. Los Angeles hotel workers have similarly turned to pensions to supply helpful pressure in the union's efforts to organize the Terranea luxury resort, operated by Lowe Enterprises.[21]

The interface between public pension funds, labor union funds, and private equity funds is the most fraught relationship described in this book. Private equity would be a shadow of its current self were it not for public pension investments. Estimates vary, but somewhere between one-third and just under one-half of all private equity assets under management come from public pension funds.[22] As with hedge funds, pension funds have only recently recognized the problem of fees charged by private equity—both the size of those fees and their transparency. CalPERS has become so alarmed by private equity fees and lack of transparency that it is actively considering funding and staffing its own private equity fund or, worse, outsourcing it entirely to BlackRock.[23]

But the latest development in the relationship between public pensions and private equity is considerably more promising. In

2017, New York City comptroller Scott Stringer's office negotiated an arrangement between the NYC funds and KKR in which
the private equity fund would not collect any fee on investment
gains until those gains exceeded 7 percent. With a $3 billion in-
vestment in KKR, the NYC funds had the leverage to impose such
an arrangement, the purpose of which was to "at least match the
public markets."[24] That means the NYC funds won't pay fees on
investment gains until those gains exceed performance of an S&P
500 index fund. This is yet further illustration of the basic point.
The substantial stake that pension and union funds have in private equity means that they can shape the funds' investment strategies in more labor-friendly ways, if pension and union funds
actually make use of that power. Nowhere is that power more
important than when it comes to the question of jobs.

In many cases, public pension funds are directly funding their
own job losses via private equity's takeover of public activities.
Public ambulance drivers, firefighters, teachers, prison guards, engineers, and others have their own retirement funds invested in
companies that take away their jobs and give them to lower-paid,
private equity–funded private-sector workers with no benefits.
Such investments raise profound questions about whether the
trustees who have made these decisions are truly fulfilling their
legal duty of loyalty to the workers and their retirement savings.[25]
Here, too, formidable resistance is emerging, with many funds beginning to boycott such investments, imposing restrictions on
such investments to protect workers, and, better yet, using their
investment power to create jobs. Such jobs lead to more contributions to the fund. Still, the meaning of the law that governs pension investments is itself a political football and has flipped back
and forth between the administrations of Presidents Bill Clinton,

George W. Bush, Barack Obama, and maybe Donald Trump too. But before addressing the legal and policy challenges facing working-class shareholders, there is one more crucial topic to be covered. In the next chapter, I describe how working-class shareholders have increasingly used their shareholder power to bring lawsuits against CEOs, bankers, accountants, and others on charges of securities fraud.

6

The New Sheriffs of Wall Street

Fighting Fraud

Not long before the Great Recession of 2007–8 taught the world about collateralized debt obligations and mortgage-backed securities, another financial fraud was the talk of markets everywhere: stock-options backdating. The backdating problem was first discovered by a Norwegian professor of finance, Erik Lie, of the University of Iowa. Lie uncovered rampant stock-options backdating, which eventually led to dozens of SEC enforcement actions and investor lawsuits, making him a minor cult figure. Lie's students told the press he looked like Kevin Bacon in *Footloose*. *Businessweek* reported that he loved academic life because he could cross-country ski after class and spend summers with his family at his parents' vacation cabin in Norway. Lie would never be *Time*'s Person of the Year, but he would place eighty-fourth in the Time 100 for 2007, his profile written by Eliot Spitzer. What Lie did was quite straightforward in the world of finance academia: he collected years of data and analyzed it. In Lie's case, he focused on stock options, specifically when and how companies granted them to their executives. Lie published his first findings in 2005 in an academic finance journal called *Management Science*. As he stated in the article: "I document that the predicted returns are abnormally low before the [stock option] awards and abnormally high afterward." Summoning up what cannot quite be described as sarcasm, Lie concluded, "Unless executives possess an extraordinary ability to forecast the future marketwide movements that drive these predicted returns, the results suggest that at least some of the awards are timed retroactively."[1] Translation: these stock options were not actually being granted when companies said they were being granted. They were being granted and then illicitly backdated to some earlier date that would make them much, much more valuable. Lie's data lay there in *Management Science* for about a year, a loaded gun.

The gun fired on March 18, 2006, when the *Wall Street Journal* published an article called "The Perfect Payday." The *Journal* reported that William McGuire, the CEO of UnitedHealth, one of the largest health insurance companies in the world, had been granted stock options by the company in 1997, 1999, 2000, and 2001. The fact of these grants was not extraordinary; what mattered was their timing, which followed the pattern described by Lie in his academic research. As "The Perfect Payday" revealed, in all four years, McGuire's options were granted on dates that just happened to be the most valuable for McGuire, when United-Health's stock price was at its lowest for the year.[2] (Since a stock option is the right to buy the company's stock for its current low price when the stock is trading at some higher price in the future, the lower the "strike price" of the option, the more valuable it is. More on this below.)

In 1997, 1999, and 2000, McGuire's options were granted on the date the company's stock price traded at its absolute lowest for the year. In 2001, his options were granted on a date that was nearly the lowest. This is an extraordinary coincidence, so extraordinary that the *Wall Street Journal* calculated the probability of it happening by chance as 1 in 200 million.[3] In short, this didn't look like chance. It looked an awful lot like fraud. To understand why, and why stock options backdating is a problem, we have to understand a bit about how stock options are supposed to work.

Companies regularly use stock options to pay their employees. If the company's stock price closes at $25 per share, a stock option granted that day (known as the "grant date") would give the grantee the right to purchase company stock in the future for that price (known as the "strike price"). If the stock then drops to $24 per share, the stock option becomes worthless; it's irrational to pay $25 for a $24 stock. But if the price rises to, say, $35 per share, you can still purchase that stock for just $25 per share from the company. Each option is then "in the money," in this case worth $10, the difference between the value of the stock and the discounted purchase price. Of course, instead of stock options, the company could give you one $25 share; if the stock goes up to $35, you've made an additional $10. But a company can give you many more stock options for the same price as one share of stock, since an option to purchase a stock is always cheaper than the stock itself. If you get a few stock options with a strike price of $25, then you make a lot more money when that stock hits $35. But if it drops to $24 (and stays there), the options are worthless.[4] If, instead, the company handed you one $25 share and the price dropped to $24, you would still own one share worth $24 instead of a bunch of worthless stock options. This basic math illustrates an effect of being compensated with options: they provide very significant upside if the future stock price rises and significant downside if it falls below the strike price.

The reason why companies grant stock options to employees, from the CEO down, is to incentivize hard work and *future* performance. If employees work hard and improve the future value of the company, then they will be handsomely rewarded by those options. But if they do not and the stock price drops, the value of their options will be zero. This is one reason why stock option compensation is commonplace in startups with little cash to pay salaries but significant future growth potential. Stock option grants are higher risk and higher reward than stock grants. But in order to make this work—in order to get the incentives right—it is crucial that the strike price for the option be the closing price on the grant date. So if the stock price closed at $25 per share on May 15, the strike price for options granted to employees on May 15 should be $25 each. If you make the strike price $20 on May 15, even though the stock closed at $25 per share, then you just handed the grantee $5. That's a reward for past performance (or nonperformance), not future performance. That's no different than handing your employee cash, and it should be accounted for (and taxed) accordingly.[5] For this reason, companies always have stock option policies that set the strike price for those options at the company's closing stock price on the date of the grant. What Lie found and what the *Wall Street Journal* reported was that companies were actually granting the options on May 15 but backdating them to make it look like they were granted on, say, March 1, when the stock was trading at $20. And when I say, or anyone says, the "companies" were doing this, it's a bit misleading. It's not the "companies." It's the CEOs and CFOs and Audit Committees and Compensation Committees that were making the companies backdate these options to themselves and others. Who bears the cost of these manipulations? The companies' shareholders. As former SEC chair Arthur Levitt described it, backdating "represents the ultimate in greed. . . . It is stealing, in effect. It is ripping off shareholders in an unconscionable way."[6] It's a form of stealth compensation or, more bluntly, theft.

That brings us back to the options granted by UnitedHealth to William McGuire in 1997, 1999, 2000, and 2001. The timing of these grants was so suspicious that it strongly suggested they were actually granted later but then backdated to make them look like they were granted on the lowest date of the year to have maximum value to their recipient. Helpful as the *Journal* article was, there was only one real way to find that out what happened. That was by suing McGuire, the company, and the other executives who might have engineered and benefited from the backdating.

You might think that in the face of such strong circumstantial evidence of fraud, investors of all types would run to court. But that's not what happened. In fact, that's almost never what happens. Mutual funds are some of the largest investors in the marketplace and had billions of dollars invested in UnitedHealth. They manage the 401(k)s and 403(b)s of millions of Americans, not to mention institutions. If the allegations against McGuire were true, then they were being robbed by McGuire and others at the company. How many mutual funds brought suit against UnitedHealth over stock-options backdating? Zero. What about hedge funds, the investment masters of the universe? Zero. If companies are going to be held accountable by their investors when they commit fraud, it will only happen if they are sued by working-class shareholders like pension funds and labor union funds.

Mutual funds, hedge funds, and other large investors effectively never sue companies that commit securities fraud. This remains true even when these investors are badly harmed by the fraud. They do nothing about it for several reasons. These reasons overlap with why they engage in little shareholder activism generally, as suggested in Chapter 2, but they are worth amplifying here. First, mutual funds face several conflicts of interest in bringing shareholder lawsuits against companies. As noted, one of their most important businesses is managing the 401(k) retirement funds of the employees of large, publicly held companies. Corporate management selects which mutual funds it offers to its employees for their retirement funds. If you're a mutual fund trying to get on, or stay on, a company's platform of funds offered to its employees, then suing its corporate management is an unsuccessful marketing strategy. CEOs may look askance at your presence on the company's retirement fund platform when you're suing them, or their accountants, or their bankers.

A second reason relates to how investment analysts employed by mutual funds obtain information. Investment analysts are assigned certain companies to track and analyze, usually by market sector. Mutual fund analysts make buy, sell, and hold recommendations to clients. They are constantly trying to predict what their covered companies' earnings will be in the next quarter. In an ongoing dance that comes perilously close to insider trading but is perfectly legal, these investment analysts want to communicate with company CFOs, to check their information against that of the CFOs, to try to figure out if their predictions for the coming quarter are accurate or not. Suing the company is a great way to get that CFO to stop taking your calls, yet another reason for mutual funds to remain passive in the face of fraud. Social network effects may also contribute to the problem. Mutual fund managers travel in the same social circles as corporate managers; they have often attended the same universities and business schools, and may seek to avoid confrontation for that reason alone. Conversely, union and pension trustees, lacking such social networks, may need to turn to more confrontational, activist methods to attain their aims.[7]

Finally, mutual funds face serious free-rider concerns that keep them on the litigation sidelines. Mutual funds compete with each other. This fact is important when one remembers that most of these lawsuits are brought as class actions on behalf of all investors who were harmed by the misconduct. If a mutual fund steps forward to sue, they incur some of the costs of the litigation.[8] If a mutual fund invests time and money in bringing a lawsuit for fraud, it incurs those costs, but any benefits are shared equally with the rest of the investor class, including competing mutual funds that also were defrauded by the same company. It's the free-rider problem again. So mutual funds are reluctant to step forward to bring suit. They'd rather let someone else do it and passively collect their pro rata share of the class-action settlement.

Hedge funds face similar social network and free-rider constraints, and they have still other reasons to avoid litigation. Hedge funds market themselves to investors by claiming that they will beat the market. They have to perform better than the market; they have to outwit other investors to be worth the additional fees they charge. As I noted in Chapter 3, they rarely succeed in their core mission. When you sue for securities fraud, you have to reveal your ownership stake in the target company, what you bought, and when you bought it, so that the court knows you actually lost money in the fraud and have standing to bring the case.[9] Hedge funds claim to be sensitive about making such disclosures because it might reveal their trading strategies. I think that's largely an excuse. Perhaps disclosure will reveal their lack of trading strategies. But I think the main reason hedge funds stay away from lawsuits is to avoid drawing attention to the fact that they lost a lot of money in a fraud. There's no shame in being defrauded, and hedge funds are genuinely not responsible when they've been lied to. But still, it's hard to look like a Master of the Universe when you loudly proclaim, "I've been robbed!"

The only investors in the marketplace who lack these conflicts of interest are working-class shareholders: public pension and labor union funds. These entities have no business relationships with defendant companies beyond investing in the company. They are not trying to manage the 401(k) money of defendants. They are not trying to get the CFO on the phone to check their numbers. The math teachers, nurses, and police officers, or the state and local politicians who sit on pension boards, rarely travel in the same social circles as corporate CEOs. These funds are also diversified investors, like mutual funds but unlike hedge funds. They have no stake in trying to claim they beat the market; they're only trying to match the market. They claim no genius strategy other than to bet comparatively small amounts on a broad swath of companies, and face no stigma, perceived or otherwise, from bringing suit when they have been lied to. They also don't care about free riders because they don't have true competitors. CalPERS doesn't lose money if it confers a benefit on NYCERS; CalPERS invests for California public employees, NYCERS for New York City employees; these employees can't switch their pension funds back and forth from one to the other, so one fund incurs no risk by conferring a benefit on another. They can work together, or not, without

fear of harming themselves. Finally, there is a public-spirited cul-
ture in these funds that distinguishes them from much of the rest
of the marketplace. When I asked Bobby Deal, a police sergeant,
why he and his fund—a retirement fund for police and firefighters—
sued UnitedHealth over the stock options backdating scandal, he
said, "Half of my guys carry axes and the other half carry guns.
We put bad guys in jail for a living. We are not about to sit back
and let someone steal from our members and the investing public.
We are going to do something about it."[10] And they do.

About 40 percent of all U.S. securities fraud class actions (and
mergers and acquisitions class actions) are brought by public pension funds and labor union funds. The other 60 percent are led by
individual investors. Hardly any other institutions get involved.
Empirical research has shown overwhelmingly that public pension
fund leadership in securities fraud and mergers and acquisitions litigation correlates with better outcomes for shareholders. My own
empirical scholarship has demonstrated this, as has the work of
several others. Public pension funds correlate with both higher
recoveries and lower attorneys' fees in both securities fraud class
actions and deal cases.[11]

On March 29, 2006, eleven days after publication of "The Perfect Payday," the St. Paul Teachers' Retirement Fund Association,
the Public Employees' Retirement System of Mississippi, the Fire
and Police Pension Association of Colorado, the Jacksonville Police and Fire Pension Fund, the Louisiana Municipal Employees'
Retirement System, the Louisiana Sheriffs' Pension and Relief
Fund, the Public Employees' Retirement System of Ohio, the
Connecticut Retirement Plans and Trust Funds, and the Service
Employees International Union Pension Plans Master Trust filed
what's called a "derivative" lawsuit against UnitedHealth and

McGuire.[12] (A derivative suit is a lawsuit where investors step into the shoes of the company to sue the company's management on behalf of the company, since corporate management is highly unlikely to decide to sue itself.) They also sued Stephen Hemsley, the company's chief operating officer and president, who would take over as CEO after McGuire was forced to resign because of the lawsuits; David Lubben, the company's general counsel; two of the company's chief financial officers (who served at different times); and its entire board of directors. Notable among the board members was William Spears, chairman of the Compensation Committee, which oversaw McGuire's compensation.[13] Several months later, CalPERS and other pension funds would step in with a securities fraud class action against the company, a different form of lawsuit than a derivative suit.[14] Predictably, no mutual or hedge funds helped lead either case.

Necessary as it was to find out what happened with McGuire's stock options, these lawsuits were not quests for truth alone. Lawsuits never are. If McGuire and others were backdating their stock options, the money they were pocketing would have come from the company and, by extension, its shareholders. That's why these UnitedHealth investors sued. They were ultimately the ones who would get stuck paying McGuire and others for their seemingly backdated stock options. One final point: just because these derivative and class actions were brought by working-class shareholder institutions does not mean these shareholders would be the only ones to benefit from the suit. All shareholders benefit—all shareholders get their pro rata share of any result. It's just that the investors named above took the lead in bringing the suits.[15]

At the time of these UnitedHealth lawsuits, I was a midlevel, bag-carrying, law firm associate working for one of the firms that represented these shareholders. One of the clients I worked with on the case was the Fire and Police Pension Association of Colorado, whose general counsel, then and now, was Kevin Lindahl. I asked him about his recollections of the case. Lindahl told me that his fund, a classic diversified public pension that owns a broad swathe of the market, had been on the lookout for cases "where policing was needed in the market." "The deeper value of this to me and the board was to send a message that we would defend ourselves against the titans running these corporations," he said. When the fund's outside counsel brought the UnitedHealth case to their attention, Lindahl's reaction, and the reaction inside his fund, was "Are you kidding me? We thought it was shocking that someone could think backdating was ok." So they sued.[16]

Because I worked as a lawyer on this case, I saw many documents produced under a confidentiality agreement, and I was privy to conversations and negotiations that I am barred from disclosing publicly. These documents were reviewed and turned over by the plaintiff pension funds' counsel to the special litigation committee of two judges appointed by UnitedHealth to review the backdating allegations. (The case itself was filed in federal court in Minnesota.) I have limited my entire discussion of this case to information that is in the public record.

Enormous effort went into crafting the allegations in the amended complaint, which spanned seventy-six pages and was filed on September 21, 2006, six weeks before the case settled. Here is a fraction of the allegations detailed in the complaint:

> The [backdating] scheme was implemented by delegating to McGuire unilateral power to choose the dates for his own (and effectively the other Officer Defendants') option grants,

in direct violation of the Company's stock option plans. As set forth more fully below, in violation of state and federal law and the Company's stock option plans, McGuire repeatedly picked the dates of the grants that were the best for him and the other Officer Defendants and the worst for the Company, cheating the Company out of billions of dollars for the benefit of the Officer Defendants. None of these facts were disclosed to UnitedHealth's shareholders so this fraudulent scheme continued for at least nine years.[17]

The complaint also reviewed the timing and amount of numerous stock options grants to McGuire and the other officers. For example, the complaint reported that McGuire was granted 325,000 UnitedHealth stock options on March 8, 2000, with an exercise or base price of $47.63 per share. That date was "the lowest market close for the entire year, and, yet again, at the bottom of a large trough in UnitedHealth's stock price. . . . During the fifteen days preceding the purported grant, UnitedHealth's stock price declined by 20% and during the fifteen days following the purported grant, it increased by 17%."[18]

The complaint detailed the process by which McGuire's stock options grants were awarded. McGuire's 1999 employment agreement with the company, "granted to McGuire the ability to set the dates of his own stock option grants through oral notification to Director Defendant William G. Spears. The Director Defendants also knowingly or recklessly permitted McGuire to abuse his power to set grant dates by allowing McGuire to fraudulently backdate the option grants." The complaint similarly made the following allegation about Spears, the chairman of the Compensation Committee: "Assets of McGuire's family foundation are also managed by the New York firm Spears Grisanti & Brown LLC, of which Director Defendant Spears is a Senior Principal, and to which the foundation pays significant fees."[19] In other words, Spears—who as compensation committee chairman set McGuire's pay and was the only person from whom McGuire needed approval to set the grant dates for his stock options—was simultaneously managing McGuire's family money. Spot the conflict of interest if you can find it.

According to the complaint, the conduct of McGuire, Spears, and the other director defendants violated the company's own stock options policies, which required the option price not to be less than the closing price on the date of the grant.[20] These are the provisions that were designed to prevent the company from granting, say, a stock option with a strike price of $20 on a date when UnitedHealth stock traded at $25, never mind backdating the stock options to accomplish the same objective.

The UnitedHealth stock options backdating case settled on December 6, 2007, less than twenty-one months after it was filed, which is lightning speed in the world of securities fraud litigation.[21]

As is standard, UnitedHealth, McGuire, and the other defendants settled the claims against them without admitting or denying wrongdoing. But McGuire paid the highest sum ever by any individual in a derivative or securities fraud lawsuit up to that time—over $615 million—and the second highest sum ever paid by an individual in civil litigation of any kind. Only billionaire international arms trader Adnan Khashoggi paid more to settle a case, to his ex-wife over their divorce. Chief Operating Office Stephen Hemsley, who had similarly received backdated stock options, paid $240 million; David Lubben, the general counsel, paid $30 million; and the remaining officer defendants paid another $35 million combined.[22] Consider the size of these settlements and then draw your own conclusions about the merits of the allegations in the complaint.

Despite the record-setting damages, the settlement didn't stop there. As is almost always the case, the pension funds and labor union funds remained invested in the defendant company even after the fraud was committed. As diversified investors, that makes sense. Dropping a major health insurance company from your portfolio only complicates your ability to remain properly exposed to, in this instance, the health insurance business. Moreover, selling your stake in protest can be a pointless gesture. The fraud has already been exposed, and the harm to shareholders incurred. Large pension funds run the risk of hurting themselves by exiting. Their ownership stakes may be large enough that if they sell, it would put even more downward pressure on the stock price, inflicting further losses on the funds on the way out the door.

This point, about the potential costs of exit, is extremely important in understanding why the interests of large, diversified investors like working-class shareholder institutions are so well-aligned with the long-term growth of the market overall. It used to be that shareholders who were unhappy with corporate performance, ranging from incompetence to fraud, would take the "Wall Street Walk," that is, sell their stakes. The threat of the walk, and the downward pressure that could put on stock prices, was supposed to be enough to discipline management. But diversified investors can't easily do the Wall Street Walk for the reasons just described: it may undermine their diversification and can cause them harm as they disinvest. The funds remain locked into their investments. Therefore, an alternative strategy is to turn to activism, to hold companies accountable, to transform them from within through many of the tools described in earlier chapters, and through litigation.

This explains why the pension and labor union fund clients insisted that any settlement be accompanied by corporate governance reforms designed to avoid the toxic governance breakdowns that allowed the malfeasance in the first place. Working with expert Lucian Bebchuk, these funds and the legal team devised a proposed set of comprehensive corporate governance reforms to be adopted as part of the settlement. These reforms were substantially adopted and altered the internal functioning of United-Health for the better. They included separating the role of CEO and chair and making the chair independent, empowering shareholders who owned 3 percent of the company for three years to nominate a director (almost a decade before proxy access became widespread), enhancing the company's standards for who is considered an independent director, altering the executive compensation rules, limiting board member service to no more than four other corporate boards, requiring directors to attend shareholder meetings, and requiring executives to retain at least one-third of their share in the company upon vesting. The company also adopted a policy forbidding "related-person" transactions unless they are approved by the Audit Committee. Such transactions refer to business dealings between the company and company leaders like board members, executive officers, significant shareholders, or their immediate families.[23] The company also adopted a clawback policy that allowed it to recover cash and equity awards given to senior executives "in the event of fraud."[24] In short, the case led not only to substantial investor recovery and one of the largest individual payments ever made in civil litigation but also fundamentally transformed the internal governance of UnitedHealth in ways designed to reduce the risk of future fraud. Since the case was settled and the reforms adopted, UnitedHealth has not been sued by either the SEC or its investors.

The UnitedHealth case might never have happened absent the *Wall Street Journal*'s "Perfect Payday" article, but its coverage of the settlement omitted mention of the role played by the public pension funds that brought suit. Its sub-headline announced, "UnitedHealth, SEC Settle with McGuire on Options Backdating." It incorrectly gave most of the credit to the SEC. The SEC did indeed deserve credit for a $7 million fine it imposed on McGuire, and for banning him from serving as an officer or director of a public company for ten years. But the SEC played little or no role in the massive settlement of the derivative action. The newspaper's coverage made no mention of the pension funds, or their lawyers, who brought that action, only referencing in passing that "shareholder representatives" approved the settlement. In contrast, the *New York Times* noted the role of the pension funds and their lawyers.[25]

Given the positive role played by public pension funds in shareholder litigation, backed up by several empirical studies, it is clear that enforcement of our securities laws would be seriously undermined if these funds disappeared, or if their ability to act in the face of fraud were hampered.

History is constantly repeating itself when it comes to securities fraud. In 2016, the Consumer Financial Protection Bureau (CFPB)—the brainchild of Senator Elizabeth Warren, created by Dodd-Frank and ably led by Richard Cordray—announced that it was fining the Wells Fargo bank $185 million. The CFPB, the

Los Angeles City Attorney, and the Office of the Comptroller of the Currency alleged that Wells Fargo had opened or applied for more than 2 million credit card or bank accounts between May 2011 and July 2015 without their customers' knowledge or permission. The Wells Fargo scandal led to a massive $22.5 billion loss for the company's shareholders. Following the historical pattern, hedge funds and mutual funds took no legal action against Wells Fargo despite the clear harm they suffered. But there is one investor lawsuit against the company, co-led by the Colorado Fire and Police Pension Association, under the auspices of its general counsel, Kevin Lindahl. As of this writing, the suit is making its way through the court system.[26]

7

The Law of Fiduciary Duty and the Risk of Capture

In Whose Interests Should We Invest?

For twenty-two years, Rick Thorne worked as a custodian in the Chelmsford, Massachusetts, public schools. He earned twenty dollars an hour and made payments every other week to his local public employee pension fund. In December 2007, a statewide investment trust invested Massachusetts public employee retirement funds, including those of Thorne and his colleagues, in a company called Aramark Corporation. Aramark is a facility management and food-service company that competes with public employee unions to win contracts from states and cities to service public entities like prisons and public schools.[1] Aramark, which was owned by a private equity pool invested in by the Massachusetts trust, then underbid Thorne's custodians' union for the Chelmsford schools contract. The company offered to retain Thorne and his fellow custodians if they would accept a 56 percent salary cut to $8.75 an hour. Thorne declined the offer and spent the next year and a half looking for another job. Put simply, Thorne's own retirement funds were used to invest him out of a job. Once let go, he ceased contributing to the fund. Because his career was cut short, he wound up collecting a reduced pension from his local pension fund.[2]

Thorne's plight is not a solitary one. The Teachers' Retirement System of Louisiana also invested in Aramark. In the aftermath of Hurricane Katrina, the company was hired to run schools in New Orleans. It cut pay for fund participants like Carol Sanders, who had worked as a cook for Orleans Parish since 1982. Before the Aramark contract, Sanders earned fifteen dollars an hour plus benefits. Aramark cut her time in half, assigned her to excruciatingly inconvenient split shifts, and reduced her pay to nine dollars an hour. Sanders "went without medical insurance and began drawing $200 a week in food stamps." Eventually, she was fired. According to Phil Griffith, executive director of Louisiana Teachers, in weighing an investment like the fund's in Aramark:

> We take a kind of hands-off approach, which is from a fiduciary responsibility. . . . We manage [the fund] for return and for our own constituents. We don't get into, 'Does that mean it lays off public workers?' The only thing we look at is the security of the trust, not whether or not it creates jobs or takes away jobs, whether it be public employees in Louisiana or public employees throughout the country. . . . Our responsibility is to the trust.[3]

What Griffith is really talking about is called "the duty of loyalty," one of the core trust law duties. The duty of loyalty requires trustees to prioritize the interests of their charges above all other concerns, including their own interests and those of third parties. The question here is whether the duty of loyalty means that trustees must maximize returns to the fund, or whether it means they should also directly consider the welfare of the workers who contribute to it. It's a narrow legal question with profound real-world consequences. Griffith was expressing one widely shared view that the duty of loyalty did not run to the workers themselves, that it did not include consideration of whether the funds' investments hurt their jobs, and did not even include whether the fund itself might be hurt by loss of contributions from those workers. That view of fiduciary duty has a number of implications.

First, if Louisiana Teachers had screened out the Aramark investment because of its potential to negatively impact the jobs of fund participants, that would have breached this interpretation of the duty of loyalty, because it would have favored Louisiana Teachers' contributors' jobs over fund returns. Second, if Louisiana Teachers divested from Aramark in favor of a slightly less profitable investment that had no negative impact on participant jobs, that would also have been a breach in this view because the first investment was better for the fund. Third, if Louisiana Teachers had negotiated to protect their participants' jobs at some cost to returns, that too would have been a breach of Griffith's idea of fiduciary duty. That would be true even if it would have improved the investment's net economic benefit to fund participants and beneficiaries, because it would have reduced returns to the fund.[4] But each of these violates the goal I set out at the beginning of the book: that pensions should assess the effects of their investments on their workers, including their jobs. It is an errant view of fiduciary duty that locks labor into using its investment power to undermine its worker interests and overall economic interests.

The law can reasonably be interpreted to accommodate the consideration of worker jobs in making investments, whether it be avoiding job losses or creating job gains. To my mind, this is not just the correct understanding of the law but the right policy choice. And I argue that purely moral considerations may lawfully be taken into account, particularly if given cover under state law.

Pension Fund Investments and the Duty of Loyalty

This next section is addressed particularly to shareholder activists, lawyers, judges, and policymakers working in the field. The take-home message is that the law can reasonably be interpreted as accommodating the consideration of worker jobs in making investments, whether it be avoiding job losses or creating job gains. That view stands in contrast to an interpretation of the law that these funds must maximize returns at the expense of all other considerations.

The starting place for legal analysis of the fiduciary duties of pension trustees is the Employee Retirement Income Security Act (ERISA) of 1974. ERISA is derived from trust law, which in some respects is a shame. Legal duties under trust law tend to be more narrow than the same duties under its cousin, corporate law, which is often more flexible and permissive. Today, pension funds have become so vast and complex that, in many respects, the more lenient duties of corporate law would be more appropriate. Regardless, ERISA relies on the traditional trust law duty of loyalty. The duty of loyalty under both trust law and corporate law requires trustees or fiduciaries to manage a trust in the interests of its beneficiaries, not in their own interests or that of third parties. Let's start with the text of ERISA. It states, "A fiduciary shall discharge his [or her] duties with respect to a [pension or retirement] plan solely in the interest of the participants and beneficiaries and—(A) for the exclusive purpose of: (i) providing benefits to participants and their beneficiaries; and (ii) defraying reasonable expenses of administering the plan."[5] Read that again. In 2008, the Bush Department of Labor (DOL) issued guidance for interpreting this language. It said that this language means that "in the course of discharging their duties, fiduciaries may never subordinate the economic interests *of the plan* to unrelated objectives, and may not select investments on the basis of any factor outside the economic interest of *the plan* except in very limited circumstances."[6] Where this Bush DOL guidance leads us is to what I call the "returns-only" view of fiduciary duty, the one expressed by Griffith, a view that I think is wrong.

The first thing to observe about this interpretation from the Bush DOL is that it effectively reads "participants and beneficiaries" out of the statute, substituting the word "plan." That's a subtle chess move that has significant consequences. Once you've made that substitution, you're a half step from arriving at the returns-only view of fiduciary duty. The next step is for proponents of that view to hang their interpretation on the language "for the exclusive purpose of providing benefits." These proponents argue that if the exclusive purpose of these investments is to provide benefits, then fiduciaries must maximize the value of the plan's investments without regard to considerations like jobs and fund contributions, which are "outside the economic interest of the plan." According to their view, for the Massachusetts pension funds to reject the investment in Aramark because of the potential impact on Thorne and his fellow custodians, or for it to even *consider* that impact, would be to "subordinate the economic interests of the plan to unrelated objectives, and . . . [to] select investments on the basis of [a] factor outside the economic interest of the plan."[7] That is a bizarre jump, because it's easy to argue that worker contributions, and employer contributions, are within the interests of the plan. But the jobs consideration is often dismissed, as it was by Louisiana Teachers' Phil Griffith, and as it has been in certain academic treatments.[8] Frequently it is simply rejected as a collateral social consideration rather than a core economic one.[9] It may also be dismissed under the mistaken belief that the job loss is a wash: when a worker loses her job, the loss of her and her employer's contributions to the fund is offset by lower liabilities to that worker. This is not correct, and neither is the "returns-only" view of ERISA.

First, as noted, the actual words of the statute say that trustees must invest "solely in the interests of participants and beneficiaries"—in the *workers'* interests, not the interests of the *plan*. These interests are often but not always the same. See Rick Thorne. If Congress meant in the interests of the plan, it could have used that word, as it did in the second clause, "defraying reasonable expenses of the plan."[10] It is a leap to say that because trustees must defray reasonable plan expenses, they must also maximize returns to the plan even if so doing harms participants and beneficiaries, precisely the people the statute is designed to protect. Likewise, the phrase "for the exclusive purpose of providing benefits" does not mean considering "returns only" or even the "plan only" to the exclusion of other imperatives. Again, consider Rick Thorne. What happened to his benefits when he lost his job? They were reduced. One can hardly describe that as "providing benefits." And not only were Thorne's benefits reduced but so were his contributions to the pension plan. That is because the jobs of public pension fund participants are inextricably linked to their pensions. Typically, a worker's pension is a direct function of her job title and length of service. Workers also make contributions to pension plans that are proportional to their compensation. For fund fiduciaries to consider the impact of the funds' investments on its workers' jobs is entirely consistent with making investments "for the exclusive purpose of providing benefits." Funds cannot provide the same level of benefits to workers who have lost their jobs, and those workers also contribute financially to the plan, a source of income that is separate from investment performance.[11]

This should mean, at the extremes, that a fund could select a less-profitable investment that has no negative jobs impact over a more profitable one with a negative jobs impact, as long as the trustees reasonably believe that the avoidance of job losses and therefore maintenance of worker contributions can outweigh the profit reduction. And it also means that funds should be able to make less-profitable investments that create jobs for people who will pay into the fund, as long as the trustees credibly conclude that there is a reasonable chance that the benefits in the form of jobs or increased contributions would outweigh the reduced profits and increased liabilities. This is especially true because pensions have bulges or bottlenecks of retirees who may occasionally require contributions from younger members to shore up the fund's ability to pay benefits to those retirees.[12] That is why it is incorrect to conclude that any drop in contributions from job loss cannot hurt the fund because of offsetting liability reductions. It can. Moreover, these decisions need not take place on an unwieldy, investment-by-investment basis. They may instead form the basis for investment policies adopted by the funds. Some funds might rationally conclude that investments that kill public-sector jobs are simply never worth the economic tradeoff, in the near or long term.

I am not suggesting that funds should always prioritize employment and contributions over returns. Sometimes, loss of jobs can hurt the fund through loss of contributions. Other times it might help because of loss of liabilities. But the point is, as a trustee, you have to look before you invest. The impact of fund investments on jobs and contributions to the fund is effectively ignored under a maximize-returns view, and it should not be. Also, under the same reasoning and perhaps of most significance in the real world, pensions should be able to make investments and then use their investment power to enhance the jobs and job security of workers, even if that means some reduction in returns, as long as the net economic benefit is higher.

Setting aside "plain language" arguments, two courts have rejected the "returns-only" view of fiduciary duty.[13] In fact, these courts have implicitly embraced a "worker first" view of fiduciary duty that allows trustees to consider economic benefits to workers directly, not just to their pensions, whether it be via returns or contributions from jobs. In *Brock v. Walton,* the U.S. Department of Labor sued the Operating Engineers Local 675 Pension Fund for offering below-market-rate home loans to workers who contributed to the fund. The DOL argued that this breached the duty of loyalty to the fund. By offering below-market-rate loans to its members, the fund was accepting lower returns on investment in exchange for a purportedly extraneous benefit, in this instance, greater home affordability for fund contributors.[14] Instead, the pension fund should have offered these loans at market rate, to its contributors or to anyone else. The U.S. Court of Appeals for the

Eleventh Circuit rejected the DOL's argument, finding no breach of the duty of loyalty. In so doing, it declined to find that the home loan program constituted a per se breach of duty just because it failed to maximize returns. Instead, the court focused its analysis on the board's comprehensive deliberation. That is a classic way to analyze fiduciary duties, focusing on process, not outcomes.

Similarly, in *Bandt v. San Diego County,* San Diego County requested that the trustees of San Diego's public employees' pension fund agree to a new pension calculation formula that would reduce San Diego's required contributions to the fund.[15] If the trustees failed to agree, the county would fire workers. The trustees agreed to the new formula, a decision that harmed the fund by reducing employer contributions. The trustees were sued by two pension contributors claiming that the trustees breached their duty of loyalty by acting to benefit workers at the expense of the fund. The court rejected that argument, ruling in favor of the trustees. Both *Brock v Walton* and *Bandt v. San Diego County* support the argument that the law does not command trustees to ignore other economic benefits in favor of an exclusive focus on the fund.

I do not mean to suggest that the weight of case law favors this broad interpretation of fiduciary duty. There are cases that come out the other way.[16] My point is that there is enough flexibility in the law to permit the interpretation I advocate. Trustee discretion is broader under my view than under the maximize returns view but is still constrained by the command to invest "for the exclusive purpose of providing benefits." My view would have allowed the Massachusetts or Louisiana funds to consider avoiding the Aramark investment by directly weighing its potentially negative jobs impact, doing so "for the exclusive purpose of providing benefits." The pension funds also need not have waited until Aramark was actually taking their own workers' jobs to do so. I am not arguing that investing in, screening out, or divesting from Aramark would be required, simply that it is allowed.

It may sound like there is little at stake in these legal niceties, but they are enormously consequential, and likely to become massively more so should a large-scale infrastructure investment plan emerge under the current or a future presidential administration, or from privately financed sources, or both. At stake is the question of whether pension funds investing in infrastructure may also pursue the hiring of union labor, or the payment of prevailing wages to the workers on those projects. A narrow returns-only advocate would say no or would at least argue that prioritizing labor would have to be justified in purely investment terms. I would say yes. Under my approach, labor would have massive leverage using its pensions to its advantage in hiring and future pension contributions. That leverage could administer an adrenaline shot to the working class that could keep it off life support and send it back into the political arena in the twenty-first century.

Several public pension funds have already adopted policies either outright banning investments in privatization of public services or requiring that such investments maximally protect the jobs of public workers, more or less along the lines I describe. Not surprisingly, New York City's is among the boldest: "The System will not entertain proposals that have the potential of eliminating public sector jobs." Note that's not just the funds' own contributors' jobs but all public-sector jobs. Other funds are less decisive but at least address the concern. For example, the Ohio Public Employees' Retirement System (OPERS) has adopted the following investment policy:

OPERS does not aim to promote privatization of public sector jobs through its Private Equity investment program. It is highly unlikely that OPERS Private Equity investments would be dependent on privatization strategies. In evaluating private equity Investments, the Staff shall use its best efforts to limit circumstances where privatization may have an adverse actuarial impact on OPERS. If such limitation is not possible, the Staff shall seek guidance from the Board before proceeding.[17]

The California State Teachers' Retirement System (CalSTRS) has a similar policy that it applies to "public-private partnerships" or to bidding on "public offers for the sale, lease or management of public assets." The policy states that when entering into such arrangements, the fund's investment staff must obtain a written commitment from the investee, typically a private equity fund, that "the investment vehicle shall make every good faith effort to recognize the important role and contribution of public employees to the development and operation of such assets." In so doing, "the investment vehicle shall make good faith efforts to ensure that such transactions have a de minimis adverse impact on existing jobs."[18] CalPERS has a similar policy.[19] Smart pension funds have become sophisticated about using their shareholder power to negotiate separate deals with private equity funds that require private equity to protect worker jobs or to use union labor for everything from constructing new buildings to sending their mail via unionized UPS instead of FedEx.

But other pension funds have used the returns-only rationale to ignore these investment conflicts, claiming that it is illegal for them to consider potentially negative investment impacts on their own workers' jobs. Worse yet, some pension funds appear to have been forced into such investments by hostile politicians. For example, after teachers' unions in Florida opposed the reelection of Governor Jeb Bush in 2004, a victorious Bush turned around and invested teacher retirement money in Edison Schools, a private company that replaces public-sector school employees. Under the returns-only view of the law, there was little to constrain Bush and the Florida State Board of Investment from buying Edison. This investment also demonstrates the weaknesses of the "investments of equal value rule." That rule allows trustees to select one investment over another for any reason, as long as the choice is between two investments of equal value. Such a rule gives labor some sway over even profitable hedge funds that do other things to harm workers. But the same rule allows a hostile pension actor to select an investment of equal value *because* it harms workers.

The view of the law that purportedly requires pension trustees to ignore the negative jobs impact of pension investments reached its apex in the DOL interpretive bulletin issued under President George W. Bush. That guidance was eventually rescinded by President Barack Obama's Department of Labor in November 2015. The new guidance reinstated a more flexible interpretation instituted in 1994 during the Clinton administration, when Robert Reich was secretary of labor.[20] The old-and-now-new-again interpretation is more flexible in letting fund fiduciaries consider environmental, social, and governance factors in making investments, including worker jobs. As this book goes to print, it is still not clear what, if anything, Donald Trump's Department of Labor might do with this issue. Lobbyists will likely push to reinstate the Bush view.

There is one final legal wrinkle to this debate. ERISA does not actually apply to the public pension funds whose activism is described in much of this book. ERISA only covers private pensions like labor union funds, not state and local public pension funds like CalPERS, CalSTRS, NYCERS, and all the rest.[21] That's because these pension funds are created by states and cities—not the federal government—and therefore are governed by state, not federal, law. What the Bush, Obama, or Trump Labor Departments have to say about their fiduciary duties under ERISA—or almost anything else—is not binding on these funds, because they are not bound by ERISA.

So why spend several pages discussing it? Because most state pension codes have the same or similar fiduciary language as ERISA. There are fifty separate state pension codes, and each of those states' courts and attorneys general can make up their own minds about what that language means, even if the language is identical to or varies just slightly from that of other states or federal law. But ERISA interpretations issued by the DOL are influential in an informal way, because many pension lawyers think of ERISA as "best practices." Lawyers advise their clients to do what ERISA says, which often means whatever the current administration says ERISA says.[22] There also has been relatively little litigation over these issues, and consequently, few legal opinions by which to guide judges and lawyers in making decisions, leaving discussions of ERISA to fill the void.[23] The meaning of these fiduciary duties can and has been captured, and recaptured, and will likely remain a political football for some time.

Harkening back to Chapter 1, Safeway implicitly accused Sean Harrigan of violating the returns-only view of fiduciary duty. It implied that he was breaching his duty to CalPERS by steering the fund into a fight with Safeway to support Safeway's workers, rather than to maximize returns to CalPERS's investment in Safeway. I suspect that this is why Harrigan retreated to the background in the Safeway shareholder campaign and was coy about it afterward. Because he had been involved with the strike, his overt participation in the shareholder campaign might strengthen Safeway's argument that he was breaching his duties to CalPERS by having it fight on behalf of Safeway's workers instead of maximizing returns. That is also why CalPERS and other pensions depicted their actions against Burd as being focused on Safeway's management and performance, which were, after all, inseparable from what led the company to cut its workers' benefits. Basically, the law punishes you if you frame your conduct as benefiting workers, and rewards you if you frame it as benefiting shareholders. For workers, these interests are not mutually exclusive. In our current system, you are always on stronger legal ground when you can find an investment rationale for your conduct. Whenever there is a significant labor issue at a company, there will inevitably be a significant investment issue too. So it's wiser to couch it as an investment issue.

Of course, the campaign against Safeway was entirely defensible even under the returns-only view, on account of Safeway's deeply flawed governance and company performance. The same might not be true of Aramark. The company might have performed quite well as an investment, while directly undermining the economic well-being of its worker-investors. That is the context in which "worker-centric" becomes essential.

The legal question of whether pension funds can consider other factors in making investments is separate from the question of whether it should do so, as a matter of policy. There are more than four thousand public pension funds in the United States. Whether to pursue one course or the other necessarily depends on the specific circumstances of particular funds, which invest the savings of different types of workers, in different jurisdictions, facing different funding statuses, and governed by fifty different state pension codes. Returns only versus worker-centric may not have a one-size-fits-all solution. There is still much more that can be done to advance the interests of workers even entirely within the returns-only framework, from cutting fees to maintaining value-enhancing shareholder activism to considering jobs and pension security, even if just as a collateral benefit. I briefly outline here some of the policy tradeoffs between these two approaches.

Returns-only advocates argue that maximizing returns to the fund is not just the law, it's the right policy choice, the right thing to do even from the perspective of workers. For one thing, it lets you judge fund investment performance objectively, enabling cross-firm comparisons of performance. And there are legitimate concerns about trustees being given too much leeway to invest funds in their favored projects, or to support pet political causes, deviating from their primary goal: to fund the retirement of the workers who contribute to them.[24] In the very worst-case scenario, deviating from maximizing returns could mean a fund winds up not just with lower returns but with insufficient offsetting economic benefits in the form of jobs and contributions, accelerating the downward spiral for workers. There is evidence of similar investments having gone awry. For example, some state pensions have been required to prioritize in-state investments over return-maximizing investments. Some research suggests that these have not performed well, though as always, the studies only look at the investment returns on such investments and do not examine other economic benefits to investors, thereby rendering them only marginally relevant to this debate. And there is a significant difference between requiring investments to benefit your state and requiring them to benefit your own members in a form other than just returns.

Going further, some returns-only advocates argue that these investments by public pensions in companies that privatize public worker jobs are actually in the interests of workers, as a hedge. The theory is that public-sector jobs may be doomed anyway, and therefore, their retirement funds ought to make a profit on their own demise.

All of this leaves us with an argument about which approach leaves workers better off. Even the fundamental terms of the debate are not as clear as they might seem. There is substantial evidence that policies to maximize returns do not always in fact maximize returns. That evidence shows that investment portfolios filtered through an environmental, social, and governance (ESG) lens outperform portfolios striving to maximize returns with no filters.[25] Examples of ESG investments include screening for reductions in greenhouse gas emissions, using fair labor practices in the supply chain, or pursuing proxy access. Of course, there is also evidence that cuts against the idea that ESG investments outperform.[26] But the evidence favoring such portfolios on purely investment grounds is broad and deep and cannot be completely dismissed.

At first blush, the results are counterintuitive. Why would investments that value ESG factors have better outcomes than ones just looking for the highest returns? For one, companies that institute ESG-friendly policies may attract more consumers, increasing sales.[27] They also may attract more investors, lowering the cost of capital.[28] The "G" in ESG, like proxy access, majority voting, destaggered boards, and splitting the role of CEO and chair, could perhaps decrease business and legal risks or improve accountability. Investors focused on ESG may perceive real risks ahead of the rest of the marketplace, like the investment risks of climate change or reputational risks like harm to a corporate brand because of business practices that violate human rights.[29] A worker-centric approach may match or outperform maximize returns portfolios for similar reasons. But I do not base my argument for worker-centric on the claim of higher returns.

I favor the worker-centric approach based on several distinct, but related, intuitions. The first is that, all things being equal, one should expect better outcomes from directly accountable agents than from indirectly accountable agents. The second is that participant and beneficiary board members and unions have a better grasp of the jobs and benefits impact of investments than investment managers do. That not only affects employment but fund contributions. The third intuition is based on the well-worn cliché that we manage what we measure. In my view, the worker-centric approach is stronger than the maximize returns approach under each of these criteria. I should also note that there will be many instances in which both methods will lead to the same outcome, especially in situations where the investment has no direct job implications, which is often. Where the difference really matters is in managing the threat of privatization or making investments that create worker jobs.

One effect of favoring worker-centric over returns only is that it empowers trustees over investment managers in deciding the fate of pension funds. Returns only effectively empowers Wall Street to decide the fate of pensions. If the stated goal of the funds is to prioritize returns, that automatically favors the expertise of, and decision making by, investment managers, who focus exclusively on, and calculate, risk and returns. They are ranked annually and quarterly on the basis of returns, and funds flow in and out of their portfolios based on those rankings. If they were to make 10 percent on an investment instead of 11 percent, they would get paid less, even if the 10 percent investment spared fund participant jobs or created new ones. Because portfolio managers are compensated primarily on returns and assets under management, they are frequently blind to the actual economic impact of their investments on their investors beyond those metrics. This explains why pension funds wind up in investments that kill their own workers' jobs. Trustees may not even be aware of it until they receive an outraged call from a plan participant. Under returns only, the issue is legally invisible. And because investment managers are compensated on fund performance, they prefer a fund-first legal regime. Public pension fund trustees have repeatedly told me that when they have tried to raise the jobs issue with investment managers, they are told by those managers—and often by their own legal counsel—that even to raise the jobs issue is a breach of fiduciary duty, and that it would be a breach of duty for these investment managers to take jobs concerns into account. This may help explain why the Bush DOL embraced returns only. Did Bush's DOL advocate that approach because it really believed this was in the interests of workers? Or was it rather that it was in the interests of a traditional Republican constituency, investment managers?

A broader view of fiduciary duty empowers pension fund trustees to consider how these investments actually impact their worker-contributors, not just what investment managers want them to focus on. Trustees are the ones directly accountable to fund participants. They can shift the focus to the actual interests of their participants and beneficiaries by devising investment policies that must be adopted by investment managers, like the privatization policies of the NYC funds, OPERS, and CalPERS. That makes trustees, not investment managers, the center of the investment calculus.

As noted, pension trustees are a combination of elected officials and fund participants and beneficiaries elected by their peers to the board of trustees. Often, unions have great say in how these latter trustees end up on the board. Overall, both sets of trustees, particularly ones who are themselves fund participants elected by their peers, are more accountable to fund participants than Wall Street investment managers over whom fund participants have only indirect influence. Plan participants unhappy with their trustees can vote them out in the next election.

Moreover, unions are better placed than investment managers to understand the jobs impact of investment projects. They have a better grasp of compensation, labor standards, and the work that is required from particular projects. They also have more experience than investment managers on the benefits side of the equation, such as how benefits are distributed to members, in what quantities, and for what reasons. Thus, the worker-first approach shifts the locus of investment decision making from investment managers to trustees.

My third intuition favoring a broader economic view than maximizing returns is based on the well-worn market cliché that we manage what we measure. If pension funds and labor union funds do not have a way of measuring and accounting for the jobs impact of investments, then no one in the market will. Corporations, hedge funds, and private equity funds analyze the question from the perspective of investment returns and do not incur the costs of reductions in jobs and pay. If anything, they often benefit from such losses. If pension funds can't consider the jobs issue directly in their investment portfolios, then the jobs calculation disappears entirely from investment consideration. Arguably, that is exactly what has happened in America in the last forty years. Markets are blind enough to this issue as it is. But if there is a market player such as these labor's capital institutions making investment calculations incorporating some assessment of their participants' jobs and fund contributions, then the marketplace begins to consider these jobs. Investment managers interested in managing the capital of these pensions will have incentives to create investment products and strategies that reflect these interests. Some unions have created their own investment managers for precisely these reasons.

That leads to another argument, the "hedge" argument that says public workers are dead anyway so they might as well profit from their own demise. First, there is a good argument that these investments aren't just a hedge. As noted, public pensions account for between one-third and just under one-half of all private equity assets under management.[30] If tomorrow they all adopted policies severely limiting investments in privatization the way the NYC funds or OPERS did, they could seriously undermine, if not eliminate, private equity privatization of public services. In other words, privatization is not inevitable and might be undermined if pensions stopped participating in it. Second, the worker-first view would still permit these investments, as long as trustees had good reason to believe that the investment returns were so strong that their workers would be better off making them, even at the risk of their own jobs. I am skeptical about such a calculation but concede it is possible. There are many good reasons to shun privatization. It's not necessarily a binary choice, to either invest in privatization or boycott it. Under a more flexible legal interpretation, one implicitly adopted by many funds already, workers could shape privatization in their own interests, for example, by having these funds hire union labor or create jobs for their members, or otherwise aid the public sector.

Finally, there remains the possibility raised in the first chapter, which is to treat labor issues as a moral trump card outside the economic calculus, as some European funds do. To the extent this presents a legal conflict with American fiduciary duties—particularly under a returns-only view—that legal question gets resolved by blending the moral motive with a business one, as CalSTRS did with its gun divestment. The legal issue can also be resolved by the state and local sponsors of pensions explicitly authorizing or even commanding consideration of labor issues, as many states and municipalities did with apartheid divestment in the 1980s and 1990s, and as many states have done again today, counterboycotting Israel boycotters.[31] That kind of legal pronouncement from a governor or a state legislature removes the issue from fiduciary consideration. I am sympathetic to the prioritization of labor issues in this way. But it also must be noted that so doing opens the door to all sorts of controversial political and moral issues that may have little to do with the economic security of workers, itself a crucial moral and political issue, especially for pension funds that invest these workers' retirement savings. In the U.S. context, widespread implementation of an economically holistic worker-centric view would itself be such a significant advance that, if nothing else, I would start there first as a matter of tactics.

Where Working-Class Shareholder Power Lives

The fact that ERISA is influential but does not actually control public pension funds is consequential for one overriding reason: the highest concentration of public pension fund assets is in Democratic states and cities with strong public sectors and comparatively sympathetic political leadership and courts. That provides some insulation for these funds from whoever happens to control Washington.

The largest U.S. public pension funds are among the largest funds of any kind in the world. In size order, they include, among the top fifty worldwide, CalPERS, CalSTRS, the New York State Common Fund, the New York City Employees Retirement System, the Florida State Board of Administration, the Texas Teachers Retirement System, the New York State Teachers Retirement System, the State of Wisconsin Investment Board, the North Carolina Retirement Systems, the Ohio Public Employees Retirement System, the University of California Retirement System, the Oregon Public Employees Retirement Fund, the State Teachers Retirement System of Ohio, the Minnesota State Retirement System, and the Michigan Retirement System. The California and New York funds alone oversee close to $1 trillion in pension assets.[32] Almost by itself, their engagement can sustain the shareholder activism described in this book. They are not going to listen to interpretations of their pension codes if they perceive them to come from a hostile Department of Labor in Washington. And note that, among the pensions in so-called purple or red states, they are disproportionately teacher funds, which may tend to be more politically liberal than the states they reside in, as is true of public employees generally.

Other massive pension funds include the Massachusetts Pension Reserves Investment Management Board (which invested in Aramark), Pennsylvania School Employees (still blue though Pennsylvania voted for Trump), the Los Angeles County Employee Retirement Administration, Colorado Public Employees Retirement Association, Maryland, Illinois Teachers, and the Missouri Schools. If you add the Los Angeles fund to the California / New York tally above, you have well in excess of $1 trillion from those two states alone. Note who is not on this list: smaller, red, anti-union "right to work" states that have maximally whittled down their public sectors. As a result of the so-called right to work, these states have surrendered the field of shareholder activism to larger, more liberal states with large public sectors. From the perspective of markets, these right-to-work red states are irrelevant, a collective rounding error. They have just the amount of clout they've paid for. Contrast that with smaller blue states like Colorado, Massachusetts, Maryland, and Oregon, which have robust public sectors and substantial pensions that give them outsized say with investees. The same trend is discernible in comparing large states like New York and Texas. Texas has a larger population, but New York's pensions trounce Texas's.[33] New York is a far more significant shareholder.

The concentration of pension power in blue states, and the fact that they are governed by state law, makes it relatively challenging for any administration in Washington to rein in the power of these pension funds, short of nationalizing them—an extreme step that is risky and likely unconstitutional. Federal politicians might also try to rein in these funds with aggressive use of antitrust law, which may have constitutional problems, and even if it were deployed by a hostile administration to reduce coordination of activity among funds, would still be relatively limited in its ability to undermine shareholder activism generally. Undoubtedly, the SEC could try to limit certain investor rights, though it is relatively limited in what it can do absent new legislation, and much of what it can do on its own, it can reverse when the political winds change. Overall, when it comes to these funds, what happens in Albany and Sacramento may matter more than what happens in Washington. But that does not mean that these blue-state pension funds are safe. They remain vulnerable to the Koch brothers, Charles and David, billionaire oil magnates who have funded a wide array of libertarian causes in the United States, and their allies. Together they have directly targeted many of the pension funds identified in this book, as detailed in its final chapter.

The fateful question then becomes who controls these pension funds and how they can be moved in one direction or another. Will private equity funds and other investees continue to take public pension money and invest it against public workers' own interests? Or will pension funds gain the upper hand, using their investment power to force concessions that shape these investments in their workers' interests? How should these funds navigate the tension between boycotting investments, and thereby possibly undermining them, and losing the ability to shape them? To what extent can funds deploy their investment power to create jobs for their own workers? We have already seen how some leaders like New York City comptroller Scott Stringer have answered such questions. Where will everyone else fall on the spectrum? And perhaps of greatest consequence in the near term, how will these struggles play out in the potentially trillion-dollar infrastructure program advocated by the Trump administration and backed by Democrats in Congress, possibly over Republican objections? How will these funds affect whether, and to what extent, pensions should invest in the massive infrastructure spending plan that President Trump promised during his campaign and that has already been embraced by Senate Democrats, whether it manifests now or under a future administration?[34] Or even just massive private infrastructure spending absent a significant Washington plan, which is already under way? It's not hyperbole: the fate of trillions of dollars in assets, entire industries, and millions of jobs are at stake in these questions.

One aspect of resolving them is the debate just covered, the struggle over the definition of the fiduciary duty of pension trustees. Another has to do with a related organizing drive that is as consequential as any in recent memory—the drive to train pension fund trustees to spot these issues and conflicts of interest, to understand the scope of their fiduciary duties, and to fully grasp the consequences of the investment policies they adopt. Multiple activists told me that the gold standard for this trustee organization drive has been set by Vonda Brunsting, who leads the Capital Stewardship Program of the Service Employees International Union.[35]

Organizing the Trustees

Vonda Brunsting began her career as a community organizer before becoming involved in working-class shareholder activism. She spent a decade working for the Industrial Areas Foundation (IAF), founded by Saul Alinsky in 1940. (Perhaps unsurprisingly, Brunsting never heard of Alinsky while earning her master's degree in public policy at the University of Chicago. She learned about him in church.) The IAF deploys a philosophy of congregation-based power building, working with churches, synagogues, temples, and mosques to advance change. One of IAF's organizational theories was to work with existing collective bodies like these congregations, rather than create them from scratch. Through it, she participated in the "Justice for Janitors Campaign," as had Dennak Murphy. Eventually, Brunsting met John Adler, who was then working at the SEIU. It was Adler who pitched Brunsting on the idea of joining the SEIU's budding Capital Stewardship Program, and she agreed. She started at the SEIU in 2004 as an international representative, working her way up through the ranks to coordinator, then assistant director, then deputy director, and now director of the program.[36]

In this capacity, Brunsting oversees one of the most powerful working-class shareholder institutions in the country. The SEIU has 2 million members who work primarily in healthcare, property management, and government service. They participate in forty-eight public pension funds and nineteen private funds with roughly $1.5 trillion in assets. Brunsting herself serves as a trustee on the SEIU Master Trust Pension Plan and sits on the board of the Council of Institutional Investors, the pension coalition that lobbied for proxy access and other key elements of Dodd-Frank. She oversees a staff of fifteen people devoted to training SEIU members to be effective pension trustees.[37]

Brunsting views her primary task as helping to turn her trustees into leaders. The core problem is that SEIU pension trustees often find themselves isolated and unsupported. Pension staff try to exert control over fund decisions, keeping trustees at arm's length. This dynamic also explains why many of these pension funds have wound up in investments that finance their own workers' demise. Brunsting says that her trustees are frequently treated with intense disrespect, usually because they don't come from the finance industry; they are "lawyers, social workers, accountants, auditors for the state, mostly professionals operating outside of finance." When they find themselves serving as trustees on a large pension fund, "it's very intimidating." They are often told, "let the experts take over."[38]

The experts invest them in hedge funds and private equity funds. The experts buy AAA-rated mortgage-backed securities that are not actually AAA quality. The experts don't push back when their investment managers demand 2 and 20 regardless of performance. The experts don't want to vote against executive pay packages. The experts think it's irrelevant if their outside investment managers take worker money and invest in charter schools or privatization schemes. The experts don't care about the CEO-worker pay ratio. The experts think shareholder voting rights are pointless. The experts are hoping to get a job at Goldman Sachs. The experts think the CEO should also be the board chair. And when the non-expert trustees question the experts, the experts respond with two magic words, often with the assistance of fund counsel: "fiduciary duty." The experts tell the non-experts that their job is to maximize returns. The experts say that they understand the fee structures. The experts know what to consider, and not consider, when making investments. The experts know that taking losses, sometimes large losses, sometimes large losses year after year under the auspices of outside investment managers making huge sums of money, are just what grownup market participants should expect. The experts say, "just sign here."

Fundamentally, what Brunsting does is teach trustees how to deal with the blight of these experts. Bringing trustees in for training by yet another panel of experts who talked at them all day and handed them a three-inch binder of "useful information" helped slightly, at best, but didn't get to the core of the problem. What trustees really needed was a few days a year, more than once a year, to sit around a table and talk to each other about their experiences and their challenges, to develop a base of collective knowledge from the ground up, to learn from each other and to be their own experts. Brunsting sought "to knit them together. To make them feel supported." Thus, she became a key player in the founding of the Trustee Leadership Forum, situated inside the Initiative for Responsible Investment at the Kennedy School of Government at Harvard under the auspices of David Wood. The forum was founded by Brunsting, along with Nancy McKenzie of the National Education Association; Paul Quirk, formerly of the Massachusetts Pension Reserves Investment Management Board; Lisa Lindsley, then still at AFSCME; Jim Sando, a trustee of the Pennsylvania State Employees Retirement System; Dan Pedrotty, then at AFL-CIO; author and consultant Randy Barber; Allen Emkin of the Pension Consulting Alliance; and Jack Marco of Marco Consulting. Michael Musuraca, a former NYCERS trustee, and Jay Youngdahl, a lawyer / trustee and publisher of the *East Bay Express,* were also involved in early conversations about the group. It is one of many such forums under the auspices of different organizations, including the Labor and Worklife Program and the National Conference on Public Employee Retirement Systems.[39]

The Trustee Leadership Forum holds meetings multiple times a year around the country. It "draws on the experiences of these trustees to identify the core issues they face in developing strategies for long-term sustainable wealth creation—how they grapple with and react to the role that portfolio theory, fiduciary duty, agency issues among trustees, staff, consultants, legal advisors and fund managers, and challenges to the very idea of defined benefit pension plans." In Brunsting's view, a few slight changes from the normal conference setting decisively changed the dynamics. They sat at a round table. The trustees themselves set the agenda for the meeting. It was not about people from labor or academia telling them what to do, what the important topics are, what they should be talking about. The occasional outside expert would be invited to speak, but ample time would be left for discussion.[40]

The two most important, tangible developments to emerge from these meetings were the pushback against fees and the retreat from hedge funds. Perhaps these topics sound mundane, but they cut to the very heart of a corrupt financial system. As David Wood, the director of the Initiative for Responsible Investment, said to me, the question of fees "was the lowest common denominator" for everyone in the group. He continued, "Fees also enabled a conversation about whether finance should serve society or whether it was all about rent seeking." What the trustees discovered in these meetings was that they were all having different versions of the same conversation. The staff pushes them into the most "sophisticated," "alternative" investments like hedge funds and private equity funds, and the returns are miserable, trailing the market year after year, the fees astronomical. Trustees felt they were being "raked over the coals" on fees. "There was always this God-given truth that 2-and-20 is just what you pay," said Brunsting. That's what staff would tell them, and when trustees would try to push back, to urge some form of negotiation, or, even worse, to switch to new fund managers, they would be told by fund counsel that they might be breaching their fiduciary duties.[41]

Some simple examples illustrate how trustees began to organize and push back. We already read about one in Chapter 3, Dennak

Murphy's push to get CalPERS to divest from hedge funds. Another example comes from Brunsting's work with Chicago treasurer Kurt Summers. Prior to serving as treasurer, Summers had worked at McKinsey and Company and then at Grosvenor Capital Management, where he led its Emerging and Diverse Manager business investing over $2 billion with minority- and women-owned firms. In his capacity as treasurer, Summers served as a trustee on several different Chicago funds, much in the way that Scott Stringer oversees the five New York City funds. Summers quickly made a straightforward observation: his funds were using the same investment managers for the same products for which they were charged separately. Brunsting worked with Summers to get the Chicago-area funds (combined assets of $59 billion) to share investment manager fee data and work to lower fees.[42]

Similarly, the Trustee Leadership Forum became a place for discussing not just lowering investment manager fees but reassessing whole asset classes like hedge funds. I was in attendance at a forum meeting at the Kennedy School to watch a presentation by Simon Lack, a former industry insider, discussing his book *The Hedge Fund Mirage: The Illusion of Big Money and Why It's Too Good to Be True*. Lack offered a devastating, data-driven argument that

> In fact, in 2008 the hedge fund industry lost more money than all the profits it had generated during the prior 10 years. . . . It's likely that hedge funds in 2008 lost all the profits ever made. By the end of 2008, the cumulative results of all the hedge fund investing that had gone before was negative. The average investor was done. . . . And perhaps most damning of all, if all the investors had not bothered with hedge funds at all, but had simply put their hedge fund money into Trea-

sury bills, they would have done better, earning 2.3 percent. And this doesn't include the cost of investing in hedge funds.

The conversations about hedge fund divestment produced the American Federation of Teachers' "All That Glitters Is Not Gold" report. It has also led to another report by the AFT, "The Big Squeeze: How Money Managers' Fees Crush State Budgets and Workers' Retirement Hopes," on what returns to pension funds would look like if they paid 1 and 10 instead of 2 and 20. Both of these reports have played a role in the current retreat from hedge funds.[43]

Brunsting's work is a straightforward application of decades of union know-how about organization, albeit applied outside the usual context. Rather than organizing communities, religious groups, or workers, she is organizing pension trustees who oversee, collectively, trillions of dollars in assets. The principles are largely the same: helping isolated individuals converge to explore their shared interests and increase their effectiveness by "knitting them together" into groups with more power and more knowledge. This organization often bears fruit in the real-world actions that follow it. The skills of people like Brunsting and her trustees will be sorely tested going forward as they try to fend off an enormous backlash against these funds and the work they do. That is the subject of the final chapter.

8

The Retirement "Crises" and the Future of Labor's Capital

Labor's capital can become one of labor's most powerful mechanisms for advancing the interests of twenty-first-century workers. We have seen how activists deployed it to challenge incompetent CEOs trying to shift the costs of their mistakes onto workers. We have seen it used to open up the corporate election process, to push back against hedge funds and private equity funds that take worker money and use it to undermine workers, to curtail the power and compensation of imperial CEOs, to track down and expose private equity funds that would rather hide in the regulatory dark, and to sue companies for committing fraud. We have seen how traditional union strengths like organizing and educating workers have been deployed to focus fund trustees on the conflicts of interest their funds face, and to avoid being captured by their investees. These same tools can be used, and are already being used, to shape future infrastructure spending initiatives to favor workers.

Despite this evidence of strength, there are also profound threats to labor's capital. Billionaire conservative activists Charles and David Koch and their organization Americans for Prosperity, as well as Enron billionaire John Arnold and his Laura and John Arnold Foundation (LJAF) and other allies, are determined to reform public pension funds in ways that would destroy labor's shareholder activism.[1] This threat takes three primary forms. The first and most dangerous is to fracture the massive public pension funds driving shareholder activism into tens of millions of individual investor accounts that end up being outsourced to mutual funds. That would undermine and probably destroy pension funds' leverage with companies, hedge funds, and private equity funds. This decentralization and outsourcing of pension management could undermine, if not extinguish, activism, depending on how it is structured. The second threat is the "shop floor" equivalent: the elimination of collective bargaining for public employee unions and the targeting of agency fees through litigation before the Supreme Court. This threat is real and enormously dangerous to labor generally, but a less direct threat to shareholder activism than the first. And the third is an overly restrictive definition of fiduciary duty that would choke off some of labor's shareholder activism, as discussed in Chapter 7. This chapter focuses on the first two threats. There is good reason to believe that the first can be beaten back in one way or another, and in some ways counterbalanced by other positive developments. The second threat is less immediately dangerous but much more likely to manifest. Both offer existential challenges to labor and are very, very well-funded by the Kochs, Arnolds, and others.

Dividing and Conquering the Pension Funds: Defined-Benefit versus Defined-Contribution Funds

One of the primary effects of the campaign by Americans for Prosperity and the Arnold Foundation against pensions would be to cripple their capacity to engage in shareholder activism by breaking them up.[2] That would be accomplished by transforming these pensions from centrally managed "defined-benefit" funds to individually managed, outsourced "defined-contribution" funds like 401(k)s. For example, Michigan shifted its public school employees from a defined-benefit pension system, to a hybrid defined-benefit and defined-contribution system, to a system in which new employees default into a defined-contribution system. These plans are managed by Voya (formerly ING), a private mutual fund company.[3] Scaling up that shift nationwide would have many consequences for worker retirement, and for state budgets, in addition to shareholder activism. And it would mimic the shift that already took place years ago in the private sector, a shift that has set millions of Americans on the path to retirement catastrophe.

Earlier, I briefly noted some of the differences between defined-benefit and defined-contribution funds, but some more detail is required here to understand how this otherwise dull topic of pension structures has such massive implications for all of the activism described in this book. In many respects, the difference between a defined-benefit and a defined-contribution pension plan is analogous to the difference between a unionized and a nonunionized workforce. The former empowers workers; the latter leaves them isolated and exposed. The same forces that attack unions attack defined-benefit funds, and for the same reasons.

The defined-benefit pension plan is the gold standard in retirement funds, one that has been slowly eroded for decades in favor of the less-secure defined-contribution fund, whose most popular forms are the 401(k) or the Individual Retirement Account (IRA), in which employees can make tax-advantaged contributions that are sometimes matched by their employers.[4] Roughly 40 million Americans depend on defined-benefit plans, a figure that has remained flat for decades.[5] About 30 million of these U.S. workers are public employees who participate in public pension plans. Defined-benefit plans once dominated the private sector too, but they have almost disappeared there.[6]

There are two main differences between defined-benefit and defined-contribution plans. Defined-benefit plans are centrally managed by trustees. The larger funds often have their own staff of investment professionals, whereas smaller funds may hire outside managers.[7] That means some minimum level of professional skill is being applied to these investments. More importantly, centralized management means that fund participants have significant leverage vis-à-vis investment managers in negotiating fees and overseeing investment performance. A threat by a centrally managed defined-benefit plan to shift billions of dollars—the collective retiree funds they manage—from one asset manager to another quickly gets the attention of that asset manager. These funds have not always exercised that authority, but it exists, and one of the purposes of this book has been to tell the stories of the activists who figured out how to use it. In contrast, in a defined-contribution plan, individual account holders have no leverage to negotiate anything with their investment managers. Account holders manage their retirement funds on their own and are told what their fees will be. The most they can do is switch from one fund to another, depending on what options are made available by their employers.

A second difference is that defined-benefit plans guarantee a fixed payment to workers in retirement. That means that the fund itself or the employer bears the market risk; for defined-contribution plans, the employee bears the market risk. For example, if you owned a 401(k) or IRA during the 2008 financial crisis, you probably saw the value of your retirement fund drop by more than half, although those plans have since recovered with the market. But if you participated in a defined-benefit plan, you were still entitled to the same retirement even when the market collapsed. It was promised to you by your employer, and therefore, your employer still owed you that sum regardless. The employer must find a way to make up the difference. In defined-contribution plans, workers are not guaranteed a penny. They get whatever they still have in their individually managed accounts when they retire, and if that means they lost half of their retirement savings in a market collapse, too bad.[8]

All of the activist pension funds that we have read about in this book are centrally managed defined-benefit funds. That's not a coincidence. CalPERS, CalSTRS, NYCERS, and the other funds collect employer and employee retirement contributions, invest those contributions, and pay out benefits to these workers when they retire. As the vehicles for managing those collective retirement assets, they have become immensely powerful shareholders, monitoring corporate and Wall Street misconduct through shareholder activism and litigation.

In contrast, defined-contribution plans were never designed to function like pensions, that is, to actually support people in retirement. Instead, they were meant to supplement, not substitute for, traditional pensions.[9] Thrust into the role of pensions, they have performed poorly. Even the inventors of the 401(k) have conceded that these plans have failed, most recently in an article in the *Wall Street Journal,* "The Champions of the 401(k) Lament the Revolution They Started." "The great lie is that the 401(k) was capable of replacing the old system of pensions," Gerald Facciani told the *Journal.* Facciani fought for the 401(k) back in the 1980s. "It was oversold," he said.[10]

There are many problems with individually managed accounts like 401(k)s.[11] One of the most glaring is the excessive fees charged to unwitting individual holders who lack the skill or leverage to keep fees low. Wall Street has made huge sums off of those fees. Such fees may be earned in multiple ways. They may direct investors toward actively managed funds that charge more than index funds while underperforming. One study showed that 16 percent of 401(k) plans charged fees that exceeded the tax benefit of contributing to the plan. In such plans, workers would have been better off forgoing the tax benefit and putting their money in a savings account. Some plans also offer two essentially identical plans with one charging significantly higher fees than the other. It's like a restaurant offering the same dish twice on its menu under different names, one for ten dollars and one for twenty. No rational person chooses the second option, and yet the market is filled with investors making that choice, conveniently furnished to them by their employers and mutual fund managers. It is certainly true that pension funds have also paid excessive fees, but at least they have belatedly begun to take action on that issue, and they have the investment clout to knock fees down, unlike individual investors. On top of high fees, individual 401(k) holders have contributed too little to these funds over the years. Significant market crashes in 2001 and 2008 hurt them too. Underfunded 401(k)s are one of the main reasons more than half of all Americans risk running out of funds in retirement, even accounting for Social Security. According to the Employee Benefit Research Institute, the median 401(k) holds just over $18,000, which is nowhere near enough to support a worker in retirement.[12]

But that hasn't stopped their proliferation. According to statistics from the U.S. Department of Labor, 88 million Americans participate in defined-contribution retirement plans, twice the number enrolled in such plans since 1975.[13] Employers embraced these plans because they shifted the market risk to employees. Although the 401(k) has its defenders, the weight of the evidence suggests that they will result in millions of Americans facing significant economic constraints in their postemployment years. In short, there is ample reason to believe that 401(k)s are in real crisis.[14] It is both astonishing and utterly predictable that, as I write this, Congressional Republicans are debating significantly *reducing* the tax benefit of 401(k)s, making them an even less viable source of retirement security than they are now. (The proposal would shift the tax treatment to favor IRAs over 401(k)s. For purposes of my analysis, there is no difference between a 401(k) and an IRA. They are both individually managed retirement accounts that deprive investors of the capacity to act collectively).[15]

Traditional pensions and individually managed accounts also differ on the investor side. Centralized, defined-benefit plans are capable of engaging in shareholder activism in ways that are almost impossible to do with 401(k) plans or the like. That's not inherently the case, but it works out that way in the American context. To illustrate, let's imagine what were to happen to CalPERS if it were converted overnight from a defined-benefit plan to an individually managed defined-contribution plan.

Today, CalPERS is a highly effective shareholder activist because it sits on more than $300 billion in assets and speaks with one voice for its 1.8 million plan participants.[16] It owns a substantial stake in thousands of companies, giving it significant influence with each investee. It can bargain over fees with investment managers, achieving economies of scale. But if CalPERS were broken up into individually managed accounts, each worth on average about $166,000, the effect would be eerily similar to what happens to unions when they can no longer bargain collectively. One individual shareholder with $166,000 in total diversified retirement assets, and maybe at most a few hundred dollars in any particular stock, loses all of her leverage with investees. Most of us atomized 401(k) or IRA holders don't undertake shareholder activism. First, we are indirect owners anyway, because through our own funds we own mutual funds that in turn own companies. The mutual funds therefore exercise shareholder rights, not us. Even if we were direct owners, we do not have the time, money, expertise, or incentives to rally our fellow individual investors to actively engage the CEO of a company in which we have a small investment. As individuals, we could potentially become active within our mutual funds, but that is quite rare. Very, very few individual investors file their own shareholder proposals, with the notable exception of investors like John Chevedden and James MacRitchie, who have become famous in shareholder activist circles for making this their life's work. And these investors are currently being targeted by the Business Roundtable's efforts to effectively ban individual investors from filing shareholder proposals, despite recent research suggesting that the net effect of their activism has been positive.[17]

Of course, the mutual funds could become active on behalf of all the new 401(k) money they would be managing. But as discussed earlier, mutual fund activism ranges from mild to nonexistent because of all of the business conflicts that constrain them.

The point is that it's hard enough to wield influence even when you're CalPERS. As individual shareholders, there are currently very few opportunities to exercise our voice, and our mutual funds aren't likely to exercise it for us. In fairness, there have been some recent efforts to raise awareness among individual investors about how to exercise voice inside mutual funds. For example, the Center for the Study of Responsive Law, founded by Ralph Nader, has undertaken efforts to teach individual mutual fund investors about how mutual fund managers vote their proxies in ways that are highly regressive on corporate governance and executive compensation issues. I would not rule out the possibility that some organization will arise to organize individual investors on a meaningful scale. Organizations like As You Sow already do such work.[18] That also raises another possibility: the creation of labor-friendly mutual funds. If the existing mutual funds are unwilling to act, it is possible that new entities could. But as it currently stands, conversions from defined-benefit to defined-contribution or hybrid plans involve the outsourcing of 401(k) plans to existing mutual funds with their usual sets of conflicts.

Under any circumstance, it would be difficult to organize individual investors to function with the cohesion and power of a CalPERS. This is not a bug of pension reform, it's a feature. The destruction of shareholder activism is one of the main effects of these proposed changes, a fact that has been almost totally ignored by the media, the public, academics, and even labor and pension activists.

Conservative activists like the Koch brothers' Americans for Prosperity and the LJAF are pushing the public sector to adopt individually managed defined-contribution funds. The pretext for such action is, as always, crisis. Some experts have argued that defined-benefit public pension plans are in crisis. Although the average individual public pension is worth approximately $26,000 annually, that sum is actually more "generous" than what most people have in their 401(k)s. (The small sums of money in most public pension funds did not stop Americans for Prosperity California from offering a "Lifestyles of the Rich and Famous on a Government Pension Tour," hiring a chauffeur and limousine to drive around the state pretending to be ferrying purportedly overcompensated public employees.)[19]

One would think that the underfunding of 88 million Americans' retirements via 401(k)s would attract more attention than the comparatively generous—though still quite measly—defined-benefit pensions of public employees. The truth is just the opposite. The 401(k) crisis has received relatively little attention from the media and in Washington compared to the public pension crisis. To use one crude measure of this attention gap, a Google search of "401(k) crisis" (in quotes) yields 649 results, but a search of "public pension crisis" yields 41,200 results, roughly 63 times as many hits.[20] What explains the attention given to purportedly generous public pension plans and not underfunded 401(k)s?

The answer is money, of course. The cost of paying for underfunded individual retirement funds falls exclusively on the individual atomized saver, who suffers the lack of resources alone. But the costs of underfunded defined-benefit plans fall on the states and municipalities that sponsor them. Taxpayers, especially wealthy ones, assume the burden of covering those pension gaps. One way out of this legal obligation is through bankruptcy, as was almost the case for Detroit, but that is not a viable option for states (which are ineligible for bankruptcy under federal law) and most municipalities. Another way is the path taken by Americans for Prosperity and the Arnold Foundation, which is to attack public sector unions' right to bargain collectively and to eliminate legal protections for pensions.[21]

My CalPERS hypothetical above was not a pure hypothetical. California's pension funds have been under unrelenting assault for nearly a decade. "It's every two years, like clockwork. Every election," said Jennifer Baker, a legislative advocate for the California Teachers Association, the California teachers' union. Most recently, pension critics have proposed the Voter Empowerment Act, a ballot initiative initially proposed for 2016 and now potentially to be placed before California voters in November 2018.[22]

The proposed act would change the California constitution to end defined-benefit pension plans for all California public employees hired on or after January 1, 2019. As the proposal states, "Government employers shall not allow new government employees to enroll in a defined benefit pension plan unless the voters of that jurisdiction approve enrollment in such a plan." It also prohibits, absent voter approval, government employers from paying more than half of the benefits of new employees. In addition, the Government Pension Cap Act could accompany the Voter Empowerment Act. This proposed law would limit the government's contribution responsibility for most employees' retirement benefits to 11 percent of employee base compensation. If these proposals were adopted, particularly the Voter Empowerment Act, they would impair the long-term ability for CalPERS, CalSTRS, the Los Angeles County Employee Retirement Association, and other California pension funds to engage in shareholder activism. The effect would not be overnight, because existing employees would still participate in these plans. It would be like the slow leak from a tire, diminishing pension shareholder power over time. A 2018 California initiative might fail, as it has for the past decade. But it only takes one win. "They just keep changing the words," said Baker, but the goal is always the same. "They claim they're just about reforming pensions, but they're not. The goal is not reform. The goal is elimination."[23] If they fail in 2018, we can expect them to return again in 2020.

Who is behind this CalPERS initiative? Who is funding it? As I write this, it is technically impossible to say. But in 2014, a slightly different pension proposal by one of the Voter Empowerment Act proponents, former San Jose mayor Chuck Reed, received a $200,000 contribution from John Arnold, which constituted 100 percent of the campaign's funding. That proposal would have changed the California constitution "to give state and local governments authority to alter future pension formulas for current employees."[24] That cuts against a widely held view that the California constitution bars state and local governments from changing bargains with workers after they have already struck.[25] Reed has publicly expressed the hope that Arnold will contribute to his next initiative.[26]

Arnold made his billion-dollar fortune as an oil and gas trader, beginning his career at Enron before moving on to start his own hedge fund after the company collapsed in the largest accounting fraud in U.S. history.[27] In the book, *The Smartest Guys in the Room,* the authors described Arnold praising his team for "learning how to use the Enron bat to push around the market."[28] The fraud cost Enron employees $2 billion in lost pensions and another $1.5 billion to public employee pensions invested in the company. (There is no allegation or evidence that Arnold was involved in the Enron fraud. He did not work for the division that led to the company's demise.) Not surprisingly, after the malfeasance was revealed, many of these public pension and labor funds, like the Washington State Investment Board, the San Francisco City and County Employees' Retirement System, Teamsters Locals 175 and 505, the Hawaii Laborers Pension Plan, and the Central States Southeast and Southwest Areas Pension Fund, along with the Archdiocese of Milwaukee and lead plaintiff University of California Regents, brought suit against Enron and other defendants, ultimately recovering over $7 billion for defrauded shareholders.[29]

With the money he made from Enron, Arnold established the $1.3 billion LJAF. Arnold has since become a leading crusader in favor of pension reform, with significant emphasis on transforming pensions from defined-benefit to defined-contribution funds. (Although the Arnold Foundation website maintains that it is open to defined-benefit funds, much of its work to date has been to undermine them.) Arnold's efforts with the Pew Foundation and others on pension issues have been well-documented, including in a recent report, "The Plot against Pensions."[30]

While Arnold hotly contests it, according to the National Public Pension Coalition, he had spent $53 million through the end of 2014 on pension reform efforts. These efforts have taken many forms. In 2014, he donated $1 million to a ballot initiative in Phoenix, Arizona, that would have required the city to abandon defined-benefit pensions for future hires. Arnold's contribution constituted almost 75 percent of all donations for the initiative, which lost. That same year, he donated $200,000 to a SuperPAC that supported the election of Democrat Gina Raimondo as Rhode Island governor; upon election, she instituted painful pension reforms. Arnold has funded reform efforts in Chicago, Colorado, Oklahoma, and, as we saw above, California. And policy has been inching in his direction. Before the financial crisis of 2008, just two states—Michigan and Alaska—required new employees to participate in a defined-contribution plan. The remaining states offered defined-benefit plans and optional, additional defined-contribution plans. Since the crisis, seven states have moved to hybrid plans, including Georgia, Michigan, Pennsylvania, Rhode Island, Tennessee, Utah, and Virginia. These hybrid plans retain a defined-benefit component but also offer individualized defined-contribution components, reducing the assets that are centrally managed by the pension fund.[31] In theory, this should reduce state and local pension obligations, while undermining the retirement security of workers. In fact, there is some evidence that it has not helped states save money. West Virginia switched to a defined-contribution plan and then switched back after realizing that the costs of the plan were prohibitive and the benefits to workers too paltry. And when public employees face salary and benefit cuts, they often turn to public assistance, burdening taxpayers anyway. That's what happened to Carol Sanders, the cook who lost her job when Aramark took over Orleans Parish school services. She turned to food stamps.[32]

Another force behind pension reform efforts has been the Koch brothers' Americans for Prosperity. Americans for Prosperity has opposed strengthening pension protections in New Jersey, advocated pension cuts in Illinois and Kentucky, and opposed a federal bailout of the United Mine Workers of America pension fund.[33]

The main message in all of these pension reform efforts is always the same: pension funds are in crisis and threaten to overwhelm state and city budgets. One recent example from a law school conference that appears to have been indirectly funded by the Arnolds, the Kochs, or both: "Underfunded public employee pensions are one of the major fiscal crises confronting American states and municipalities. It is estimated that the shortfall is as much as $1 trillion and payments to retirees increasingly are diverting funds for necessary services, including police, fire, schools, roads, and other core services."[34]

The underfunding of pensions remains hotly contested by economists, finance academics, and actuaries. Mere underfunding alone is not necessarily a problem—pensions are widely considered healthy if they are 80 percent funded. According to a recent study by the National Conference on Public Employee Retirement Systems, pensions nationwide have hit a 76 percent funding level, up from 74 percent post-financial crisis. And the Center for Retirement Research at Boston College projects that pensions will hit 78 percent funding by 2020. In comparison, corporate pensions are 84 percent funded. Critics repeatedly predict that fulfilling pension obligations will force states and municipalities to divert resources from schools, roads, and other public services.[35] But nationwide, pension obligations constitute, on average, only 4.5 percent of all state and local public obligations.[36] In addition, most of the state and municipal sponsors of these purportedly underfunded public pension funds have seen little or no negative effects in the bond market, with the notable exception of Illinois and, to a lesser extent, New Jersey.[37] That fact is of considerable significance. Financial economists and others regularly argue that we have no better means of pricing risk than market forces. It was the bond market that pushed Greece into a sovereign debt crisis in 2009, ultimately requiring a European bailout. It nearly did the same to Italy and Spain. Investors began demanding ever higher bond yield for taking the risk of funding Greece, for fear that Greece's public-sector debt was unsustainable on account of pensions and other spending. The unsustainability of pensions and public debt is the same argument being made in the United States by pension critics. If the critics are right, why have we seen no comparable pressures in the bond market here? Yes, there have been local bankruptcies, and Illinois is in a class by itself, though the state recently raised taxes to begin dealing with the issue. But overall, we are not seeing troubles approaching the scale and scope of what we saw in Greece, Italy, and Spain post-crisis. That strongly suggests that the market has examined pension issues and concluded not that everything is perfect but that the risks are manageable, that investors will be repaid, and that they do not need to demand excessively high yields to invest.[38]

In contrast to the Koch / Arnold view of pensions captured in the above conference announcement, the Center for Retirement Research at Boston College, led by economist Alicia Munnell, offers up a checklist of "Myths and Realities about State and Local Pensions," based on Munnell's 2012 book, *State and Local Pensions: What Now?* (Pensions were in much worse condition in 2012 than they are today.) Among these myths:

> *Myth:* Most state and local pensions are in crisis.
>
> *Reality:* While plans were thrown seriously off course by the twin market downturns of the past decade, their finances have begun to stabilize, and most now face a manageable challenge.

Myth: Public sector unions are responsible for today's pension shortfalls.

Reality: It is impossible to find a link between a plan's generosity or funding level and the strength of unions.

Myth: The high discount rates that plans use to value future benefits explain the shortfalls.

Reality: Discount rates do not explain funding levels either. Pension funding is simply a story of fiscal discipline—developing a reasonable plan and sticking to it.

Myth: Plans should always use a riskless rate of return to discount obligations.

Reality: A riskless rate is appropriate for reporting purposes, but not for guiding investment or contribution decisions.

Myth: State and local pensions are busting government budgets.

Reality: In 2009, overall pension contributions were 4.6 percent of total state and local revenues; this share will rise to 5.1 percent if plans realize their assumed returns. [As noted, today they are 4.5 percent of budgets.]

Myth: Public workers are overpaid compared to their private sector counterparts.

Reality: State / local and private sector workers, on average, receive about the same in total compensation, with public workers' lower wages roughly offset by higher benefits. Higher-paid public workers get less than their private sector counterparts while lower-paid workers get more.[39]

At bottom, the debate over whether public pension funds are currently underfunded comes down to a debate over what is a fair and accurate estimated rate of return for these funds. That is, how much is it safe to assume they will earn in the future on their investments?[40] Economists and actuaries are divided over this question; a few percentage points difference on these estimates has a significant impact on the perceived health of these funds.

Some finance economists have taken the position that because defined-benefit pension funds are a guaranteed payment, pensions must assume a "risk-free" rate of return. That is what an investor would expect to make on an investment basically guaranteed to be repaid, in short, very little return on investment in exchange for the certainty of payment. The closest to a truly risk-free investment remains U.S. treasury bills, bonds issued by the government to fund U.S. government activity, because the solvency of the United States remains the world's safest economic bet (for now). Such an investment earns close to nothing, at the time of writing, but investors can be quite certain that they will get paid.[41] Proponents of this approach argue that only by investing in U.S. treasury bills or their close equivalent can we be certain to keep pension promises.

Other economists and academics argue that applying a risk-free rate of return to a guaranteed future payment might make sense inside a classroom on a whiteboard, but that real-world investors making real-world investment decisions would not assume a risk-free rate of return, even for a guaranteed future payment. That's why economist Alicia Munnell, in her "myths and realities," states that "a riskless rate is appropriate for reporting purposes, *but not for guiding investment or contribution decisions.*" The basic reason is because the actual performance of a diversified investment portfolio is likely to outperform the risk-free rate. According to online data reported by Professor Aswath Damodaran of the Department of Finance at New York University's Stern School of Business, from 1928 to 2016 the S&P 500—widely considered the best barometer of U.S. stock market performance—returned, arithmetically, 11.42 percent per year. Over the same period, the safest and most conservative U.S. treasury bill, the three-month bill, returned 3.46 percent annually, while the ten-year bill—which is riskier than the three-month bill because it locks up your investment for a full ten years—paid 5.18 percent. Economists arguing in 1928 in favor of applying a risk-free rate of return for guaranteed future payments would have argued for an assumption much closer to 3.46 percent than 11.42 percent. As of 2014, the average annual rate of return assumed by most pension funds was 7.69 percent, a number that has been reduced from a pre-crisis high of closer to 8 percent, and a number that has likely dropped even further since.[42] The *Wall Street Journal* recently published an opinion piece that assumed a 7.4 percent rate of return for a retirement account.[43] Pro-risk-free rate economists counter that these stock market numbers reflect the economic performance of the United States over the past ninety years, arguably the most successful record of economic growth in world history, and that it is unreasonable to assume that the next ninety years will match that performance. And so the academic tennis match continues.

The immediate political implications of the debate are easier to tease out than the question of how markets will perform in the coming decades, which, to state the obvious, we will only learn over time. If we assume a 7.69 percent rate of return, then most pensions are healthy. But if we assume a risk-free rate of return going forward, then pensions are badly underfunded. That would require states and cities to contribute far more to them than they currently do, which could lead to both tax increases and reduced spending on other needs like infrastructure and education. Paying higher taxes for worse services infuriates taxpayers and creates an angry constituency in favor of gutting pensions.

Despite the uncertainty over the appropriate rate of return to assume going forward—after all, we are talking about the future—the panic is useful to those who want to cut pensions. It is true that the risk-free rate of return argument is a principled academic argument. But it is also true that many of the real-world players pushing that argument do so not because they are interested in seeing pensions adjust to a risk-free rate of return but because they want to gut pensions. And that's because there is another way to deal with financing "guaranteed" future payments like pensions: come up with legal arguments as to why they are not guaranteed at all and then simply not pay them. It's amazing how effective novel legal arguments become before judges faced with a newly roused and angry public.

That brings us back to the law school conference announcement noted above. I recognize that discussing a law school conference sounds like very, very small potatoes in the grand scheme of these debates. But it illustrates the larger point about the pervasiveness of the forces aligned against pensions.

The Henry G. Manne Law and Economics Center at the George Mason University School of Law, recently renamed the Antonin Scalia Law School, announced that it would host a conference on "The Economics and Law of Public Pension Reform," later renamed the "LEC Public Policy Conference on Solving the Public Pensions Crisis for Law Professors," in December 2016. George Mason has received significant funding from the Koch brothers, the LJAF, and others, including $10 million from the Kochs to re-name the school after the late Supreme Court justice. Despite the complexity and contested nature of the pension "crisis," the an-nouncement, as noted, assumes the Koch / Arnold line in defining the problem: pensions are underfunded and will inevitably lead to tax increases and service cuts without immediate action. The announcement simultaneously included a call for papers, that is, a call to the academic community to submit papers to the confer-ence. Eight papers would be accepted, workshopped, and then presented at the conference. It further suggested that papers be submitted on "topics of interest," including "whether public em-ployees pay for their pensions in forgone cash wages . . . the legal nature and limits of pension rights, whether gratuity, contract, or positive constitutional right, . . . the Illinois Constitution's Pen-sion Non-impairment Clause . . . [and] legal analysis of various pension reform proposals."[44] Each of these proposed topics reveals the conference's underlying goal: to find arguments to undermine legal protections for pensions. To question "whether employees pay for their pensions in forgone cash wages" is to question whether pension obligations must be honored. To ask whether pension rights are a "gratuity" as opposed to a contract or positive right is to suggest they can be abrogated. No one is owed a gratuity, not even a waiter. Questioning Illinois's crystal clear "Pension Non-impairment Clause" is more of the same.

For each of the accepted papers on these topics, "authors will receive a $12,000 total honorarium (inclusive of travel expenses)." That's $96,000 for eight papers undermining the economic and legal foundations for pensions. In addition to the $12,000 paid to each of the paper authors, the call for papers noted that confer-ence *attendees* would get paid $1,000 each along with covered costs.

Perhaps most importantly, the conference was also advertised as the "Policy Conference on Solving the Public Pension Crisis for *Judges* and *Attorneys General*."[45] Judges and attorneys general were especially invited to be in attendance to learn about this new research. Out of curiosity about these arguments, and in anticipation of writing this book, I attended the conference, though I did not submit a paper. There were around two hundred people there.

Not surprisingly, the papers presented were, for the most part, of excellent quality. They were not strident, hysterical presentations offered in a highly politicized tone. The organizers had curated a set of sober and rigorous academic presentations on pension issues from a right-of-center perspective. That's precisely what makes such conferences effective. But overall, there was no questioning whether there truly was a pension crisis, or assessing its depth and scope. The crisis was taken as given. Speakers repeatedly depicted labor as a narrow special interest group thwarting sensible solutions. The possibility of raising taxes to cover pension shortfalls was never seriously considered. In fact, raising taxes was only mentioned once. Steven Malanga, of the conservative magazine *City Journal,* mocked an Illinois Supreme Court opinion for suggesting that the state could raise taxes to cope with its pension shortfalls, a suggestion that elicited loud laughter in the room. (Subsequently, Illinois did just that.)[46] The lunchtime speaker criticized the Detroit bankruptcy proceedings for offering greater protection to worker pensions than it gave to the city's bondholders.

In fairness, there was at least one invited dissenting voice—my Boston University law colleague Jack Beermann—who made two basic points. First, he argued that taxpayers who might have to pay for pension shortfalls had zero moral standing to complain, because they were being asked to pay for public services they had already consumed, ranging from garbage collection to the education of their children to the policing of their streets. Second, he argued that the real reason why reformers want to cut pensions is because corporations want an insecure labor force that will keep wages down. As Beermann spoke, I overhead one judge sitting behind me say to another, in a deep southern accent, "Jack Beermann is a smart guy."[47]

Obviously, the academic piece of this story is only a small one, but it illustrates the larger forces at work. The anti-pension forces are not content merely to facilitate favorable academic legal arguments and deliver them straight to judges and attorneys general. They target legislators too, and voters. The American Legislative Exchange Council, or ALEC, is similarly working on pension reform. In an editorial, "The Big Money behind State Laws," the *New York Times* described ALEC as "a little-known conservative organization financed by millions of corporate dollars . . . its big funders include Exxon Mobil, the Olin and Scaife families and foundations tied to Koch Industries." The editorial describes the net effect of ALEC's work as "making it harder for minorities and other groups that support Democrats to vote, obstructing health care reform, weakening environmental regulations and breaking the spines of public- and private-sector unions."[48]

As with so much of ALEC's work, it is dry and technical, flies below the public radar, and is deadly effective. For pension reform, ALEC maintains model legislation in the form of the Pension Funding and Fairness Act. This proposed legislation illustrates how ALEC and other groups hope to use the pension crisis to completely transform the taxing and spending power of states. It would create "a Spending Growth Index of inflation plus population growth which is used as a limit on state spending each year." It would establish "a Taxpayer Relief Fund, which will issue refunds to taxpayers annually according to the number of exemptions filed on their most recent tax return." Increasing state spending or taxes beyond the limits set in the act would require the "three-fifths supermajority vote of all members of each House of the Legislature; and approval by a majority of voters," with some very narrow exceptions. Any surplus funds in the state budget above a certain low threshold would go into this taxpayer relief fund.[49] And all of this handcuffing of the state's power to tax and spend would be in exchange for what? For paying off the state's unpaid debt on its pensions.

All of this effort and massive mobilization of resources focuses just on labor's pensions. But these same forces are also working to undermine the core foundation for unions generally by targeting their funding and their right to bargain collectively.

The Threat to "Fair-Share Fees" for Public Employee Unions

Another threat to labor's shareholder activism, at least in the long term, is a threat to labor itself: the elimination of agency fees or "fair-share fees" for public employee unions. Fair-share fees are paid by non-union members to unions for the benefits they derive from the union bargaining with the employer for wages and benefits. I will say at the outset that this fight will likely be over shortly after this book is published. Unless Justice Anthony Kennedy or perhaps Justice John Roberts changes his mind, both unlikely, the Supreme Court is poised to deliver a sharp blow to public-sector unions.[50] Because unions and their pensions are related, that blow will indirectly hurt public employee pensions and shareholder activism. Although it would not be an immediately devastating, existential blow in the way that mass conversion to individualized 401(k) funds would be, the two threats are connected.

Collective bargaining empowers a union to negotiate compensation, benefits, working conditions, and workplace rights on behalf of all employees. The capacity to bargain collectively is crucial to union power and legitimacy, and it is precisely this ability that enables unions to improve wages and working conditions for workers. Getting paid to do so by the workers you represent is the lifeblood of unions. Without collective bargaining, workers are on their own to negotiate individually with their employers, and have little or no leverage, resulting in lower wages, lower benefits, and worse working conditions. And without the fees generated from all of the workers who benefit from such bargaining, the union purse would be even emptier than it is already. It is no exaggeration to say that labor avoided a devastating blow in a 4–4 Supreme Court vote in *Friedrichs v. California Teachers Association,* one that would have been 5–4 against labor if Justice Antonin Scalia hadn't died of natural causes on a Texas hunting trip in February 2016.[51] But this same blow is set to be delivered all over again anyway, with the appointment of Justice Neil Gorsuch to the court.

In *Friedrichs,* Rebecca Friedrichs and nine other California teachers claimed that their obligation to pay a fair-share fee to the union that bargained collectively on their behalf, the California Teachers Association, violated their First Amendment rights. (The California Teachers Association is the same union that has spent the past decade fending off attacks on California pensions.) These teacher plaintiffs did not bring the suit on their own. They were represented by the Center for Individual Rights, a conservative legal rights organization funded by—do I need to say it?—a series of foundations connected to Americans for Prosperity and the Koch brothers.[52]

For forty years, ever since the Supreme Court decided *Abood v. Detroit Board of Education,* the rule had been clear: public employees cannot be forced to pay for their union's political activity but they can still be required to pay a fair-share fee to cover other union costs from which they benefit, like the cost of collective bargaining. The logic is straightforward: forced subsidy of political activity would violate the workers' First Amendment rights, but forced subsidy of the economic activity from which they profit—like the wages and benefits negotiated by the union with the state—is perfectly appropriate. As the Supreme Court itself stated in an earlier case, "The primary purpose of permitting unions to collect fees from members . . . is to prevent . . . free-riding on the union's efforts, sharing the employment benefits obtained by the union's collective bargaining agreement without sharing the costs incurred."[53]

In *Friedrichs,* some California public school teachers claimed that the fair-share fee they paid to the California Teachers Association violated their First Amendment rights, squarely challenging the holding in *Abood.* They had been invited to make that challenge by Justice Samuel Alito in another case. Ultimately, in *Friedrichs,* Justices Alito, Kennedy, Roberts, and Clarence Thomas voted to reverse *Abood* and strike down agency fees as unconstitutional. Justice Scalia would almost certainly have been the fifth vote. The transcript of the oral argument reflects Scalia's hostile questioning of the solicitor general, Donald Verrilli, who was defending the precedent that protected agency fees.[54]

But with Scalia's passing, the Supreme Court deadlocked 4–4, keeping the old rule in place and preserving fair-share fees, at least briefly. Had the Senate confirmed President Barack Obama's Supreme Court nominee, Merrick Garland, or had Hillary Clinton won the presidential election of 2016 and had the chance to nominate a Supreme Court justice, it is highly likely that the Court would have upheld the *Abood* precedent, 5–4. But Scalia's replacement, Neil Gorsuch, nominated by President Donald Trump, is widely perceived to be even more conservative than the justice he replaced. It is highly likely that he will vote with the other four conservatives to strike down agency fees in the next case to raise the issue, *Janus v. AFSCME,* a similar lawsuit.[55]

If the Supreme Court strikes down agency fees in the *Janus* case, as expected, the reaction nationwide could be similar to what happened in Wisconsin after the Republicans eliminated collective bargaining for state employees. The two leading teachers' unions in the state saw their memberships drop by one-third and one-half respectively, and the state public employees union saw its membership drop by 70 percent. In anticipation of a negative ruling, unions have undertaken extraordinary efforts to recruit new workers and to recruit existing workers to stay in the union, even if they can no longer be required to pay agency fees should they leave it. Hopefully, those efforts will bear fruit. Still, we could see an enormous decline in public-sector unions nationwide. This would itself have profoundly negative consequences in a variety of ways. For the purposes of this book, however, the question is how this will affect shareholder activism. It cannot be good. But would it be an existential threat?[56]

In the short term, no. First, there has been no discernible negative effect on Wisconsin's pension funds since the state abolished collective bargaining. That makes sense. The loss of collective bargaining may well devastate the public employee unions, but it does not automatically abrogate union contracts, nor does it make the pensions disappear. Some research suggests that pension benefits may be lowered prospectively because nonunionized workers will have less leverage to negotiate good deals for themselves. That is likely true. But that still leaves these pension funds in place, and still leaves workers contributing to them, even if they no longer contribute to the unions that negotiated the benefits in those pensions. As the NYC funds' Michael Garland told me, they have plans to remain active going well into the future.[57] The bigger, more indirect threat to pensions and shareholder activism stemming from the loss of collective bargaining is that unions will have fewer resources to invest in shareholder activism, or to defend pensions when they are assaulted in legislatures or statewide ballot initiatives.

Let's tally up the score. The Koch brothers, the Arnolds, and their many lower-profile allies are lobbying legislators, judges, and attorneys general; they are funding state- and city-level ballot proposals and academic research they transmit directly to the powers that be. Although difficult to calculate, the sums of money must be astronomical. One estimate, calculated as of 2014, puts them at a minimum of $50 million for the Arnold Foundation alone.[58] (It is true that liberal and progressive organizations engage in most or all of the above activity, but they do so in far less systematic fashion, with fewer resources, on a smaller scale.) All of this for an issue that has only barely registered with the American people: the funding and legal status of pension funds.

The question is, Why? Why do the Kochs and the Arnolds think this issue is worth the multifaceted campaign; the comprehensive, state-by-state assault targeting voters, lawyers, judges, attorneys general, and academics; the vast expenditure of resources?

The answer is because they perceive, correctly, that fully funded shareholder activist pension funds pose a significant threat to their ideology. What other voice in our society elicits the same level of responsiveness from inside corporations, hedge funds, and private equity funds? Not the government, post–*Citizens United,* with elected officials beholden to the largest donors. Maybe, on rare occasion, a roused voting public—at most every two to four years—and only then for brief periods of time, before inattention returns and the lobbyists get back to work.

These pension funds, with the assets and power they have accumulated, represent something new under the sun. They operate inside the private sector, inside the market, as shareholders. They benefit from rules designed to keep power and resources marshaled there. Shareholder empowerment empowers them. Perversely, these particular shareholders are more powerful than most because they operate in the private sector unencumbered by business conflicts of interest that keep other shareholders quiet when their rights are violated or their interests subverted.

More worrisome, from the perspective of Koch et al., has been the ability of these shareholders to build broader alliances that enhance their power by focusing beyond their own parochial interests. When the *Wall Street Journal* editorial page slammed the SEC's proxy access rule with the headline "Alinsky Wins at the SEC," the writers likely believed that other "normal" shareholders would never sign on for proxy access. But those shareholders supported it in droves, riding largely behind working-class shareholder institutions such as Scott Stringer's NYC funds. When it made sense, these shareholders aligned with large, powerful, often passive, diversified mutual funds ranging from Vanguard to Fidelity to TIAA-CREF and BlackRock. When it made sense, they aligned with socially responsible investors, endowments, foundations, and environmental investors. And when it made sense, they aligned with each other, or operated alone.

Working-class shareholders have built alliances with other shareholders by exposing boards to elections with real consequences, or by stepping forward to litigate fraud cases on behalf of all shareholders, as in the UnitedHealth stock options backdating case.[59] They have also demonstrated the ability to advance worker-friendly agendas, sometimes on their own, sometimes with others, by making companies rethink the true cost of firing workers or by pushing hedge funds and private equity funds to avoid funding the privatization of jobs and to invest in projects that create union jobs. Working-class shareholders have also demonstrated their ability to build mutually beneficial alliances with environmental activists and with advocates of diversity.

The question is, where does it go from here? What is the future of labor's capital and what role does it have to play in the future of labor itself? In these final pages, I outline some thoughts on what comes next for the working-class shareholder.

The Future of Labor's Capital

The first thing that labor's capital must do is survive long enough for the Democratic Party to regain strength at the national level and, more importantly, at the state and local levels. If you live in a state or city with such a fund, you must pay attention to statewide ballot initiatives designed to destroy pensions, assuming such initiatives exist. By destroy, I mean convert them from centrally managed defined-benefit pension funds to individually managed defined-contribution funds. The justification for doing so will be saving taxpayers from the "crisis" of underfunded pensions. The reality will be stealing previously earned public worker money and crippling the capacity of the pension funds to negotiate Wall Street fees or to police corporate or investment manager misconduct. The biggest prize in this fight is California. If a statewide initiative passes that enables California's public pensions to be converted into individualized accounts, that would be a sharp blow to labor's capital, and to the shareholder activist movement more generally. But every single state counts, every city counts, and both states and cities have been drifting in the wrong direction. The more likely challenge for state and city pensions, including California, would be the *prospective* conversion into individualized defined-contribution funds, meaning that all future pensions would be individualized and then outsourced to mutual funds. That would preserve the status quo for the time being but be devastating in the long run, a dangerous, slow leak in the tire rather than an immediate collapse.

If I were a union leader, a pension trustee, or a politician who sits on a pension board, I would fight to protect centralization and to defend defined-benefit funds. Defined-benefit offers a much more secure retirement than defined-contribution funds do.[60] In fact, one of the real risks of defined-contribution funds is that it becomes a kind of tax arbitrage. States and cities that think they will save money not having to fund underfunded defined-benefit pensions may instead find they are spending money on Medicaid, disability, and other welfare benefits required by people with defined-contribution funds who have outlived their savings.

That said, in the face of a truly fierce onslaught from the Kochs, Arnolds, and their allies, there is a fallback position. Hybrid plans have emerged that retain a defined-benefit component while also introducing defined-contribution funds. Most recently, Pennsylvania reformed its pensions so that new hires default into such a hybrid plan. Preservation of some defined-benefit component would not only assure workers a basic level of retirement security but would preserve the collective element that is so crucial for these worker-investors to be able to protect themselves from Wall Street and its corporate pathologies. Another alternative is managing defined-contribution funds in-house, rather than outsourcing them to mutual funds, in ways that could preserve the independence and integrity of public pension funds. These centrally managed defined-contribution funds still create enormous, collective shareholder power. But workers are not guaranteed a specific sum in retirement; they just get what's in their accounts. That protects taxpayers from having to make up large shortfalls in the event of market downturns.

The economist Teresa Ghilarducci and Blackstone president Tony James have recently proposed an overhaul of U.S. retirement policy that would abandon much of our current system in favor of guaranteed retirement accounts. These accounts would be pooled, unlike 401(k)s.[61] Although Ghilarducci and James don't discuss the governance side of their proposal—that is, who would vote proxies or make litigation decisions—their proposed pooling would retain at least some of the shareholder power described in this book. Such funds could reduce the potential risk to taxpayers from shortfalls or defaults while retaining the capacity for investors to stand up for themselves, fight for their rights, police markets, make sensible, informed investments, and have leverage to negotiate fees and asset allocation. They could be another fallback position. While they would not be quite as generous as defined-benefit plans, they would be much better than the worst-case scenario, turning all pensions into individualized 401(k)-like funds that are outsourced to mutual funds, with no hybrid, defined-benefit component. So I say it again and for a final time: the conversion of these pension funds into exclusively individualized, outsourced 401(k)-like funds is unacceptable and should be fought to the end. That would be the death of activism, and it would condemn tens of millions of Americans to an inadequate and impoverished retirement.

A second challenge for pension advocates is to maintain the labor movement's commitment to shareholder activism. Labor must continue to fund shareholder activist entities like the AFL-CIO's Office of Investment, or the capital stewardship programs of the SEIU, AFSCME, North America's Building Trades, UNITE HERE, and others. Some years ago, around the time of Lisa Lindsley's departure, AFSCME cut back its program. If and when the *Janus* case kills off agency fees, many public sector unions will have fewer resources to allocate. Some unions have already cut back on expenses because of declining unionization and in anticipation of *Janus*.[62]

I do not mean to oversimplify the brutal choices that will have to be made in the face of resource scarcity. But I hope this book has made the case that the loss of, or even a significant reduction in, the resources allocated to shareholder activism will have a devastating effect on workers. Most directly, it would leave them vulnerable to attacks on their pensions, to high fees, to self-serving managers, to fraud in the marketplace, to fund managers who "simultaneously solicit and betray" them, to privatization of their own jobs using their own retirement money. The rest of the market will feel this loss keenly too. This is another way that *Janus* could indirectly hurt labor's capital. Yes, it will lead to reduced benefits in the long run stemming from reduced bargaining leverage, but it could also force lower investment in shareholder activism. If you are a union member, or if you contribute to or participate in a state or local pension fund, call them and tell them you want them to maintain activism as a priority.

Maintaining centralized defined-benefit pensions and continuing to support activism should be priorities in the near term. This is how labor and others can help labor's capital. How can labor's capital help labor while still helping itself?

President Donald Trump has advocated for $1 trillion in infrastructure spending, and Senate Democrats have issued their own proposal for such spending. Public pension and labor union funds were talking about infrastructure and acting on it even before Trump or the Senate Democrats. Ironically, infrastructure spending was also much discussed and facilitated by the Clinton Global Initiative. For labor and labor's capital, the logic of infrastructure spending is apparent. There is an enormous need to refurbish vital, outdated U.S. infrastructure including roads, bridges, tunnels, schools, broadband networks, railroads, train stations, seaports, and airports. The American Society of Civil Engineers has estimated that the United States needs over $2.2 trillion in infrastructure spending. Pension funds like CalPERS, CalSTRS, and others have already committed billions of dollars to such projects. As noted, Blackstone has committed $100 billion to infrastructure and agreed to prioritize hiring union labor for such projects. Apart from there being a clear investment need and potential profits to be made, infrastructure represents a true "virtuous circle" opportunity for labor. Investments in infrastructure can be a stimulus package for labor. It could put millions of men and women back to work, hopefully unionized workers earning respectable "prevailing" wages.[63] Those workers could in turn constitute a new group of pension contributors, helping to shore up those pensions through both investment and new participants. This is why Congressional Republicans and the Koch wing of the party will never support it.

Organizations like the Union Labor Life Insurance Company (ULLICO) and the National Electrical Benefit Fund (NEBF) have significant expertise in funding their own construction projects in ways that advance the bottom line of their pension funds and the interests of their workers. ULLICO was founded in 1927 by Samuel Gompers, the American Federation of Labor's first leader, to offer life insurance policies that were otherwise unavailable to union members. Today, the company is owned by union pensions and unions themselves, and continues to offer insurance and other financial products to unions and their members. ULLICO also does considerable work as an investor. For example, it has a $2.7 billion "J for Jobs" investment fund, which finances construction and development projects. As a requirement of securing a loan from the fund, developers commit to using exclusively union labor on their projects. As Brain Hale, ULLICO's senior vice president and chief operating officer, explained, "We're not a nonprofit. We do everything for a market rate of return, and we pass that along to our pension fund investors. But our work has significant collateral benefits. Unionized construction workers get hired. All of our contractors and subcontractors must be members of the building trades. The workers then make contributions to their pension plans, which makes them stronger."[64]

ULLICO also maintains an infrastructure investment fund. On such projects, even if ULLICO is a minority investor, the entire project must use union labor or ULLICO can't invest. For example, ULLICO has only a $75 million investment in a $1 billion water treatment project, but because of that investment, the entire plant is being built with union labor. And in contrast to the colonization of public services by private equity funds described in Chapter 5 and in the *New York Times*'s "Bottom Line Nation" series, ULLICO does not necessarily demand outright ownership of the public asset. They can instead take a long term lease. An "8, 9, 10, 11 percent rate of return for our pension funds investors who have a long term revenue stream is fair, it beats their expected rate of return [of approximately 7.5 percent]." ULLICO has spoken with the Trump administration and with Democrats on Capitol Hill about infrastructure investments.[65]

Similarly, the NEBF was capitalized by, and spun off from, the International Brotherhood of Electrical Workers (IBEW) as an independent investment manager. This setup can help avoid the myriad problems faced by other pension funds when dealing with managers from hedge funds and private equity funds. Instead, the IBEW works with an investment manager it controls. In the words of the fund's executive director for investments, Monte Tarbox, working with such an investment manager "makes sure our values are respected." That includes hiring unionized electrical workers on construction deals they invest in. It is unusual for pension funds to create their own investment manager in the United States, although CalPERS is reportedly considering capitalizing its own private equity fund. But pension funds in Canada, the Netherlands, and the United Kingdom have done so. British Telecom's establishment of Hermes, noted earlier, is such an example.[66]

Potentially the most significant deployment of labor's capital to generate unionized jobs and pension contributors is also the most recent. It involved a tag-team effort between two of the main players in this book, Scott Stringer's NYC funds and Dan Pedrotty, the former head of both the AFL–CIO Office of Investment and Capital Strategies for the American Federation of Teachers, now in his third activist incarnation as director of capital strategies for North America's Building Trades Union. As noted in Chapter 5, the NYC funds have adopted a muscular Responsible Contractor Policy that not only bars investments that harm public sector jobs but strongly prefers that such contractors be hired for fund investments. A Responsible Contractor "is a contractor or subcontractor who pays workers fair wages and benefits as evidenced by payroll and employee records. 'Fair benefits' may include, but are not limited to, employer-supported family health care coverage, pension benefits and apprenticeship training programs. 'Fair wages' and 'Fair benefits' are based on relevant market factors that include the nature and location of the project, comparable job or trade classifications, and the scope and complexity of services provided."[67]

The $160 billion NYC funds will not invest without a Responsible Contractor Policy in place. They will not become a limited partner in a private equity pool without it. The list of people who helped institute the policy features many of the players already discussed. Pedrotty and others spent months urging the NYC funds to adopt the policy. Stringer pushed for it. John Adler (the director of the New York City Mayor's office of pensions and investments and chief pension investment advisor to Mayor Bill DiBlasio), and Antonio Rodriguez (senior pension and investments officer) helped push it from inside DiBlasio's office. So did Michael Garland, Stringer's deputy in the proxy access fight, as well as Stringer's pension director, Suzanne Vickers.[68]

Once the policy was adopted, Pedrotty, with the backing and involvement of the Building Trades Union president, Sean Garvey, set his eyes on the world's juiciest target for that policy: private equity powerhouse Blackstone's $100 billion infrastructure fund, the largest private infrastructure fund ever created. Pedrotty entered into negotiations with Blackstone's Tia Breakley and others in an effort to get it to adopt the same policy. Although not a NYC funds representative, Pedrotty was able to use its Responsible Contractor Policy as leverage in these negotiations, pointing out how much more capital would be available to Blackstone if it adopted these rules. Contacts between the Building Trades and Blackstone also took place at a more senior level, between Garvey and Sam Klimczak, the head of Blackstone's infrastructure investment fund.[69]

On September 5, 2017, Blackstone announced the result of these negotiations: "Blackstone (NYSE:BX) today announced that its dedicated infrastructure business has adopted a Responsible Contractor Policy that includes an agreement to cooperate with the North America's Building Trades Unions ('NABTU') to include 'responsible contractors' in the bidding and selection process for its investments. Through this policy, Blackstone will promote fair benefits, wages, working conditions, and training opportunities for construction workers on projects for Blackstone's dedicated infrastructure business." Blackstone had two excellent reasons for adopting this policy: access to capital and access to labor. By adopting the policy, it obtained access to the NYC funds' capital and those of other funds that require such a policy before investing. And it obtained access to labor for its infrastructure projects via the agreement with the Building Trades Union.[70]

Now, the scramble is on for other infrastructure players to catch up, and for additional working-class shareholders to adopt similar policies. The Building Trades already has agreements with TIAA-CREF, MassMutual, and Deutsche Bank, and is targeting other players like private equity powerhouse Carlyle Partners and Brookfield Properties. It is also pushing for the aid of other allies like the Ontario Municipal Employees' Retirement System and the Australian labor movement through its superannuation funds.[71]

Of course, much work remains to be done in monitoring Blackstone and others for compliance with these policies, and in making sure these infrastructure projects actually get built. Such spending programs could have huge risks for both labor and its capital. It could be structured in a way that lets private funds skim billions off the top in fees, it could offer low-wage work to nonunionized workers with no benefits, and it could leave much of our public infrastructure in private hands, hands with veto rights over future public spending. If the investments and projects are poorly designed, it could leave these pensions in bad shape. That said, entities like ULLICO, the NEBF, and now the Blackstone–Building Trades agreement offer a solid alternative means of building these projects, and monitoring them for proper execution.

This is where the work described in these pages could help build labor's future. There are many people inside the labor movement, inside union and pension funds, or within sympathetic foundations or even mutual funds, who have been fighting these fights for a dozen years of more. They understand the issues. They know how deals are structured. They know how their investees work. They have learned to monitor and set fee structures. They can shape investments. They can force the hiring of unionized workers and payment of prevailing wages. They can do so using the investment leverage in their retirement funds. If Trump lives up to his rhetoric, a big if, he could create a massive infrastructure investment plan with Democratic support. If not, then a truly big initiative on infrastructure, and pension security, might have to await the next time Democrats control the House, Senate, and White House. Until then, much of this work will be done privately, or at the state and local levels.

In the longer term, there are additional steps these funds and their sponsors can take to further enhance their leverage and improve the retirement security of workers nationwide.

First, upward of 55 million people in the United States have no retirement plan other than Social Security. Hank Kim, the executive director of the National Conference on Public Employee Retirement Systems, devised a plan targeted at that population. Kim proposed Secure Choice Pensions, a state-created, defined-benefit pension plan for people who do not have retirement plans, mostly for employees of small businesses.[72] Some percentage of employee income, around 3 percent, would be deposited into a state-run retirement fund for the employee. Employers would face no fiduciary obligations or liabilities, other than to pay in the requisite employee percentage of income. The plan's trustees would assume all the fiduciary duties and liabilities. Funds would be conservatively invested under conservative investment assumptions.

Versions of Kim's plan spread rapidly to numerous states and cities, including California, Connecticut, Illinois, Maryland, Oregon, New York City, and Philadelphia, which either adopted or were considering legislation to create them.[73] Unfortunately, some of these plans did not retain a centralized investment component. Regardless, with help from a favorable legal interpretation from the Obama Department of Labor exempting these funds from federal law, tens of millions of people were on the verge of obtaining a retirement plan for the first time.

But less than one month into the Trump administration, two Republican congressmen introduced legislation to overturn the

Department of Labor ruling that enabled creation of these accounts. Congressmen Tim Walberg (R–Mich.) and Francis Rooney (R–Fla.) argued that the Labor Department regulation "will discourage small businesses from offering private-sector plans," forcing them "into government-run plans with fewer protections and less control over their hard-earned savings."[74] Of course, these small businesses weren't offering private sector plans to begin with, which explains the need for state plans. The U.S. Chamber of Commerce came out against Secure Choice, as did the 401(k) community, which rationally feared what would have happened to its business when lower-fee state run plans outperformed theirs. The whole debate is reminiscent of the debate over Obamacare, reminiscent of every debate over state-sponsored plans designed to help people who are not getting what they need from the private sector. The Republican Congress quickly voted to override the Labor Department's regulatory interpretation. They did so under the same Congressional Review Act that would have allowed it to reverse the CEO-worker pay ratio with a hand wave had Senator Elizabeth Warren and Heather Slavkin Corzo not pushed hard for issuance of the rule sooner.

Fortunately, in spite of loss of the safe harbor created by the federal government's regulation, it appears that all of these states are proceeding with their Secure Choice Pension plans anyway. Vermont has since added its name to the list. As a result, tens of millions of Americans may still obtain a massive benefit in spite of Republican opposition. At the moment, some of these plans may be managed in-house by state entities, which should retain some of the centralization benefits discussed above. Others appear set to outsource management to private-sector mutual funds, which would be unfortunate for the reasons already described, unless state leverage could be used to encourage these mutual funds to give these workers some collective shareholder voice. But it seems clear that the next time the Democrats take the White House and/or Congress, they can give these plans a significant boost, and potentially encourage them to become part of state pension plans, as Kim initially envisioned. If such plans could be managed centrally, instead of individually, either within existing public pension plans or in some other form, they could serve as a new voice for working- and middle-class people in markets. Centralization would empower these funds to protect themselves from rapacious fees, destructive investments, or self-serving corporate managers.

Another idea worth exploring for labor's capital, particularly as the SEC turns over to hostile hands under the Trump administration, is to revive the exit option, that is, the option to sell their stakes in underperforming companies. One of the assumptions undergirding much shareholder activism today is that labor's capital is locked into its investments because of diversification requirements. But that's not quite right. It is true that these funds must remain diversified, and that furnishing a secure retirement for their beneficiaries remains their highest objective. But portfolios can remain diversified without holding every stock in every market sector, as long as the fund retains some exposure to each sector. Substantial empirical evidence demonstrates that a manager can construct a diversified investment portfolio from even just twenty or thirty stocks. Yet many of these pension funds own thousands of different stocks. The ability to exit private equity funds and hedge funds has been a significant source of power for pension funds, and the same could be true for investments in public companies, especially if parallel exits occurred. And while I would not necessarily advocate pensions slimming down from thousands of stocks to twenty, any reduction would necessarily increase funds' shareholder stakes in the companies they continue to hold. That could make them more effective monitors of such companies and potentially aid their ability to overcome barriers to shareholder proposals or litigation. Of course, exit has costs of its own. The trick, as always, is not to hurt yourself on the way out the door, because your selling can put downward pressure on the stock price.

Thus, I think working-class shareholders and their allies should do the following: (1) Protect the status quo for centrally managed defined-benefit pension plans. As a fallback position, they can settle for hybrid plans, or perhaps centrally managed defined-contribution plans. Under no circumstances should any labor organization consent to individually managed defined-contribution funds that are just pass-throughs to mutual funds. (2) Dump recalcitrant investment managers who cannot fall into step with pension funds' investment priorities. Pension funds should also consider creating their own investment managers, like ULLICO and NEBF did, or pursuing agreements like that between the Building Trades and Blackstone, that favor the use of union labor. CalPERS is reportedly considering creation of its own private equity fund, a step I would strongly encourage it to explore over outsourcing it. (3) Continue to invest in shareholder activism and in the staffing and resources required to support it, even in the face of budget cuts. (4) When the political opportunity presents itself, support and seek expansion of Secure Choice Pensions in pooled form, preferably making them part of existing public pension funds, even if done in a way that eliminates liability for taxpayers. (5) Explore reviving exit as a meaningful strategy in the face of renewed efforts to limit shareholder voice in the near term.

All of this is in addition to continued work on many of the issues sketched out in earlier chapters. That includes advancing and using proxy access, continued expansion of shareholder voting rights like promoting a universal proxy card (to allow shareholders to ticket split, rather than be forced to choose one slate or another in a proxy fight, which is the status quo), and continuing the fight on executive compensation. This near and midterm agenda is not an exclusive list, but it goes to the core concerns for labor's capital.

Conclusion

The shareholder activists described in this book have fought to give voice to working-class people with modest pensions. These activists have fought for corporate accountability by making shareholder elections meaningful. They have sought to take back control from hedge funds and private equity funds that take their money and betray them. They have pushed for greater transparency over investments and fees, sued to enforce the law when defrauded, and built alliances with other shareholders and with foundations, environmental investors, mutual funds, and activists more generally. They may now have an opportunity through infrastructure investments to shape the interests of working people for decades to come.

Sketching out the work of these shareholder activists places the backlash against them in some perspective. At bottom, these attacks are about more than dollars and cents. They are about more than just stripping away the retirement security of millions of Americans in the name of ideology or self-interest. That would be bad enough on its own. But the drive to silence activism and to undermine pensions is about something more fundamental than questions of corporate authority, of tax levels and state budgets. It is about economic voter suppression.

It is about stifling economic voice, rather than just political voice. It is about snuffing out the economic voice of tens of millions of Americans, those who currently have that voice in the form of activist, centrally managed pensions, and those who have never had any voice at all. The backlash against labor's capital is about establishing and maintaining a system in which the financial and corporate elite deploy worker retirement money as they like, and give workers no say over how it is used. This backlash is about perpetuating the illusion of an open and participatory economic system without ceding the authority that meaningful participation would require. This silencing of economic voice, even more than political voice, explains much of the desperation driving our politics today. And if opponents of working-class shareholders succeed in silencing that voice, I fear that it will find some other, perhaps more vicious form of expression. In many ways, it already has.

But I conclude here with what I said at the outset of this book: of all the institutions built by and on behalf of workers in the twentieth century, these pension funds—assembled in the dullest and least dramatic fashion, with small contributions from tens of millions of modest paychecks over decades of labor—have the best chance of surviving into the twenty-first century. The activists who figured out how to pilot them are community and labor organizers, Democratic operatives, and fed up ex-bankers. None of them started out thinking they'd be shareholder activists when they grew up. No such thing existed. All found their way into this space through a combination of idealism and pragmatism, from a desire to find realistic ways to help working-class people. In so doing, they created a movement. They have labored inside that movement for years, mostly outside of public view, and without much need for help.

That has now changed. Without some larger mobilization of public support, the ability of these activists to go on working could be sharply curtailed if not eliminated. That's particularly true if the Kochs, Arnolds, and others successfully divide and conquer the pension funds, especially in California. What these opponents want from labor's capital is what they have always wanted from labor itself: fractured, passive, leaderless decentralization that deprives it of the ability to protect itself. If they get that, they will silence the voices heard in this book, and accelerate every noxious trend toward economic inequality, toward corporate and financial impunity. With the unions and the Democratic Party as vulnerable as ever, the threat is serious. But this is a campaign that can be beaten back. These pensions are defensible, tactically, strategically, and morally. There is still time, if people recognize the importance of the task and mobilize to complete it.

Too many of us have already written the obituary for traditional working-class institutions. People are moving on, convinced, with the hubris of the living, that the creations of prior generations are outdated and outmoded, that we must start the world again anew. The ignorance of that perspective when it comes to pension power is scandalous. These pensions have real-world clout of a sort that working-class institutions have not wielded in decades. They don't need to be hacked or disrupted by activists looking to attach their names to the new thing. They don't need to be fretted over by thought leaders pondering the neoliberal taint of stock ownership. And they don't need to be marginalized by progressive strategists too deeply in love with the activism of the ballot booth or the street. They just need to be defended as they are and given room to grow. It is not a big ask, and if our collective answer is anything other than yes, we will lose the only institutions and activists that have consistently delivered tangible benefits to working-class people in this country for decades.

Notes

1. Safeway

1. Freddie Mooche, "Safeway CEO Sells $21.4 Million in Shares before Union Strikes," Xcess News, October 13, 2003, https://perma.cc/SZC2 -S3FE; "2 Sides Seem Entrenched in Supermarket Dispute," *New York Times,* November 10, 2003, https://perma.cc/S2CV-DREG; Steven Greenhouse, "Wal-Mart, Driving Workers and Supermarkets Crazy," *New York Times,* October 19, 2003, https://perma.cc/52GT-JZGH; Ronald Grover and Louise Lee, "Time for Safeway's Burd to Fly Away?" Bloomberg, February 12, 2004, https://perma.cc/M5HP-PPJ8; "70,000 Grocery Store Workers Strike," CNN, October 12, 2003, https://perma.cc /CM3K-DKBD.

2. "Steven A. Burd," Reference for Business, https://perma.cc/S48G -UHDQ; Grover and Lee, "Time for Safeway's Burd to Fly Away?" See also James F. Peltz and Melinda Fulmer, "Safeway Chief at Center of Standoff," *Los Angeles Times,* October 19, 2003, https://perma.cc/89NA-THCN; "Safeway Buys Dominick's," CNN Money, October 13, 1998, https://perma .cc/5AQE-5M5X; Melinda Fulmer, "Safeway to Buy Texas Chain Randall's Food," *Los Angeles Times,* July 24, 1999, https://perma.cc/3URZ-RLA8; and Barbara Powell, "Publix Denies Talk of Safeway Buyout," *Sun-Sentinel,* January 1, 2002, https://perma.cc/QA7T-8UDN.

3. Pia Sarkar, "Safeway Loss Tops $1 Billion," SFGate, February 7, 2003, https://perma.cc/U49T-FNTJ. Burd was outmaneuvered by supermarket magnate Ron Burkle, who bought Dominick's for $700 million in 1995, sold it to Burd / Safeway for $1.5 billion in 1998, and offered to buy it back from Burd / Safeway in 2004 for $350 million. See David Whelan, "Unsafe at Safeway," *Forbes,* June 7, 2004, https://perma.cc/Z7GC-VFKR.

4. Burd traded under a legal loophole called a 10b5-1 plan. Using 10b5-1 plans, insiders plan their trades months in advance. This insulates them from claims of illegal insider trading because they have already decided to trade months before they obtain the inside information; this supposedly severs the connection between the trade and the inside information itself. Would that were true. First, insiders can cancel trades at any time, which lets them cancel

based on inside information (in short, insider non-trading). Second, insiders have some wiggle room to time the release of information, rather than timing the trade. Thus, you can hold bad news until after your preplanned trading window closes, then disclose it; similarly, you can disclose positive information shortly before you are scheduled to trade. This still gives the insider a trading advantage over the public. Academic research has found evidence showing that (1) company stock price drops consistently after 10b5-1 trades, tending to illustrate that insiders exploit this loophole to their advantage, and that (2) companies time their information disclosures around preplanned executive trading windows. See, e.g., Alan Jagolinzer, "Sec Rule 10b5-1 and Insiders' Strategic Trade," *Management Science,* February 2009, 224–39. Burd himself adopted the 10b5-1 plan under which he sold his Safeway shares on August 6, 2003, just four months before the Safeway strike. For his SEC filings, see Safeway Inc., Statement of Changes in Beneficial Ownership (Form 4), SEC, September 8, 2003, https://perma.cc /9FB6-RUAC. It seems likely that Burd might have anticipated the strike that took place shortly after, triggered by the benefit cuts he announced after completing his 10b5-1 plan trades.

5. Mooche, "Safeway CEO Sells."

6. Melinda Fulmer and Kathy M. Kristof, "Safeway Rewards 11 Top Execs," *Los Angeles Times,* January 26, 2004, https://perma.cc/6UV3-3ZZT; Janet Adamy, "Safeway Unveils New Executive Pay Plan," Bloomberg Law, January 16, 2004, https://perma.cc/B4UZ-P5BN; Grover and Lee, "Time for Safeway's Burd to Fly Away?" (quotation); Ronald D. White, "Workers Are Stopped Far from Safeway CEO's Home," *Los Angeles Times,* January 29, 2004, https://perma.cc/7DSM-VQSZ (see the note revising down the number of strikers from 70,000 to 59,000); Peltz and Fulmer, "Safeway Chief at Center of Standoff." See also "Steven A. Burd," Reference for Business.

7. "California Attorney General Sues Grocery Chains over Revenue-Sharing Agreement," Bloomberg Law, February 6, 2004, https://perma.cc /D7T8-9MHR; "Attorney General Lockyer Files Lawsuit Alleging Grocers' Agreement Violates Antitrust Laws," press release, State of California Department of Justice, February 2, 2004, https://perma.cc/RX2Y-R9BJ. See also "Safeway: California Strike Cost $103 Million in Q4," Brotherhood of Locomotive Engineers and Trainmen, February 13, 2004, https:// perma.cc/NT73-JVMR.

8. Louis Lavelle, "A Battle Zone in Safeway's Board," Bloomberg, December 24, 2003, https://perma.cc/2KSD-S2ZW: "The nine-member Safeway board has only one truly independent director."

9. "SEC Approves NYSE and NASDAQ Proposals Relating to Director Independence," FindLaw, https://perma.cc/KD2C-7UBK. One impetus for this change was adoption of the Sarbanes–Oxley Act of 2002, which imposed similar reforms.

10. Seven of the nine members on Safeway's board of directors had prior ties to KKR. Although KKR had sold its stake in the company by this time, its affiliates had ongoing business ties to Safeway. Lavelle, "A Battle Zone in Safeway's Board." Additionally, an eighth member of the board, William Tauscher, had several favorable business dealings with Safeway before becoming a member of the board. Ibid.; Yaron Nili, "Out of Sight, Out of Mind: The Case for Improving Director Independence Disclosure," *Journal of Corporation Law* (2018), forthcoming.

11. James F. Peltz, "CalPERS Blasts Safeway Decision to Retain Burd," *Los Angeles Times,* May 4, 2004, https://perma.cc/Z249-UK76; Dylan Machan, "Henry Kravis and George Roberts: All in the Family," *Barrons,* May 17, 2004, https://perma.cc/8S9M-JEM5; Melanie Warner, "Ten Years after We're a Decade Past One of the Steamiest Years in the Age of Excess, Loaded with Memorable Megadeals Cut by Jack Welch, Robert Campeau(!), and the KKR Crowd. Herewith, a Look Back at the Good, the Bad, and the Ugly of 1986," *Fortune,* February 17, 1997, https://perma.cc/3BW2-MG2C; Delroy Alexander, "Funds Challenge Safeway Chief," *Chicago Tribune,* March 25, 2004, https://perma.cc/H3QP-UR8D; Lavelle, "A Battle Zone in Safeway's Board"; "New Safeway Director; Casa Ley General Director Hector Ley Lopez to Be Nominated to Board of Directors," Business Wire, February 17, 2000, https://perma.cc/9APY-8JWZ.

12. John A. Byrne, "Who Is the Real 'Chainsaw Al'?" Bloomberg Businessweek, December 2, 1996, https://perma.cc/7RSM-CWSU; Sherryl Connelly, "Jumpin' Jack Flash: There's No Spark in Former GE Chief's Memoir," *New York Daily News,* September 23, 2001, https://perma.cc/827R-BVXB; "Neutron Jack," Bloomberg Businessweek, December 11, 2000, https://perma.cc/6DSP-QA8L; Stacie Garnett, "Shareholders: Huffy's Downsizing CEO Should Downsize His Own Pay," United for a Fair Economy, April 24, 2000, https://perma.cc/5G9Z-63FY; Grover and Lee, "Time for Safeway's Burd to Fly Away?"

13. Peltz, "CalPERS Blasts Safeway Decision"; "Oregon to Withhold Safeway Votes," *Los Angeles Times,* April 7, 2004, https://perma.cc/PVY7-4UUM; "State Pension Fund Joins Bid to Oust Safeway CEO," *Seattle Times,* April 7, 2004, https://perma.cc/9QRV-DEZE.

14. The first use of the term "labor's capital" that I am aware of was by Teresa Ghilarducci in her book of the same name. Ghilarducci, *Labor's*

Capital: The Economics and Politics of Private Pensions (Cambridge, Mass.: MIT Press, 1992). She uses the term a bit differently than I do, focusing on private pension capital. I use the term to refer specifically to capital invested by union and public pension funds.

15. Saul D. Alinsky famously predicted that pension fund shareholder activism could become a useful progressive tool in his book *Rules for Radicals: A Practical Primer for Realistic Radicals* (New York: Vintage, 1971). The topic was again the subject of two books published in the late 1970s: Peter F. Drucker's *The Unseen Revolution: How Pension Fund Socialism Came to America,* republished as *The Pension Fund Revolution* (New Brunswick, N.J.: Transaction, 1996), and Jeremy Rifkin and Randy Barber's *The North Will Rise Again: Pensions, Politics, and Power in the 1980s* (Boston: Beacon Press, 1978). Other treatments of the topic include a collection of essays edited by Archon Fong, Tessa Hebb, and Joel Rogers, *Working Capital: The Power of Labor's Pensions* (Ithaca, N.Y.: Cornell University Press, 2001); Ghilarducci, *Labor's Capital;* James P. Hawley, *The Rise of Fiduciary Capitalism: How Institutional Investors Can Make Corporate America More Democratic* (Philadelphia: University of Pennsylvania Press, 2000); and Robert A. G. Monks and Nell Minow, *Power and Accountability: Restoring the Balances of Power Between Corporations and Society* (New York: HarperCollins, 1991). Additional writings on the topic, including my own, are referenced throughout this book.

16. U.S. Census Bureau, 2016 Survey of Public Pensions: State and Local Data, https://perma.cc/R789-U7SV; Bureau of Labor Statistics, U.S. Department of Labor, Occupational Outlook Handbook, 2016–17 edition, Construction Laborers and Helpers, https://perma.cc/BA6G-NLWL; Bureau of Labor Statistics, U.S. Department of Labor, Occupational Outlook Handbook, 2016–17 edition, Police and Detectives, https://perma.cc/7VS3-6BMU.

17. David H. Webber, "The Use and Abuse of Labor's Capital," *New York University Law Review* 89 (2014): 2106.

18. Board of Governors of the Federal Reserve System, Financial Accounts of the United States, Flow of Funds, Balance Sheets, and Integrated Macroeconomic Accounts: Historical Annual Tables, 2005–15, table L.120, "State and Local Government Employee Retirement Funds," 91 (March 2016). Most of those assets ($5.2 trillion) are in defined-benefit pension plans. See ibid., table L.120.b, 92.

19. Marc Lifsher, "CalPERS to Withhold Votes on Safeway CEO," *Los Angeles Times,* April 8, 2004, https://perma.cc/Z9MD-KZFN; Burd, Reference for Business. See also Fred Schneyer, "Proxy Advisors Back Pension

Funds' Safeway Opposition," Plan Sponsor, July 5, 2004, https://perma.cc /S2N6-HLVS.

20. James F. Peltz, "Labor Leader Is Elected Board President of CalPERS," *Los Angeles Times,* February 21, 2003, https://perma.cc/SAZ8-RSXE.

21. Jeff Daniels, "CalPERS Could Put Money Back into Tobacco Stocks," CNBC, April 4, 2016, https://perma.cc/H7MP-R8S8. See also Peltz, "Labor Leader Is Elected Board President of CalPERS."

22. SWFI Institute, "SWFI Fund Rankings," June 2016, https://perma .cc/QGS5-NYLJ; Peltz, "Labor Leader Is Elected Board President of CalPERS."

23. The New York Stock Exchange went public in 2006. Oliver Ryan, "Trade Your Stock on the NYSE—But Don't Buy NYSE Stock," *Fortune,* March 29, 2006, https://perma.cc/USV3-8DYT; *New York v. Grasso, Langone, and NYSE,* complaint, https://perma.cc/8234-JRW5, ¶15.

24. Walter Hamilton and Thomas S. Mulligan, "Grasso Says He Won't Resign," *Los Angeles Times,* September 11, 20113, https://perma.cc/SF6C -6BJL; *New York v. Grasso, Langone, and NYSE,* complaint, ¶15; Patrick Mc-Geehan and Landon Thomas, Jr., "Market Chief Holds Firm in Storm over Pay," *New York Times,* September 14, 2003, https://perma.cc/U9ZQ -YQMM; Jake Ulick, "Year of the Scandal," CNN Money, December 17, 2002, https://perma.cc/F9XZ-H3XV. See also Robert Kuttner, "Wake Up, Wall Street: Eliot Spitzer Is a Hero," Bloomberg Business, May 19, 2003, https://perma.cc/X7W3-48KR.

25. Susanne Craig and Kate Kelly, "Large Investors Issue Call for Grasso to Leave NYSE," *Wall Street Journal,* September 17, 2003, https://perma.cc /5N6X-GYUU; David Teather, "The Firefighter: Sean Harrigan, President of CalPERS," *The Guardian,* September 3, 2004, https://perma.cc/U5PN -D6VS; "NYSE Chairman Grasso Resigns," CNN, September 18, 2003, https://perma.cc/DV74-VZ9L.

26. Gary Gentile, "CalPERS Critical of Eisner 'Vision,'" *San Diego Union Tribune,* February 26, 2004, https://perma.cc/8397-AT39. See also Laura Holson, "Roy Disney Resigns and Urges Eisner to Follow Suit," November 30, 2003, *New York Times,* https://perma.cc/GU87-GX22, and "Roy Disney Steps up Efforts against Eisner," *Baltimore Sun,* February 3, 2004, https://perma.cc/6Y6P-NT6C.

27. "Disney's Eisner Loses Votes of Big Pension Fund CalPERS," *Chicago Tribune,* February 26, 2004, https://perma.cc/7M2G-XRN8. See also Gentile, "CalPERS Critical of Eisner 'Vision.'" Since corporate elections are rarely contested, the best shareholders have been able to do, historically, is withhold support for unopposed candidates. Because of reform efforts led

by working-class shareholders, shareholder voting has changed dramatically since Safeway and Disney, as described in Chapter 2.

28. "Disney's Eisner Loses Votes." A withhold vote is a decision not to vote for the only candidate in the race. It is a weak tool, but if the "non-tally" is significant enough, it may embarrass a board of directors into not reseating an unpopular board candidate, even one who "won" because he or she ran unopposed.

29. Chapter 2 of this book describes the ongoing shareholder activist campaign to make corporate elections meaningful. Today, as in 2004, almost all corporate elections involve only one candidate for each board seat, hand-picked by the board itself, with voters only offered the opportunity to vote for or to withhold their vote from that one candidate. This mechanism of shareholder voting has been substantially reformed since the Disney and Safeway fights and remains the most successful achievement of labor's capital. Still, even high withhold votes can lead to a candidate's demise, as it did for Eisner.

30. Robert Trigaux, "For Eisner, the Fairy Tale Is Over," *St. Petersburg Times,* March 5, 2004, https://perma.cc/8YNE-NNW5; Phyllis Furman, "Eisner Loses Chairman Post 43% Voted Down Disney Boss," *New York Daily News,* March 4, 2004, https://perma.cc/E6L3-XYNY.

31. Furman, "Eisner Loses Chairman Post"; "Eisner and Mickey at Last Parting Ways," CNN Money, September 10, 2004, https://perma.cc/2SDR -K7RW.

32. CalPERS was not technically a shareholder in NYSE, since NYSE was not a public company at the time. But CalPERS invested heavily in companies listed on the NYSE, which was overseen by Grasso and a twenty-six-member board composed of numerous CEOs of public companies. Contemporary press reports acknowledged the role played by CalPERS in Grasso's ouster. See, e.g., Landon Thomas Jr., "Officials in 2 States Urge Big Board Chief to Quit," *New York Times,* September 17, 2003, https:// perma.cc/2DMK-4VJ6.

33. Peter Dreier and Kelly Candaele, "A Watershed Strike," *The Nation,* November 10, 2003, https://perma.cc/X2ER-ZREK.

34. United Food and Commercial Workers International Union, "Supermarket Strike Spreads as Picket Lines Begin Move to Northern California Safeway Stores," PR Newswire, November 7, 2003, https://perma .cc/JE5Q-N89U.

35. Carolyn Said, "Getting Personal Safeway CEO Finds Himself at the Center of Labor Dispute," SF Gate, January 28, 2004, https://perma.cc

/MVU5-9GM7; Michael Hiltzik, "Safeway's Merger Loss Eclipses Labor Woes," *Los Angeles Times,* October 23, 2003, https://perma.cc/AJD2-VVAJ.

36. Some analysts, like Mia Kirchgaessner of Sanford C. Bernstein & Company, wrote to their firm's clients that enduring the strike by the UFCW would be "one of the best investments food retailers could make . . . [and would] likely . . . continue to pay off over a number of years." Others, like analyst Lisa Cartwright of Smith Barney, wrote to her clients that "at best, we see Safeway as dead money for now." Other analysts were mixed in their assessment of the strike on Safeway's prospects. See James F. Peltz, "Wall Street Is Chains' Not So Silent Partner," *Los Angeles Times,* December 22, 2003, https://perma.cc/SZF4-ECWF.

37. See also Teresa Ghilarducci, James Hawley, and Andrew Williams, "Labour's Paradoxical Interests and the Evolution of Corporate Finance," *Journal of Law and Society* 24, no. 1 (March 1997): 26–43.

38. "United States Government Accountability Office Report to Congressional Requesters: State and Local Government Pensions: Economic Downturn Spurs Efforts to Address Costs and Sustainability," Government Accountability Office, March 2, 2012, https://perma.cc/4PYT-FKJV. See also James Comtois, "U.S. Retirement Assets Reach $23 Trillion—ICI," *Pensions and Investments,* March 26, 2014, https://perma.cc/2H3Q-B3JF; Phillip Vidal, *Annual Survey of Public Pensions: State- and Locally-Administered Defined Benefit Data Summary Report: 2014,* U.S. Census Bureau, report no. G14-ASPP-SL, July 2015, https://perma.cc/5MAC-P9QD; Timothy Noah, "The 1 Percent Are Only Half the Problem," *New York Times,* May 18, 2013, https://perma.cc/VA8A-T498 ("Pension funds have blurred somewhat the venerable distinction between capital and labor"); and Board of Governors of the Federal Reserve System, Financial Accounts of the United States, table L.120, 91. Most of those assets ($5.2 trillion) are in defined-benefit pension plans. See Board of Governors of the Federal Reserve System, Financial Accounts of the United States, table L.120, 92.

39. Lisa M. Fairfax, *Shareholder Democracy: A Primer on Shareholder Activism and Participation* (Durham, N.C.: Carolina Academic Press, 2011); Dalia Tsuk Mitchell, "Symposium: Understanding Corporate Law through History: Shareholders as Proxies: The Contours of Shareholder Democracy," 63 *Washington and Lee Law Review* 63 (2006): 1503; Lisa M. Fairfax, "Making the Corporation Safe for Shareholder Democracy" *Ohio State Law Journal* 69 (2008): 53.

40. James F. Peltz, "CalPERS Chides Grocers' Actions," *Los Angeles Times,* December 18, 2003, https://perma.cc/XZ4P-GFS5.

41. White, "Workers Are Stopped Far from Safeway CEO's Home."

42. Ibid.; Mike Freeman, "Grocery Workers and Safeway Back to Talking?" *San Diego Union Tribune,* February 7, 2004, https://perma.cc/JGP8 -9EVJ; James F. Peltz, "Safeway Reports $696-Million Loss," *Los Angeles Times,* February 13, 2004, https://perma.cc/QG6P-EB2L; Charlie LeDuff and Steven Greenhouse, "Grocery Workers Relieved, if Not Happy, at Strike's End," *New York Times,* February 28, 2004, https://perma.cc/EPQ6 -KZYV; "Fighting for America," press release, UFCW, February 26, 2004, https://perma.cc/U5V8-YFLT.

43. "James F. Peltz, "How the Supermarket Strike Was Settled," *Los Angeles Times,* March 8, 2004, https://perma.cc/6ER8-2Q4T; LeDuff and Greenhouse, "Grocery Workers Relieved."

44. "The Incredible Decline of American Unions, in One Animated Map," *Washington Post,* February 24, 2015, https://perma.cc/D7JQ-K97E; "American Unions Membership Declines as Public Support Fluctuates," Pew Research, February 20, 2014, https://perma.cc/BGU9-T72V; Cole Stangler, "US Workers Say They're Unhappy So Why Are They Striking Less?" *International Business Times,* February 12, 2015, https://perma.cc /Q5WF-YQXM. Stangler cites U.S. Department of Labor data showing strikes have been declining for four decades, reaching a low point in 2009.

45. "Comprehensive Annual Financial Report: Year Ended June 30, 2004," CalPERS, https://perma.cc/R6DM-VSCT, 15, 133; "Comprehensive Annual Financial Report: Fiscal Year Ended June 30, 2015," CalPERS, https://perma.cc/T9PW-NDE5, 26, 144; "Comprehensive Annual Financial Report of the Comptroller for the Fiscal Year Ended June 30, 2004," City of New York, https://perma.cc/66BG-R3MN, 110; "Comprehensive Annual Financial Report of the Comptroller for the Fiscal Year Ended June 30, 2015," City of New York, https://perma.cc/W62C-LE5Z, 177; "Comprehensive Annual Financial Report for Fiscal Year Ended March 31, 2004," New York State and Local Retirement System, https://perma.cc /YE6X-GN6E, 27; "Comprehensive Annual Financial Report for Fiscal Year Ended March 31, 2015," New York State and Local Retirement System, https://perma.cc/68K7-4QLX, 38; "Illinois State Board of Investment Annual Report 2007," https://perma.cc/9Y7R-BXWR, 9; "2015 Annual Report: Illinois State Board of Investment," https://perma.cc/3QJ2-9QBZ, 3; "Pension Reserves Investment Trust Fund Comprehensive Annual Financial Report for the Year Ended June 30, 2005," MassPRIT, https:// perma.cc/6FRG-DEXA, 14; "Pension Reserves Investment Trust Fund Comprehensive Annual Financial Report for Fiscal Year Ended June 30, 2015," MassPRIT, https://perma.cc/UF2J-R2GL, 25; "Combined Invest-

ment Funds Comprehensive Annual Financial Report for the Fiscal Year Ended June 30, 2004," State of Connecticut Office of the State Treasurer, https://perma.cc/Q45L-N5R7, 18; "Combined Investment Funds Comprehensive Annual Financial Report for the Fiscal Year Ended June 30, 2015," State of Connecticut Office of the Treasurer, https://perma.cc/B7GZ -U8CG, 19; "Oregon Public Employees Retirement System Comprehensive Annual Financial Report for the Fiscal Year Ended June 30, 2004," https://perma.cc/BRS2-9WT2, 12; "Oregon Public Employees Retirement System Comprehensive Annual Financial Report for the Fiscal Year Ended June 30, 2015," https://perma.cc/PX59-6RPV, 18; "Washington State Investment Board Twenty-Third Annual Investment Report June 30, 2004," https://perma.cc/9MLG-67SK, 5; "Washington State Investment Board Thirty-Fourth Annual Report Overview Two Thousand and Fifteen," https://perma.cc/RM69-HKAS, 24, although according to the "Message from the Chair," the fund ended 2015 with $107 billion in assets under management.

46. Alexander, "Funds Challenge Safeway Chief."; David Goll, "Safeway a Longshot for Pension Funds," *San Francisco Business Times,* April 1, 2004, https://perma.cc/3RNL-5Q6L.

47. Alexander, "Funds Challenge Safeway Chief."

48. Ibid.

49. 29 U.S.C. § 1104(a)(1)(A)(i): "Subject to sections 1103(c) and (d), 1342, and 1344 of this title, a fiduciary shall discharge his duties with respect to a plan solely in the interest of the participants and beneficiaries and for the exclusive purpose of providing benefits to participants and their beneficiaries."

50. Whelan, "Unsafe at Safeway."

51. "Safeway Leadership under Fire," *Washington Post,* March 26, 2004, https://perma.cc/JSN7-RAF6. The shareholder campaigners undoubtedly would have liked to throw out the entire board but that was not possible at the time. Safeway had a so-called staggered board, that is, only one-third of the board—three directors—was up for election each cycle. (In response to shareholder pressure, Safeway's board agreed to destagger itself, letting all of its board members face election every year, but it made that decision effective for 2005—the year following this fight. I discuss the issue of staggered boards in Chapter 2. "Safeway Moves to Eliminate 'Staggered Board' Structure," *San Francisco Business Times,* January 5, 2004, https://perma.cc /7GJH-XLRS; Lifsher, "CalPERS to Withhold Votes on Safeway CEO."

52. Robert D. Hershey, "A Little Industry with a Lot of Sway on Proxy Votes," *New York Times,* June 18, 2006, https://perma.cc/PT78-AQP7.

53. Hershey, "A Little Industry with a Lot of Sway on Proxy Votes"; Charles Nathan, James D. C. Barrall, and Alice Chung, "Say on Pay 2011: Proxy Advisors on Course of Hegemony," *New York Law Journal: Corporate Governance,* November 28, 2011, https://perma.cc/Z768-2QST.

54. Schneyer, "Proxy Advisors Back Pension Funds' Safeway Opposition"; Michael Liedtke, "Advisers Want CEO of Safeway off Board," *San Diego Union-Tribune,* May 7, 2004, https://perma.cc/UH5Y-AD8V.

55. "Edward M. Smith Executive Profile," Bloomberg, https://perma.cc /C8P6-KTNG; Ed Smith, telephone interview, January 21, 2015.

56. Ed Smith, telephone interview, January 21, 2015.

57. "Safeway Removes Two Directors," *Las Vegas Sun,* May 3, 2004, https://perma.cc/F52N-G4MW.

58. Mary Ellen Walsh, "State Pension Officials Accuse Safeway Leaders of Conflict," *New York Times,* March 25, 2004, https://perma.cc/Q7BX -DWSD; Liedtke, "Advisers Want CEO of Safeway off Board"; Andrew Ross Sorkin, "Safeway Is Expected to Name 3 New Independent Directors," *New York Times,* May 3, 2004, https://perma.cc/A2BF-FNT8; James F. Peltz, "Investors Lose Bid to Oust Safeway Chief," *Los Angeles Times,* May 21, 2004, https://perma.cc/J26B-M3FH.

59. Greenhouse, "The Nation; Wal-Mart, Driving Workers and Supermarkets Crazy."

60. Ibid.

61. "Comprehensive Annual Financial Report California Public Employees' Retirement System Year Ended June 30, 2003," https://perma.cc /892H-G9Q5, 77, 10; "Comprehensive Annual Financial Report New York State and Local Retirement System for Fiscal Year Ended March 31, 2004," https://perma.cc/VKT3-57VD, 56.

62. "Comprehensive Annual Financial Report California Public Employees' Retirement System Year Ended June 30, 2003," 77; "Comprehensive Annual Financial Report: Year Ended June 30, 2004," CalPERS, 79.

63. Stock prices obtained from Yahoo! Finance.

64. U.S. Securities and Exchange Commission, form 13-F, CalPERS, report for Quarter Ended June 30, 2004.

65. Michael Flaherman, e-mail correspondence, August 7, 2015.

66. Andrew Ang, "The Norwegian Government Pension Fund: The Divestiture of Wal-Mart Stores Inc.," Program for Financial Studies, The Sanford C. Bernstein & Company Center for Leadership and Ethics Case Series, Columbia Business School, Spring 2008, https://perma.cc/4SE3 -PRSG; "Two Companies—Wal-Mart and Freeport—Are Being Excluded from the Norwegian Government Pension Fund–Global's Investment Uni-

verse," press release, June 6, 2006, https://perma.cc/FM2E-EJ5A; Bill Baue, "Norwegian Government Pension Fund Dumps Wal-Mart and Freeport on Ethical Exclusions," Business Administration School of São Paulo at the Getulio Vargas Foundation, June 16, 2006, https://perma.cc/3PEY-2EJZ.

67. Madison Marriage, "Seven European Pension Schemes Ditch Ryanair Stock," *Financial Times,* May 8, 2017, https://perma.cc/6ZYQ-R3PZ.

68. "CalSTRS Divests of Certain Firearms Holdings," press release, CalSTRS, April 12, 2013, https://perma.cc/T24Q-22GU; Joe Pinsker, "Why Investors Bet on Gun Sales after a Mass Shooting," *The Atlantic,* October 3, 2017, https://perma.cc/G8U3-N3BZ.

69. David H. Webber, "Protecting Public Pension Fund Investments," *Washington Post,* November 20, 2014, https://perma.cc/PFN9-7SW6; Webber, "The Use and Abuse of Labor's Capital"; Hazel Bradford, "Pace of Pension Reform Ebbs after 49 States Change Laws," *Pensions and Investments,* April 14, 2014, https://perma.cc/64F5-6ZCB.

70. 29 U.S.C. § 1104 (a)(1) (2006); Interpretive Bulletin Relating to Exercise of Shareholder Rights, 73 Fed. Reg. 61,731 (October 17, 2008), https://perma.cc/8WGU-FNFB.

71. *Brock v. Walton,* 794 F.2d 586 (11th Cir. 1986); *Bandt v. Bd. of Ret. of San Diego Cnty. Emps. Ret. Sys.,* 136 Cal. App. 4th 140 (Cal. Ct. App. 2006).

72. Nicholas Greifer, "Pension Investing: Fundamentals and Best Practices," Government Finance Officers Association, 2002, https://perma.cc /5KZM-CQ97.

73. Lauren Gardner, "Why Trump's $1 Trillion Infrastructure Plan Could Wind up in a Ditch," Politico, April 10, 2017, https://perma.cc/YA3J -LYEG.

74. Iris J. Liv and Elizabeth McNichol, "Misunderstandings Regarding State Debt, Pensions, and Retiree Health Costs Create Unnecessary Alarm," Center on Budget and Policy Priorities, January 20, 2011, https://perma.cc /MP7C-KLQ2; Americans for Prosperity, "Public Pensions: Underfunded and Unaffordable," October 25, 2016, https://perma.cc/F4T8-RCCV; Laura and John Arnold Foundation, "Pension Reform," https://perma.cc /C9ED-HMDA; Lydia DePillis, "401(k)s Are Replacing Pensions. That's Making Inequality Worse," *Washington Post,* September 3, 2013, https:// perma.cc/F3RK-ULQ3.

75. Leslie Patton, "Safeway Names Robert Edwards CEO to Replace Steven Burd in May," Bloomberg, April 29, 2013, https://perma.cc/69B2 -NRH9; George Avalos, "Shareholders Approve Safeway's $9.2 Billion Sale to Albertsons," *East Bay Times,* July 25, 2014, https://perma.cc/A3CK -XH97. See also William Alden, "In Safeway Buyout, a Reminder of a

Painful Takeover Years Ago," *New York Times,* March 7, 2014, https://perma .cc/F9X7-CETR.

76. Burd's six-year average compensation was $16.63 million, or $99.78 million from 2006 to 2011. Neil R. Austrian and Marcel H. M. Smits, "CEO Compensation," *Forbes,* no. 418, Steven A Bird, https://perma.cc /9QWR-QTHD. Burd also received $19.5 million in 2004. "Safeway Chairman Bags $17.1M Despite Turbulent 2004," *Forbes,* April 13, 2005, https://perma.cc/7BYA-FBXJ. See also Avalos, "Shareholders Approve Safeway's $9.2 Billion Sale to Albertsons."

77. Scott Morrison, "CalPERS' Activist Head Ousted," *Financial Times,* December 2, 2004, https://perma.cc/CN7C-Y5T7; "Assessing the CalPERS Shake-Up," *Los Angeles Times,* December 3, 2004, https://perma.cc/C2Q8 -W9KA; Holly Hubbard Preston, "But Ouster of CalPERS Chief May Not Scuttle Fund's Efforts: Setback for Corporate Goad," *New York Times,* December 23, 2004, https://perma.cc/YDS8-E5LL; Sean Harrigan, "The Corporations Couldn't Tolerate My Activist Voice," *Los Angeles Times,* December 5, 2004, https://perma.cc/B62C-6UD2.

78. David Zahniser, "Villaraigosa Pension Board Appointee Quits in SEC Inquiry," *Los Angeles Times,* May 8, 2009, https://perma.cc/P3ER-RABX.

79. "Proxy Access, SEC Uncertainty and Related Issues in 2015," Harvard Law School Forum on Corporate Governance and Financial Regulation, February 24, 2015, https://perma.cc/W2FL-XHRX; "SEC Adopts Rule for Pay Ratio Disclosure," press release, Securities and Exchange Commission, 2015, https://perma.cc/8PPJ-KZM4.

2. The New Suffragists

1. Sean Lengell, "Powerful D.C. Circuit Court Has Democratic Majority Bench for First Time since Reagan," *Washington Examiner,* December 10, 2013, http://perma.cc/7XHT-6UTX; "Supreme Court—Frequently Asked Questions," U.S. Supreme Court, https://perma.cc/HBB2-HZ9K. Cases terminated by the D.C. Circuit Court of Appeals by year: 2014 (1069), 2013 (954), 2012 (1189), 2011 (1113) 2010 (1189). Federal Court Caseload Statistics, Cases Terminated, 2006–16, Official Federal Courts' Website, http:// perma.cc/8ZSP-ZUBB.

2. William A. Galston, "President Barack Obama's First Two Years: Policy Accomplishments, Political Difficulties," Brookings, November 4, 2010, http://perma.cc/2YXV-79BN.

3. *Business Roundtable v. SEC,* 647 F.3d 1144 (D.C. Cir. 2011), https://www .cadc.uscourts.gov/internet/opinions.nsf/89BE4D084BA5EBDA852578D 5004FBBBE/$file/10-1305-1320103.pdf.

4. Sean Harrigan, "The Corporations Couldn't Tolerate My Activist Voice," *Los Angeles Times,* December 5, 2004, https://perma.cc/B62C -6UD2.

5. Kaja Whitehouse, "Shareholders Threaten Boards over 'Proxy Access'," *USA Today,* January 27, 2015, http://perma.cc/WD26-LKTT; Mark Fahey, "Yahoo Will Likely Pay Millions for Proxy Fight," CNBC, April 14, 2016, http://perma.cc/569S-WHVB.

6. *Citizens United v. Federal Election Commission,* 558 U.S. 310, 370 (2010).

7. Whitehouse, "Shareholders Threaten Boards over 'Proxy Access'."

8. U.S. Chamber of Commerce, "Proxy Access Legal Challenge: Issue Backgrounder," Business Roundtable, September 29, 2010, http://perma.cc /R3US-AJTY; Rich Ferlauto, telephone interview, April 20, 2016.

9. Lyrics from "Guns and Ships," *Hamilton: An American Musical,* words and music by Lin-Manuel Miranda © 2015 Hamilton Uptown Limited Liability Company.

10. Rich Ferlauto, telephone interview, April 20, 2016.

11. Ibid.; *AFSCME v. AIG,* 462 F.3d 121 (2d Cir. 2006).

12. Rich Ferlauto, telephone interview, April 20, 2016.

13. 15 U.S.C. § 78n(a)(2)(A).

14. Stephen M. Bainbridge, "The Corporate Governance Provisions of Dodd-Frank," UCLA School of Law, Law-Economics Research Paper no. 10–14, October 27, 2010, 10, http://perma.cc/WTJ2-QUG5, citing S. Rep. no. 111–176, 146: "By adopting § 971, however, Congress did preempt an expected challenge to any forthcoming SEC regulation." As *Business Roundtable v. SEC* illustrated, the argument that congressional action preempted a legal challenge turned out to be incorrect.

15. "Roberts: 'My Job Is to Call Balls and Strikes and Not to Pitch or Bat'," CNN.com, September 12, 2005, http://perma.cc/JQG5-VSY5.

16. "Alinsky Wins at the SEC," *Wall Street Journal,* August 30, 2010, http://perma.cc/98ES-2VH8; *Business Roundtable v. SEC,* 39–40.

17. "Alinsky Wins at the SEC"; Louise Rouse, "Pension Funds That Ignore Climate Change Are Failing to Protect Savers," *The Guardian,* October 29, 2013, http://perma.cc/V2SD-N9QK.

18. Ross Kerber, "Amid Business Ties, Some Fund Firms Eased Proxy Pressure: Study," Reuters, April 18, 2017, http://perma.cc/AY3N-V86G.

19. Lucian A. Bebchuk, "Letting Shareholders Set the Rules," *Harvard Law Review* 119 (2006): 1784.

20. "White House Intervenes on Shareholder Rights," Reuters, June 17, 2010, http://perma.cc/SU3G-KA7G.

21. See Chapter 6.

22. Helene Cooper, " 'Obama Signs Overhaul of Financial System," *New York Times,* July 21, 2010, http://perma.cc/JXQ8-WXBP; Securities and Exchange Commission, "SEC Adopts New Measures to Facilitate Director Nominations by Shareholders," August 25, 2010, http://perma.cc/2REU -UYDX; "Alinsky Wins at the SEC."

23. "Alinsky Wins at the SEC."

24. David H. Webber, "The Use and Abuse of Labor's Capital," *New York University Law Review* 89 (2014): 2106; Tessa Hebb, *No Small Change: Pension Funds and Corporate Engagement* (Ithaca, N.Y.: Cornell University Press, 2008); Archon Fong, Tessa Hebb, and Joel Rogers, eds., *Working Capital: The Power of Labor's Pensions* (Ithaca, N.Y.: Cornell University Press, 2001); Stewart J. Schwab and Randall S. Thomas, "Realigning Corporate Governance: Shareholder Activism by Labor Unions," *Michigan Law Review* 96, no. 4 (1998): 1018–94; Teresa Ghilarducci, *Labor's Capital: The Economics and Politics of Private Pensions* (Cambridge, Mass.: MIT Press, 1992).

25. U.S. Chamber of Commerce, "U.S. Chamber Joins Business Round-table in Lawsuit Challenging Securities and Exchange Commission," September 28, 2010, http://perma.cc/WX87-M4GT.

26. Patrick Caldwell, "Did You Know That Antonin Scalia's Son Is Sabotaging Wall Street Reform?" *Mother Jones,* July / August 2014, http://perma .cc/475B-UYD4.

27. *Business Roundtable v. SEC.* See also the judges' biographies on the D.C. Circuit website: "Douglas H. Ginsburg," http://perma.cc/6MGZ -LRZG; "Janice Rogers Brown," http://perma.cc/26J4-DEKZ; and "David B. Sentelle," http://perma.cc/28UH-EAWK.

28. Brady Dennis, "Congress Passes Financial Reform Bill," *Washington Post,* July 16, 2010, http://perma.cc/AUP6-GFTN; "Lawmakers Agree on Ground-Breaking Financial Reform Bill," NJ.com, June 25, 2010, http:// perma.cc/3HJP-G6N7.

29. Brady Dennis, "Congress Passes Financial Reform Bill," *Washington Post,* July 16, 2010, http://perma.cc/AUP6-GFTN; "Lawmakers Agree on Ground-Breaking Financial Reform Bill," NJ.com, June 25, 2010, http:// perma.cc/3HJP-G6N7; David D. Kirkpatrick, "New Judge Sees Slavery in Liberalism," *New York Times,* June 9, 2005, http://perma.cc/7N49-7RR9.

30. Steven V. Roberts, "Ginsburg Withdraws Name as Supreme Court Nominee, Citing Marijuana 'Clamor'," *New York Times,* November 8, 1987, http://perma.cc/BR2S-RFMH; Linda Greenhouse, "Reagan Nominates Anthony Kennedy to Supreme Court," *New York Times,* November 12, 1987, http://perma.cc/U4DZ-NZWE.

31. "In Hayek Lecture, DC Circuit Judge Douglas Ginsburg Argues against Judiciary's Marginalization in Administrative Law," NYU Law News Online, October 23, 2013, http://perma.cc/DT3J-4H6Y, citing Cass Sunstein and Adrian Vermeule, "Libertarian Administrative Law," *University of Chicago Law Review* 82 (2015): 393.

32. Ibid.; Daniel Fisher, "Bureaucrats May Be the Losers if Gorsuch Wins a Seat on Supreme Court," *Forbes,* January 26, 2017, http://perma.cc/95YY-47JS.

33. "In Hayek Lecture"; *Business Roundtable v. SEC,* 35–37.

34. *Business Roundtable v. SEC*; Bainbridge, *Corporations, Securities & Antitrust,* 9n44.

35. See *Motor Vehicle Manufacturers Association v. State Farm Mutual Auto Insurance Co.,* 43 U.S. 29 (1983).

36. *Business Roundtable v. SEC.*

37. Tara Bhandari, Peter Iliev, and Jonathan Kalodimos, "Public versus Private Provision of Governance: The Case of Proxy Access," SEC staff working paper, 2015, https://perma.cc/6GZ3-HFGH (finding data supporting the hypothesis that proxy access can be value enhancing); "Proxy Access in the United States: Revisiting the Proposed SEC Rule," CFA Institute, August 2014, https://perma.cc/4JT7-ZT3C; Bo Becker, Daniel Bergstresser, and Guhan Subramanian, "Does Shareholder Proxy Access Improve Firm Value? Evidence from the Business Roundtable's Challenge," Journal of Law and Economics 56, no. 1 (February 2013): 127–60. See also Torsten Jochem, "Does Proxy Access Increase Shareholder Wealth? Evidence from a Natural Experiment," April 1, 2012, http://perma.cc/TEE5-X9VE ("Whenever proxy access was strong enough to affect firm valuations, the market valued proxy access reform positively, leading to an increase in shareholder wealth"), and Jonathan B. Cohn et al., "On Enhancing Shareholder Control: A (Dodd-)Frank Assessment of Proxy Access," *Journal of the American Finance Association* 71, no. 4 (August 2016): 1623 ("An increase in shareholder control . . . generally benefit[s] shareholders"). See, by contrast, Bernard S. Sharfman, "Why Proxy Access Is Harmful to Corporate Governance," *Iowa Journal of Corporation Law* 37 (Winter 2012): 387–97 ("Centralization of authority and its protection from shareholder[s] . . . is critical for . . . decision making"), and Thomas Stratmann, "Does Shareholder Proxy Access Damage Share Value in Small Publicly Traded Companies?" *Stanford Law Review* 64 (June 2012): 1431 ("Proxy access was a net cost to stock price returns at small firms. . . . Our results [call] into question whether proxy access is a net cost to [larger firms]").

38. Becker, Bergstresser, and Subramanian, "Does Shareholder Proxy Access Improve Firm Value?"

39. "About Scott M. Stringer," New York City Comptroller, http://perma.cc/CLY8-T847; Ari Kagan, "Comptroller Scott Stringer. Government Watchdog and Voice of New Yorkers," http://perma.cc/3ZBC-ZWU8; "Scott Stringer," CBS New York, http://perma.cc/8LNL-A7LS; "Scott Stringer," Our Campaigns, http://perma.cc/4FCT-MP3S; "Under Cover," Downtown Express, July 10, 2009, http://perma.cc/7KJR-BN28; "Bloomberg Wants to Abolish Borough Presidents, Public Advocate, and Community Boards," Vos Iz Neias, July 10, 2008, http://perma.cc/PC2X-84BK.

40. Sewell Chan, "Stringer Won't Challenge Gillibrand in Primary," New York Times, May 19, 2009, http://perma.cc/U2LL-2QWP; Kagan, "Comptroller Scott Stringer"; "The Duties of the Comptroller," New York City Comptroller, http://perma.cc/56DK-9588.

41. Ted Ballantine, "World's Largest Pension Funds, 2015 Edition," Pension360, http://perma.cc/F2DG-YVY3; New York City Employees' Retirement System v. SEC, 45 F.3d 7 (2d Cir. 1995), http://caselaw.findlaw.com/us-2nd-circuit/1456604.html; "Restaurant Bias Ban Loses," New York Times, November 24, 1993, http://perma.cc/9AAR-WBHK; Nicole Gelinas, "Corporate America's New Stealth Raiders," City Journal, Winter 2005, http://perma.cc/2SUH-Q8FS.

42. Karen Tumulty, "Eliot Spitzer Looks for Political Redemption in New York City," Washington Post, July 8, 2013, https://perma.cc/MHL9-5VJY; "Eliot Spitzer Biography," http://perma.cc/6S7R-6KMZ; Kate Taylor, "Stringer Defeats Spitzer in Comptroller Primary," New York Times, September 10, 2013, http://perma.cc/AW59-76W8.

43. Dan Strumpf, "U.S. Public Companies Rise Again," Wall Street Journal, February 5, 2014, http://perma.cc/3UPX-EL2Z.

44. "Boardroom Accountability Project," New York City Comptroller, http://perma.cc/DU2U-SEDD; Scott Stringer, telephone interview, February 27, 2017; "Michael Garland," Conference Board, http://perma.cc/765Z-S5VL; "Michael Garland," International Corporate Governance Network, http://perma.cc/483T-HYB8; Michael Garland, telephone interview, January 18, 2017; Stephen Gandel, "The Guy with the Job Spitzer Is Spending Millions to Get," Fortune, July 24, 2013, http://perma.cc/54FL-SEEN; Dan Pedrotty, telephone interview, March 25, 2016.

45. For a description of the Board Accountability Project, see http://perma.cc/DU2U-SEDD.

46. Michael Garland, telephone interview, January 18, 2017.

47. Joanna Lublin, "Investors Gain Greater Clout over Boards," *Wall Street Journal*, January 10, 2016, http://perma.cc/VX3C-76BJ; "S&P 500," S&P Dow Jones Indices, http://perma.cc/7TBB-Z3VV; Michael Garland, telephone interview, January 18, 2017; Scott Stringer, telephone interview, February 27, 2017. See also Scott M. Stringer, "2015 Shareowner Initiatives Postseason Report," 6, http://perma.cc/D7W6-8P8Y.

48. Scott Stringer, "NYC Pension Funds Launch National Campaign to Give Shareowners a True Voice in How Corporate Boards Are Elected," press release, New York City Comptroller, November 6, 2014, http://perma.cc/YY4S-A36C.

49. Michael Garland, telephone interview, January 18, 2017; Motoko Rich, "Why Don't More Men Go into Teaching?" *New York Times,* September 6, 2014, http://perma.cc/DF3R-T6PV; Patricia Cohen, "Public-Sector Jobs Vanish, Hitting Blacks Hard," *New York Times,* May 24, 2015, http://perma.cc/CFR6-Q4CL; U.S. Department of Labor, "The African-American Labor Force in the Recovery," February 29, 2012, http://perma.cc/6PY8-WVJW; Webber, "The Use and Abuse of Labor's Capital"; State Street Global Advisors, "Fearless Girl Sends Powerful Message," March 10, 2017, https://perma.cc/FJA8-JU39.

50. Shareholder proposals are comparatively easy to file. Thus, while it has historically been almost impossible to run competing board candidates because of the absence of proxy access, to place a shareholder proposal on the proxy that would allow the shareholders to institute a proxy access rule has always been easier, requiring, in effect, only a minimum $2,000 stake in the company. The reason this was not attempted earlier is because of the daunting task of filing these proposals, and running campaigns in support of them, at five thousand U.S. companies. That said, the Business Roundtable is lobbying to make it significantly more difficult for shareholders to file proposals.

51. Lublin, "Investors Gain Greater Clout over Boards."

52. Ibid.; Scott M. Stringer, "New York City Pension Funds 2016 Shareowner Initiatives Postseason Report," Office of New York City Comptroller, 7–8, http://perma.cc/Q7B3-WLJS; Jeff Green, "After 70-Year Fight, This Investor Request Is Met Left and Right," Bloomberg, March 10, 2016, https://perma.cc/8YSN-EJEX.

53. Lublin, "Investors Gain Greater Clout over Boards." Data on the seventy-three companies was supplied by TIAA-CREF.

54. See *Business Roundtable v. SEC.*

55. Bhandari, Iliev, and Kalodimos, "Public versus Private Provision of Governance," 4: "We find that the BAP announcement led to a positive,

statistically significant, 53 basis point abnormal return for the average targeted firm. Further, among the targeted firms, we find that those firms that the market expected to benefit more than others from mandated proxy access are the firms that are expected to benefit more from being targeted for private ordering." See also Cohn, "On Enhancing Shareholder Control"; Becker, Bergstresser, and Subramanian, "Does Shareholder Proxy Access Improve Firm Value?" ("Enhancing activist investors' voice . . . increases firm value. . . . Financial markets placed a positive value on shareholder access"); and Jochem, "Does Proxy Access Increase Shareholder Wealth?" See, by contrast, Sharfman, "Why Proxy Access Is Harmful to Corporate Governance," and Stratmann, "Does Shareholder Proxy Access Damage Share Value in Small Publicly Traded Companies?"

56. "Proxy Access in the United States." CFA stands for chartered financial analyst.

57. Lynn Stout, *The Shareholder Value Myth: How Putting Shareholders First Harms Investors, Corporations, and the Public* (Oakland, Calif.: Berrett-Koehler, 2012); Scott M. Stringer, "Boardroom Accountability Project," https://perma.cc/SJ26-29EW; Gianna McCarthy and George Wong, "Federal Bill Attempts to Silence Investors," Harvard Law School Forum on Corporate Governance and Financial Regulation, June 27, 2017, https://perma.cc/NFA9-M8S5.

58. "Proxy Access Corporate Governance Report," Sidley, January 3, 2017, https://www.sidley.com/en/insights/newsupdates/2017/01/proxy-access-tipping-point-dec-2016. This report concludes that just over 50 percent (251) of S&P 500 companies have adopted proxy access as of December 2016.

59. "Plurality and Majority Voting—Who Really Cares?" *Activist Investor Blog,* June 18, 2012, http://perma.cc/WF53-8BHH; "1992 Presidential General Election Results," U.S. Election Atlas, http://perma.cc/E8CR-XLSX.

60. "Plurality and Majority Voting." See also Stephen Choi et al., "Does Majority Voting Improve Board Accountability?" *University of Chicago Law Review* 83 (2016): 1119 (which finds that for some firms, the "adoption of majority voting led to more shareholder-friendly governance"); Yonca Ertimur and Fabrizio Ferri, "Does the Director Election System Matter? Evidence from Majority Voting," Social Science Research Network, May 30, 2013, http://ssrn.com/abstract=1880974 ("The adoption of [majority voting] is value-enhancing and [one] source of this value creation is the greater propensity of boards to respond to shareholder pressure under a [majority voting] standard"). But see Jay Cai, Jacqueline L. Garner, and

Ralph A. Walking, "A Paper Tiger? An Empirical Analysis of Majority Voting," *Journal of Corporate Finance* 21 (June 2013), https://ssrn.com /abstract=1491627, finding data supporting the "paper tiger hypothesis," that majority voting appears to make a firm stronger but lacks the power to do so and has no significant impact on director turnover, financial performance, or shareholder returns. See also William K. Sjostrom and Young Sang Kim, "Majority Voting for the Election of Directors," *Connecticut Law Review* 40, no. 2 (December 2007), http://ssrn.com/abstract=962784, finding that majority voting is little more than "smoke and mirrors" and documenting no market reaction to majority voting implementation.

61. United Brotherhood of Carpenters, "Issue Report: Carpenter Funds' Majority Vote Election Standard Advocacy," http://perma.cc /ZP34-MDNQ.

62. Yakov Amihud, Markus M. Schmid, and Steven Davidoff Solomon, "Settling the Staggered Board Debate," CLS Blue Sky Blog, September 18, 2017, https://perma.cc/7QR8-M4FR; "Course Catalog: Shareholder Rights Project," Harvard Law School, http://perma.cc/56ZU-6FPJ; Shareholder Rights Project, "Investors Working with the SRP Clinic," 2014, http:// perma.cc/Z9LP-6L7H.

63. Shareholder Rights Project, http://perma.cc/89AV-R7WJ; Institutional Shareholder Services, "The Latest in Governance Reform—Proxy Access," http://perma.cc/U9XM-YU8Q; Carol Bowie, "ISS 2016 Board Practices Study," Harvard Law School Forum on Corporate Governance and Financial Regulation, June 1, 2016, http://perma.cc/35SY-YXAK. See also Weili Ge, Lloyd Tanlu, and Jenny Li Zhang, "What Are the Consequences of Board Destaggering," *Review of Accounting Studies* 21 (September 2016): 808 ("This study suggests that destaggering results in potentially negative consequences for shareholders. . . . These findings are . . . consistent with the view held by proponents of keeping the previously more popular staggered board structure"); Martijn Cremers, Lubomir P. Litov, and Simone Sepe, "Staggered Boards and Long-Term Firm Value, Revisited," *Journal of Financial Economics* (2017): 1–23, https://ssrn.com/abstract=2364165 ("We find no evidence that staggered board changes are negatively related to firm value. . . . This suggests that staggered boards promote value creation for some firms by committing the firm to undertaking long-term projects and bonding it to the relationship-specific investments of its stakeholders"); and David F. Larcker, Gaizka Ormazabal, and Daniel J. Taylor, "The Market Reaction to Corporate Governance Regulation," *Journal of Financial Economics* 101 (August 2011): 431 ("The presence of a staggered board is a value-maximizing governance choice, such that banning staggered

boards decreases shareholder value"). But see also Olubunmi Faleye, "Classified Boards, Firm Value, and Managerial Entrenchment," *Journal of Financial Economics* 83 (January 2006): 501 ("Classified boards are associated with a significant reduction in firm value. . . . Classified boards benefit management at the expense of shareholders"); Lucian A. Bebchuk and Alma Cohen, "Recent Board Declassifications: A Response to Cremers and Sepe," *Social Science Research Network Electronic Journal*, May 2017, https://perma.cc/PBN8-E748 ("The results of the current study [provide] no significant evidence that declassifications are value-reducing, [and provide] some evidence that declassifications are value-increasing"); Lucian A. Bebchuk, Alma Cohen, and Charles C. Y. Wang, "Staggered Boards and the Wealth of Shareholders: Evidence from Two Natural Experiments," National Bureau of Economic Research, working paper 17127, June 2011, https://perma.cc/B2QA-UQH3 ("Our findings are also consistent with the view that the ongoing process of dismantling staggered boards, encouraged by institutional investors, could be expected to contribute to increasing shareholder wealth"); Faleye, "Classified Boards, Firm Value, and Managerial Entrenchment"; and Lucian A. Bebchuk and Alma Cohen, "The Costs of Entrenched Boards," *Journal of Financial Economics* 78 (2004): 409 ("Staggered boards are associated with lower firm value. The reduction in firm value associated with staggered boards is economically meaningful").

3. The Silence of the Lions

1. "What Is a Hedge Fund?" BarclayHedge, http://perma.cc/6ENP-NTXZ. See also SEC Rule 506 of Regulation D, http://perma.cc/P4BB-5LHE, and §230.501, http://perma.cc/5AS3-28XR.

2. §230.501(a)(5), http://perma.cc/K873-EHRV, requiring individuals to have a net worth in excess of $1,000,000 to meet the accredited investor requirement.

3. §230.501(a)(2), http://perma.cc/7QSM-47KD, allowing public pension funds and employee benefit plans with assets in excess of $5 million to participate in hedge fund investments.

4. Brody Mullins, "Teachers Union and Hedge Funds War over Pensions Billions," *Wall Street Journal,* June 28, 2016, https://perma.cc/6K52-46RH; John Gittelsohn and Janet Lorin, "Hedge-Fund Love Affair Is Ending for U.S. Pensions, Endowments," Bloomberg, November 15, 2016, https://perma.cc/T6GK-LLL7.

5. James B. Stewart, "As Hedge Fund Returns Falter, Money Continues to Flow In," *New York Times,* February 26, 2015, http://perma.cc/A9ZM-THLB: "Even as their high fees have minted scores of new billionaires,

hedge funds have now substantially underperformed a simple blend of index funds—60 percent stocks and 40 percent bonds—for three-, five- and 10-year periods." See also Tyler Durden, "Hedge Funds Underperform the S&P for the 7th Year in a Row: Here Are Their Top Holdings," ZeroHedge, February 22, 2015, http://perma.cc/76Q3-TM9X, reporting that Goldman Sachs, Goldman's composite hedge fund underperformed the S&P 500 for the six-year period of 2009–14; and Mark J. Perry, "More on Hedge Funds: Be Careful When Worshipping the 'Smart Money,'" AEIdeas, August 17, 2016, http://perma.cc/9SXK-KV6J, which notes that the Balanced Vanguard index fund has outperformed hedge funds every year since 2009.

6. Stewart, "As Hedge Fund Returns Falter"; Simon Lack, *The Hedge Fund Mirage: The Illusion of Big Money and Why It's Too Good to Be True* (Hoboken, N.J.: Wiley, 2012); Investopedia, s.v. "Index Fund," http://perma .cc/PKP8-ETD5; Investopedia, s.v. "Standard & Poor's 500 Index—S&P 500," http://perma.cc/7DTG-GUXF; Mitch Tuchman, "Hedge Fund vs. Index Fund: A Comparison," *Forbes,* July 18, 2013, http://perma.cc/3L45 -XLZN.

7. Investopedia, s.v. "Hedge Fund," http://perma.cc/5NLM-R7JG; Investopedia, s.v. "A Beginner's Guide to Hedging," https://perma.cc/J6MP -6LLQ.

8. Christine Idzelis, "Warren Buffett Is All Set to Win a $1 Million Bet with This Hedge Fund," *Business Insider,* March 1, 2017, https://perma.cc /39QL-CPF5; Lindsay Fortado and Robin Wigglesworth, "Hedge Fund Manager Who Lost Buffett Bet Feels Like a Winner," *Financial Times,* May 15, 2017, https://perma.cc/RJ9L-4CRH; "Hedge Fund Assets up to USD2.90Tn in Q4 Despite Performance Declines," Hedgeweek, January 20, 2016, http://perma.cc/F4UG-9CQZ. See also John Cassidy, "How Do Hedge Funds Get Away with It? Eight Theories," *New Yorker,* May 14, 2014, http://perma.cc/983Z-RPHG.

9. Andy Kiersz, "Here's How Badly Warren Buffett Has Beaten the Market," *Business Insider,* February 26, 2016, http://perma.cc/JG4Q-3ELA; Noah Buhayar, "Buffett Stings Hedge Funds Anew over Their 'Misbegotten' Rewards," Bloomberg, February 26, 2017, http://perma.cc/UAY6-5LSK.

10. See Eugene F. Fama, "Market Efficiency, Long-Term Results, and Behavioral Finance," *Journal of Financial Economics* 49, no. 3 (September 1998): 283–306; Eugene F. Fama and Kenneth R. French, "Size, Value, and Momentum in International Stock Returns," *Journal of Financial Economics* 105, no. 3 (September 2012): 457–72, and Michael C. Jensen, "Some Anomalous Evidence Regarding Market Efficiency," *Journal of Financial Economics* 6, nos. 2–3 (1978): 95–101.

11. Daniel Solin, "The Shocking Admission of This Shuttered Hedge Fund Manager," *U.S. News and World Report,* September 14, 2014, http://perma.cc/2CMV-JAWN. See also Juliet Chung, "Emrys Partners Hedge Fund Shuts Down," *Wall Street Journal,* July 3, 2014, http://perma.cc/V5JG -6F7P; Michael Lewis, *The Big Short: Inside the Doomsday Machine* (New York: Norton, 2010).

12. Alexandra Stevenson and Matthew Goldstein, "Battered, Apologetic and Still Pitching Their Hedge Funds," *New York Times,* December 15, 2015, http://perma.cc/GR53-9754; Solin, "The Shocking Admission of This Shuttered Hedge Fund Manager"; Katherine Burton, Saijel Kishan, and Katia Porzecanski, "Steve Eisman's Next Big Short Is Hedge Fund Fees," Bloomberg, August 28, 2016, https://perma.cc/2WRW-TW9S; Gregory Zuckerman, "Big Hit on Drug Stocks Caps $26 Billion Decline for John Paulson," *Wall Street Journal,* November 4, 2016, https://perma.cc/G6BP -RDNH?safari=1; Miles Weiss and Katherine Burton, "John Paulson Is Struggling to Hold on to Client Money," Bloomberg, June 5, 2017, https:// perma.cc/KPE6-LYHG.

13. Mikhail Tupitsyn and Paul Lajbcygier, "Passive Hedge Funds," August 10, 2015, http://perma.cc/TLX4-PMUE.

14. John Armour and Brian Cheffins, "The Rise and Fall (?) of Shareholder Activism," in *Institutional Investor Activism: Hedge Funds and Private Equity Funds, Economics and Regulation,* ed. William Bratton and Joseph A. McCahery (Oxford: Oxford University Press, 2015), 213; "The Republican Revolution," History Channel, http://perma.cc/2ART-HYK6.

15. Alexandra Stevenson, "Hedge Funds Faced Choppy Waters in 2015, but Chiefs Cashed In," *New York Times,* May 10, 2016, http://perma.cc /J9UC-ENQD; Sonali Basak and Noah Buhayar, "Buffett Says Hedge Funds Get 'Unbelievable' Fees for Bad Results," Bloomberg, April 30, 2016, http://perma.cc/L6JA-4CUR.

16. Pedrotty has since left the AFT to run the Capital Stewardship Department for North America's Building Trades Unions.

17. Rakesh Khurana and James Weber, "AFL-CIO: Office of Investment and Home Depot," Harvard Business School Case Study no. N9-407-097, May 11, 2007, citing Julie Creswell, "With Links to Home Depot Board, Chief Saw Pay Soar as Stock Fell," *New York Times,* May 24, 2006.

18. Ibid.

19. Dan Pedrotty, telephone interview, March 25, 2016; Nancy Hass, "Scholarly Investments," *New York Times*, December 4, 2009, https://perma .cc/DD2X-EY6A.

20. Hass, "Scholarly Investments"; Stephen Taub, "NYC Teachers Demonize Hedge Funds," *Institutional Investor,* June 12, 2010, https://perma.cc /X8SW-YJ5E.

21. Ed Cox, "Choking Charter Schools Is Cheating Underprivileged Kids," *New York Post,* February 28, 2014, http://perma.cc/PAJ8-Y8XB; Rachel M. Cohen, "Charter and Traditional Public Schools Fight over Money," *American Prospect,* June 6, 2016, http://perma.cc/XYY3-FXP6.

22. Allie Bidwell, "AFT, Advocacy Group Want More Accountability for Charters," *US News and World Report,* February 26, 2014, http://perma .cc/7EZV-C2EL. See also "AFT and Charter Schools," American Federation of Teachers, http://perma.cc/9WUY-8UP9.

23. "AFT Resolution—Professional Compensation for Teachers," American Federation of Teachers, https://perma.cc/6AWE-5ZGM; Mullins, "Teachers Union and Hedge Funds War over Pension Billions"; Philip Bump, "The 25 Top Hedge Fund Managers Earn More Than All Kindergarten Teachers Combined," *Washington Post,* May 12, 2015, https://perma .cc/A338-XC52; Theresa Riley, "Why Do Kindergarten Teachers Pay More Taxes Than Hedge Fund Managers?" Moyers and Company, September 17, 2015, https://perma.cc/7VS3-CTP7.

24. "Democrats for Education Reform Hail Mitchell Victory, Warn on 2015," *Illinois Observer,* March 19, 2014, https://perma.cc/TRA6-Z2LN; Rebecca Sibilia, "Challenging the Myths around Pension Reform," StudentsFirst, May 10, 2012, https://perma.cc/VG84-7EN9; Josh B. McGee and Marcus A. Winters, "Better Pay, Fairer Pensions: Reforming Teacher Compensation," Manhattan Institute, September 5, 2013, https://perma.cc /R7GH-YJ3X; Dan Pedrotty, telephone interview, March 25, 2016. See also Motoko Rich, "11 States Get Failing Grades on Public School Policies from Advocacy Group," *New York Times,* January 7, 2013, https://perma.cc/B6N6 -A5SL, and "State of Education State Policy Report Card 2013," StudentsFirst, https://perma.cc/9RPK-H7QE.

25. "Defined Benefit Plans versus Defined Contribution Plans," My Retirement Paycheck, https://perma.cc/Z72J-J22G. See Chapter 8 for more on these plans.

26. Dan Pedrotty, telephone interview, March 25, 2016.

27. Ibid.

28. "Randi Weingarten, AFT President," https://perma.cc/8T6T-YYLP; Steven Greenhouse, "Teacher Contract Ends; Giuliani Plans an Offer Soon," *New York Times,* November 16, 2000, https://perma.cc/WLR5-XQ36; Robert Kolker, "Contract Sport," *New York Magazine,* https://perma.cc /PW3D-LS6N.

29. "Ranking Asset Managers: A Retirement Security Report on Money Managers for Pension Fund Trustees 5th Edition (2015)," American Federation of Teachers, https://perma.cc/GWH2-TDFY; "Ranking Asset Managers: A Retirement Security Report on Money Managers for Trustees," American Federation of Teachers, April 19, 2013, 4, 2, https://perma.cc /ES7K-49MX; Julia La Roche, "The American Federation of Teachers Sent out a Big Watch List of Hedge Funds 'Attacking' Their Pension Plans," *Business Insider,* April 28, 2013, https://perma.cc/DER2-SCTR; Julia La Roche, "Hedge Funders Say It's 'A Badge of Honor' to Be Targeted by 'Thuggish' Teachers Unions," *Business Insider,* April 25, 2013, https://perma.cc/25YW -4FFF.

30. "Ranking Asset Managers: A Retirement Security Report on Money Managers for Trustees"; Beverly Goodman, "Teachers Turn Out to Be Tough Markers," *Barrons,* April 27, 2013, https://perma.cc/23YF-5U64; La Roche, "Hedge Funders Say It's 'A Badge of Honor.'"

31. Jim Gallagher, "Sinquefield Quits DFA Board under Union Attack," *St. Louis Post-Dispatch,* May 3, 2013, https://perma.cc/5LN8-GTVM.

32. Ibid.; Stephen Clark to Randi Weingarten, May 13, 2013; Scott Kapnick to American Federation of Teachers, December 17, 2014, both copies in author's files.

33. This raises the question of state and city budgets and public employee pensions, an issue I address in Chapter 8. The main reason why some cities are struggling to meet their pension obligations is because they underfunded those pensions, breaking decades of promises to workers, and are now facing balloon payments to catch up.

34. Dan Pedrotty, telephone interview, March 25, 2016; "AFT's Weingarten and Aon's Savacool on Decision to Remove Aon from AFT Asset Managers Report," press release, American Federation of Teachers, March 19, 2014, https://perma.cc/UYU8-PQPH; National Institute on Retirement Security, https://perma.cc/XHU6-HMSX; "NYC Retirement System Declined Investment in Greenblatt's Gotham Hedge Fund," Value-Walk, March 18, 2015, https://perma.cc/FYU5-G8V5. See also Martin Z. Braun, "NYC Pension Rejects Stake in Fund Run by Charter School Backer," Bloomberg, March 16, 2015, https://perma.cc/5DPM-VARV.

35. Matt Taibbi, "Dan Loeb Simultaneously Solicits, Betrays Pension Funds," *Rolling Stone,* April 1, 2013, https://perma.cc/V9KN-SZFA. See also "Third Point's Loeb Cancels Appearance in Face of Protest," Reuters, April 17, 2013, https://perma.cc/FWK4-32HV.

36. Tabinda Hussain, "When Dan Loeb Gets Angry He Likes to Donate to Charity," ValueWalk, June 12, 2013, https://perma.cc/H92X-JWQV;

Svea Herbst-Bayliss, "Loeb's Hedge Fund Third Point to Lose Rhode Island as Client," Reuters, January 31, 2014, https://perma.cc/622H-4PTE.

37. Randi Weingarten, telephone interview, May 9, 2017; Rachael Levy, "Something Is Missing from the Hedge Fund Industry," *Business Insider,* September 13, 2016, https://perma.cc/WX33-44FR.

38. Michael Corkery, "For the Record, KKR Loves Public Pensions," *Wall Street Journal,* April 26, 2013, https://perma.cc/X6UC-EW2B; "Sustainable Private Equity / Real Estate Investment in the Hospitality Industry," press release, UNITE HERE, March 2016, https://perma.cc/29Z7-58AD; Michael Corkery, "Blackstone Group Loves Public Workers," *Wall Street Journal,* January 20, 2011, https://perma.cc/5AGJ-XX2F; Matthew Goldstein, Kate Kelly, and Nicholas Confessore, "Robert Mercer, Bannon Patron, Is Leaving Helm of $50 Billion Hedge Fund," *New York Times,* November 2, 2017, https:perma.cc/3LM8-6ZWN.

39. "Blackstone's Infrastructure Business Adopts Responsible Contractor Policy to Promote Fair Wages and Benefits for Workers on Infrastructure Projects," press release, Blackstone, September 5, 2017, https://perma.cc/FX3W-M8KY.

40. "Laborers Wield Investment Clout on Behalf of Occupy Wall Street," press release, Laborers' International Union of North America, October 19, 2011, https://perma.cc/G292-RRXC; "A Surprise Nighttime Raid, Then a Tense Day of Maneuvering in the Streets," *New York Times,* November 15, 2011, https://perma.cc/AQ2R-8XY2.

41. 29 C.F.R. § 2509.08-1 (2013); U.S. Department of Labor, "Fact Sheet: Economically Targeted Investments (ETIs) and Investment Strategies That Consider Environmental, Social and Governance (ESG) Factors," October 22, 2015, https://perma.cc/4AKS-DZGG.

42. R. Williams, "Teacher Union's Weingarten: Let's Dump Hedge-Fund Investments," Newsmax Finance, April 14, 2016, https://perma.cc/2AK3-EWQZ.

43. Dennak Murphy, interview, June 1, 2016.

44. Dan Pedrotty, telephone interview, March 25, 2016; Dennak Murphy, interview, June 1, 2016.

45. Dennak Murphy, interview, June 1, 2016.

46. Ibid.; Emily Heil, "Costco as Political Backdrop: It's about More Than the Hot Dogs," *Washington Post,* June 16, 2014, https://perma.cc/8XR6-R7N3.

47. Svea Herbst-Bayliss, "CalPERS Move to Hedge Funds May Spark Trend," *USA Today,* November 13, 2001, https://perma.cc/WWK3-HU8L; "CalPERS Eliminates Hedge Fund Program in Effort to Reduce

Complexity and Costs in Investment Portfolio," press release, CalPERS, September 15, 2014, https://perma.cc/B56T-LBD5; Dennak Murphy, interview, June 1, 2016.

48. Dennak Murphy, interview, June 1, 2016.

49. Ibid.; "How Much Does CalPERS Pay in Fees? Only a Computer Can Say," *California County News,* May 24, 2017, https://perma.cc/8DL7 -NMH9.

50. Dennak Murphy, interview, June 1, 2016.

51. "Hedge Fund Definition," Hedge Fund Marketing Association, https://perma.cc/YUF8-VG27; Laurence Fisher and Tommy Wilkes, "Hedge Funds Enjoy Post-Crisis Popularity with 'Safe' Image," Reuters, September 27, 2013, https://perma.cc/LK9E-72SC.

52. "Priya Mathur," https://perma.cc/TL2T-Y7GL; Dennak Murphy, interview, June 1, 2016. In 2014, Mathur was fined and sanctioned by CalPERS for ethical violations because she failed to file required campaign disclosure forms on more than one occasion. When she finally and belatedly did file the forms, they revealed that she had not received any campaign contributions at all. Nevertheless, she was sanctioned for not filing the paperwork. See also Mark Lifsher, "CalPERS Board Strips Priya Mathur of Posts after Ethics Law Violations," *Los Angeles Times,* October 16, 2014, https://perma.cc/6RMP-7KN8. I am not being dismissive of these violations—it is crucial that people serving in a position of public trust make timely and accurate disclosures—but because enormously powerful interests will want to use them to discredit Mathur's work against hedge funds, I want to contextualize their comparatively immaterial nature and scope. Still, this is exactly the reason why Mathur ought to have been more careful.

53. Dennak Murphy, interview, June 1, 2016; "Curtis Ishii," https://perma.cc/5NNS-4XVQ. See also "Curtis Ishii LinkedIn," https://www.linkedin.com/in/curtis-ishii-2711a72b.

54. Dennak Murphy, interview, June 1, 2016.

55. Dan Fitzpatrick, "CalPERS to Exit Hedge Funds," *Wall Street Journal,* September 15, 2014, https://perma.cc/ZN73-BXV4; "The CalPERS Decision: A Compilation of Industry Reactions," DailyALTS, September 27, 2014, https://perma.cc/5MSU-WW3W.

56. Dennak Murphy, interview, June 1, 2016; Dan Pedrotty, telephone interview, March 25, 2016.

57. Elizabeth Parisian and Saqib Bhatti, "All That Glitters Is Not Gold: An Analysis of US Public Pension Investments in Hedge Funds," American Federation of Teachers, Roosevelt Institute, Refund America Project, and Haas Institute, https://perma.cc/BPH3-YWEJ.

58. Timothy W. Martin and Rob Copeland, "Investors Pull Cash from Hedge Funds as Returns Lag Market," *Wall Street Journal,* March 30, 2016, https://perma.cc/7VRJ-DZT6.

59. Aliya Ram, "Pension Schemes Stay Loyal to Hedge Funds," *Financial Times,* July 24, 2016, https://perma.cc/H3PJ-RA8E.

60. Janet Lorin, "Hedge Funds Are Losing Endowments after Exodus of Pensions," Bloomberg, August 15, 2016, https://perma.cc/NC5U-G82V.

61. "The Big Squeeze: How Money Managers' Fees Crush State Budgets and Workers' Retirement Hopes," American Federation of Teachers, 2017, https://perma.cc/6B4J-G8DQ.

62. *Goldstein v. SEC,* 451 F.3d 873, 874 (D.C. Cir. 2005).

4. Checks and Imbalances

1. There is a long tradition, dating to the nineteenth century and the early days of corporate law, of scholars comparing the Constitution to a corporate charter or power of attorney and describing politicians as "fiduciaries," a corporate law concept if there ever was one. To identify just a small sample of such scholarship, see, e.g., Gary Lawson and Guy Seidman, *A Great Power of Attorney: Understanding the Fiduciary Constitution* (Lawrence: University Press of Kansas, 2017); D. Theodore Rave, "Fiduciary Voters?" *Duke Law Journal* 66 (2016): 331–78; Tom C. W. Lin, "CEOs and Presidents," *University of California Davis Law Review* 47 (2014): 1351–1416; D. Theodore Rave, "Politicians as Fiduciaries," *Harvard Law Review* 126 (2013): 671–739; Robert G. Natelson, "The Constitution and the Public Trust," *Buffalo Law Review* 52 (2004): 1077–1178; Robert G. Natelson, "The Agency Law Origins of the Necessary and Proper Clause," *Case Western Reserve Law Review* 55 (2004): 243–322; and Robert G. Natelson, "The General Welfare Clause and the Public Trust: An Essay in Original Understanding," *University of Kansas Law Review* 52 (2003): 1–56.

2. Robert C. Posen, "Before You Split That CEO / Chair . . . ," *Harvard Business Review,* April 2006, https://perma.cc?YD89-8AV9. See, for example, UK Corporate Governance Code 2016, A.2.1.

3. See Stephen Bainbridge, "Separating the CEO and Chairman of the Board," September 14, 2010, https://perma.cc/Y6NE-XP7S, which argues that many analysts overstate the benefits of splitting the roles of CEO and board chair while also underestimating the costs, and Stephen M. Bainbridge, "Dodd-Frank: Quack Federal Corporate Governance Round II," *Minnesota Law Review* 95 (2011): 1779, 1800.

4. David F. Larcker and Brian Tayan, *Corporate Governance Matters: A Closer Look at Organizational Choices and Their Consequences,* 2nd ed. (Old Tappan, N.J.: Pearson Education, 2016).

5. Roberto A. Ferdman, "The Pay Gap between CEOs and Workers Is Much Worse Than You Realize," *Washington Post,* September 25, 2014, https://perma.cc/TAG3-XXS5. See also Sorapop Kiatpongsan and Michael I. Norton, "How Much (More) Should CEOs Make? A Universal Desire for More Equal Pay," *Perspectives on Psychological Science* 9, no. 6 (November 2014): 587–93.

6. Nuno Fernandes et al., "The Pay Divide: (Why) Are U.S. Top Executives Paid More?" European Corporate Governance Institute, August 2009, https://perma.cc/2RLV-7JNU.

7. "Shareholder Activism: Who, What, When, and How?" PwC Report, March 2015, https://perma.cc/3Z8Z-VETV; Joann Lublin, "Chairman / CEO Split Gains Allies," *Wall Street Journal,* March 30, 2009, https://perma.cc /LZQ2-UZYP; Yonca Ertimur et al., "Shareholder Activism and CEO Pay," *Review of Financial Studies* 23, no. 2 (2011): 535–92; "SEC Adopts Rule for Pay Ratio Disclosure," press release, Securities and Exchange Commission, August 5, 2015, https://perma.cc/MLT3-VKAF; Richard Levick, "The Pay Ratio Rule: Businesses Face Unprecedented Executive Pay Disclosure Burden," *Forbes,* February 9, 2016, https://perma.cc/9AXW -M7TZ.

8. AFSCME, About, https://perma.cc/6NWB-69DE; Lisa Lindsley, LinkedIn, https://perma.cc/3MMZ-K3NN; AFSCME, Retirement Security, https://perma.cc/65QC-MAMG; Erik Sherman, "Dell Dodges Some Governance Bullets," *Business Insider,* July 19, 2011, https://perma.cc/8ZY7 -NFY2; "Raise My Company's Taxes," *Wall Street Journal,* January 13, 2011, perma.cc / 3Q4A-4YJV.

9. Lisa Lindsley, LinkedIn; Daniel Burns, "12 Key Dates in the Demise of Bear Stearns," Reuters, March 17, 2008, https://perma.cc/K9K5-JTYE; Lisa Lindsley, telephone interview, April 6, 2016.

10. Lisa Lindsley, LinkedIn; Lisa Lindsley, telephone interview, April 6, 2016; Richard Ferlauto, LinkedIn, https://perma.cc/82L8-CM9Q.

11. Lisa Lindsley, telephone interview, April 6, 2016; "Institutional Investors Continue to Press Companies for Disclosure of Lobbying in 2016," press release, AFSCME, March 17, 2016, https://perma.cc/W642-FP2L; David H. Erkens et al., "Corporate Governance in the 2007–2008 Financial Crisis: Evidence from Financial Institutions Worldwide," *Journal of Corporate Finance* 18, no. 2 (April 2012): 389–411, https://perma.cc/4H2S -MZ44; Andrew Ross Sorkin, *Too Big to Fail: The Inside Story of How Wall*

Street and Washington Fought to Save the Financial System—and Themselves (New York: Penguin, 2010); "Shareholders Strip BofA CEO of Chairman Role," NBC News, April 29, 2009, https://perma.cc/ERT2-CJNZ; Dan Fitzpatrick, "Bank of America Chief Resigns under Fire," *Wall Street Journal,* October 2, 2009, https://perma.cc/TBQ5-ALYH; Stephen Gandel, "Shareholders Reject $15 Million Pay Raise for Citigroup's CEO," *Fortune,* April 17, 2012, https://perma.cc/32HL-JNUP; Joe Weisenthal, "Stunning NYT Report Explains How Vikrim Pandit Was Really Fired from Citi," *Business Insider,* October 26, 2012, http://perma.cc/M78S-HXD8.

12. Roger Lowenstein, "Jamie Dimon: America's Least Hated Banker," *New York Times Magazine,* December 1, 2010, http://perma.cc/LE4S -EMBC; "JPMorgan Chase & Company," Yahoo Finance, http://perma.cc /L2TV-FUV6; Kurt Badenhausen, "Full List: Ranking America's 100 Largest Banks," *Forbes,* January 10, 2017, https://perma.cc/9VWS-HHYH.

13. Investopedia, s.v. "Moral Hazard," perma.cc / A8XA-JCJG.

14. Lisa Lindsley, telephone interview, April 6, 2016; "Tracking the JPMorgan Investigations," *New York Times,* October 22, 2013, https://perma.cc /E2UY-H2A5 (focusing on foreclosure abuses); Chris Fleming, "AFSCME Plan to JPMorgan: End Dimon Double Duty," press release, AFSCME, January 17, 2012, http://perma.cc/FV7J-85RQ (referring to proposals filed in 2011 and 2012); Cheryl Kelly, "Major Investors Call on JPMorgan Chase to Name Independent Board Chair," press release, AFSCME, February 20, 2013, http://perma.cc/B48R-XK2V.

15. Lisa Lindsley, telephone interview, April 6, 2016; JPMorgan Chase & Company, proxy statement, 2012, 38–39, http://perma.cc/X9YK-AV72.

16. David F. Larcker and Brian Tayan, "Chairman and CEO: The Controversy over Board Leadership Structure," in *Rock Center for Corporate Governance at Stanford University Closer Look Series: Topics, Issues and Controversies in Corporate Governance,* no. CGRP-58, Stanford University Graduate School of Business Research Paper, no. 16–32, June 18, 2016, which argues that despite pressure from shareholder activists, there is little research to suggest the separation of the chairman and CEO materially alters firm performance or governance quality. Diane Schooley, Celia Renner, and Mary Allen, "Shareholder Proposals, Board Composition, and Leadership Structure," *Journal of Managerial Issues* 22, no. 2 (Summer 2010): 152–65, finds shareholders prefer split leadership as a way of monitoring the CEO and reducing the concentration of power in one person. "Chairing the Board: The Case for Independent Leadership in Corporate North America" (2009), Millstein Center for Corporate Governance and Performance, Yale School of Management, Policy Briefing no. 4, https://perma.cc/GDC8-UT7E,

promotes the independent chair as a means to curb conflicts of interest, allay concerns regarding CEO accountability, and foster the interests of shareowners. Aiyesha Dey, Ellen Engel, and Xiaohui Liu, "CEO and Board Chair Roles: To Split or Not to Split," Chicago Booth Research Paper, no. 09–23, December 16, 2009, warns that proposals to split the CEO and chairman may require more consideration and could have a negative effect on governance and performance outcomes. Sanjai Bhagat and Brian J. Bolton, "Corporate Governance and Firm Performance," *Journal of Corporate Finance* 14, no. 3 (2008): 257–73, https://ssrn.com/abstract=1017342, concludes that splitting the roles of CEO and chairman positively correlates with current and future operating performance. Steven Davidoff Solomon, "A Lack of Consensus on Corporate Governance," *New York Times,* September 29, 2015, http://perma.cc/6Q4A-XGQJ.

17. JPMorgan Chase & Company, proxy statement, 2012, 39–40; emphasis added.

18. Jill Schlesinger, "JPMorgan Chase: London Whale Swallows $2B," CBS News, May 10, 2012, http://perma.cc/KJ3P-XGR3; Gregory Zuckerman and Katy Burne, " 'London Whale' Rattles Debt Market," *Wall Street Journal,* April 6, 2012, http://perma.cc/KJ3P-XGR3; Dan Fitzpatrick, Gregory Zuckerman, and Liz Rappaport, "J. P. Morgan's $2 Billion Blunder," *Wall Street Journal,* May 11, 2016, https://perma.cc/25EM-BVY6; "Timeline: The London Whale's Wake," *New York Times,* March 27, 2013, https://perma.cc/ZK6J-6HZF; Simon Neville, "JPMorgan Trader 'London Whale' Blows $13Bn Hole in Bank's Value," *The Guardian,* May 11, 2012, http://perma.cc/4DGG-U8BL (this article puts the market value figure at $13 billion); "JPMorgan Chase Has Lost $20 Billion on Its Bad Trade, Taking into Account Share Price," Huffington Post, May 14, 2012, http://perma.cc/HN9E-DE5D; Jessica Silver-Greenberg, "JPMorgan Cuts Dimon's Pay, Even as Profit Surges," *New York Times,* January 16, 2013, http://perma.cc/63A6-HZPA.

19. "AFSCME Plan's McEntee to JPMorgan Chase: 'Don't Hedge on Independent Board Chair; the Stakes Are Too High to Leave Jamie Dimon Unsupervised,' " press release, AFSCME, http://perma.cc/TF67-48F9.

20. Kathryn Glass, "Dimon Safe, for Now," Fox Business, May 15, 2012, http://perma.cc/WU47-C9P3; "Dimon Apologizes to Shareholders for $2B Trading Loss," Daily Caller, May 12, 2012, http://perma.cc/7CZ3-R4VA; Eleazar David Melendez, "JPMorgan Activist Shareholders May Regret Push to Split CEO and Chairman Roles, Professor Says," Huffington Post, May 13, 2013, http://perma.cc/2UVE-W53C.

21. "In 2012, more than 46 million voters—almost 36% of the total—cast ballots in some manner other than at a traditional polling place on Election Day." Drew Desilver and Abigail Geiger, "For Many Americans, Election Day Is Already Here," Pew Research Center, October 21, 2016, http://perma.cc/HF4C-GE8C.

22. See SEC Reg 14A, 17 CFR 240.14a-1–240.14b-2.

23. Scott Winter, e-mail correspondence, April 3, 2017. Winter is the managing director of Innisfree M&A Inc., a leading proxy solicitor. Note that Winter was commenting generally on shareholder voting, not specifically on the vote to split the CEO and chair roles at JPMorgan.

24. David Henry, "Dimon Keeps JPMorgan Chairman Title after Bruising Battle," Reuters, May 21, 2013, http://perma.cc/3KH4-WL6A; Dan Fitzpatrick, "Vote Strengthens Dimon's Group," *Wall Street Journal,* May 21, 2013, http://perma.cc/NF83-W2UZ; "JPMorgan's Jamie Dimon Beats off Shareholder Revolt," BBC News, May 21, 2013, http://perma.cc/22UP-4C5C.

25. Bruce Mendelsohn and Jesse Brush, "The Duties to Correct and Update: A Web of Conflicting Case Law and Principles," *Securities Regulation Law Journal* 43 (2015): 67, 72, http://perma.cc/KY4K-4U8Z.

26. *In re JPMorgan Chase & Co.,* Second Amended Class Action Complaint at ¶328, 12-cv-03852-GBD (S.D.N.Y. April 15, 2013). For full disclosure, I once worked for one of the law firms that brought this case, years before this suit was filed.

27. Erik Larson, "JPMorgan Chase to Pay $150 Million to Settle 'Whale' Suit," Bloomberg, December 21, 2015, http://perma.cc/5DCV-YGW2.

28. Jie Cai, Jacqueline L. Garner, and Ralph A. Walkling, "Electing Directors," *Journal of Finance* 64, no. 5 (October 2009): 2389–421, https://perma.cc/4WV7-GKND; Karen McVeigh and Dominic Rushe, "JPMorgan: Justice Department Opens Investigation into $2Bn Trading Losses," *The Guardian,* May 15, 2012, https://perma.cc/F93N-L4K4; "The Board of Directors—Selecting, Electing and Evolving," AVC, March 12, 2012, http://perma.cc/LHQ9-ZK35; Karen Freifeld and David Henry, "JPMorgan, under Pressure, Gives up Vote Information," Reuters, May 20, 2013, http://perma.cc/9W5G-Q7JM.

29. Kelly, "Major Investors Call on JPMorgan Chase to Name Independent Board Chair," states AFSCME's investment at 74,984 shares, CRPTF's investment at 1,391,999 shares, and NYC funds investment at 9,747,342 shares.

30. Justin Menza, "JPMorgan Investors Propose Splitting CEO, Chairman Roles," CNBC, February 20, 2013, http://perma.cc/Y3QM-Q7C9;

Susanne Craig and Jessica Silver-Greenberg, "JPMorgan Works to Avert Split of Chief and Chairman Roles," *New York Times,* April 5, 2013, https://perma .cc/K9HL-C4M7; Dan Fitzpatrick, "Investors Seek to Split J. P. Morgan Top Posts," *Wall Street Journal,* February 20, 2013, https://perma.cc/8BYL -5F95; Kelly, "Major Investors Call on JPMorgan Chase to Name Independent Board Chair"; Hermes Investment Management, About Us, https:// perma.cc/AD49-ES98; Jay W. Lorsch and Andy Zelleke, "The Practice of Separating the Two Top Jobs Is Common in the United Kingdom and Elsewhere, but It Is Not Necessarily an Improvement over the U.S. Model of Combining the Two Positions," MIT Sloan Management Review, January 15, 2005, https://perma.cc/3YU6-BJ6G; JPMorgan Chase & Company, proxy statement, 2013, schedule 14A, proposal 6, https://perma.cc /S8Z4-XYZC.

31. Joshua Rosner, "JPMorgan Chase: Out of Control—Executive Summary," GrahamFisher, March 12, 2013, https://perma.cc/Q83Z-J2BR; Lisa Lindsley, telephone interview, April 6, 2016; Dawn Kopecki and Hugh Son, "JPMorgan Shareholders Reject Splitting CEO Dimon's Dual Roles," Bloomberg, May 22, 2013, http://perma.cc/GNE4-UUEK.

32. Kopecki and Son, "JPMorgan Shareholders Reject Splitting CEO Dimon's Dual Roles."

33. "Lee Saunders," AFSCME, Leadership, https://perma.cc/QLJ9 -ZDPZ; Nikhil Kumar, "JPMorgan: Are Investors about to Clip Jamie Dimon's Wings?" *The Independent,* May 20, 2013, https://perma.cc;6L3W -EDLH.

34. Robert Samuels, "Walker's Anti-Union Law Has Labor Reeling in Wisconsin," *Washington Post,* February 22, 2015, http://perma.cc/FJQ4 -KLYW; Reginald Fields, "Ohio Voters Overwhelmingly Reject Issue 2, Dealing a Blow to Gov. John Kasich," Cleveland.com, November 8, 2011, http://perma.cc/6EBD-ATN2.

35. See Jeffrey B. Ellman and Daniel J. Merrett, "Pensions and Chapter 9: Can Municipalities Use Bankruptcy to Solve their Pension Woes?" *Emory Bankruptcy Developments Journal* 27 (2011): 365, https://perma.cc/NWZ9 -ZDZJ.

36. See the Social Security Administration statistic on defined-benefit plans, https://perma.cc/F3W8-V69Y.

37. Lisa Lindsley, telephone interview, April 6, 2016.

38. Ibid.; Slavkin Corzo, interview, July 27, 2016; Dan Pedrotty, telephone interview, March 25, 2016.

39. See Nathan Bomey, *Detroit Resurrected: To Bankruptcy and Back* (New York: Norton, 2016).

40. Monica Davey and May Williams Walsh, "Billions in Debt, Detroit Tumbles into Insolvency," *New York Times,* July 18, 2013, http://perma.cc /L3FP-6NHD; Liz Farmer, "How Are Pensions Protected State-by-State?" Governing the States and Localities, Finance 101, January 28, 2014, http:// perma.cc/6X6J-SHU5.

41. U.S. Department of Labor, "Retirement Plans—Benefits and Savings," https://perma.cc/G86J-DWSH; Ashley Woods, "A Guide to Detroit's Chapter 9 Default and How Bankruptcy Could Change the City," Huffington Post, July 24, 2013, http://perma.cc/6Z6G-UBNR; Scott Cohn, "Detroit Bankruptcy Deal Would Limit Pension Cuts," CNBC, June 15, 2014, http://perma.cc/F8BG-H2JM; Brent Nesbitt, "Detroit's Chapter 9 Bankruptcy and the Grinch Who Stole Their Pensions," Jurist, December 23, 2013, http://perma.cc/9PHQ-2QJ8.

42. Monica Davey, "Detroit and Retirees Reach Deal in Bankruptcy Case," *New York Times,* April 26, 2014, http://perma.cc/XJX7-KFSJ. See also Ned Resnikoff, "Deal Reached to Fund Detroit Pensions, Preserve Art," MSNBC, January 14, 2014, http://perma.cc/8DQY-SKZW.

43. Davey, "Detroit and Retirees Reach Deal in Bankruptcy Case"; Steven Yaccino and Jessica Silver-Greenberg, "JPMorgan Committing $100 Million over 5 Years to Aid Revitalization in Detroit," *New York Times,* May 21, 2014, http://perma.cc/TTB5-S2BE; Nathan Bomey, "JPMorgan Chase CEO: Detroit Pensions Should Be Protected," *Detroit Free Press,* May 10, 21, 2014, http://perma.cc/K6JB-9CAF.

44. David Dayen, "Jamie Dimon's Sinister P.R. Ploy: What's Really behind JPMorgan's Detroit Investment," Salon, May 21, 2014, http://perma .cc/UPK4-GZXP. See also Roberta Romano, "Less Is More: Making Institutional Investor Activism a Valuable Mechanism of Corporate Governance," Faculty Scholarship Series, paper 1916, 2001, https://perma.cc /P7KW-BX5H: "It is quite probable that private benefits accrue to some investors from sponsoring at least some shareholder proposals. The disparity in identity of sponsors—the predominance of public and union funds, which, in contrast to private sector funds, are not in competition for investor dollars—is strongly suggestive of their presence."

45. *Business Roundtable v. SEC,* no. 10-1305, slip op. (D.C. Cir. July 22, 2011).

46. Lucian A. Bebchuk, "Letting Shareholders Set the Rules," *Harvard Law Review* 119 (2006): 1784.

47. See Chapter 2.

48. BlackRock and Vanguard voted for climate change reporting at ExxonMobil. U.S. Securities and Exchange Commission, "Annual Report of

Proxy Voting Record of Registered Management Investment Companies: Vanguard Index Funds," May 9, 2017, https://perma.cc/5KMN-KEAT; BlackRock, "Supporting a Shareholder Proposal Following Extensive Management Engagement," May 31, 2017, https://perma.cc/QWB8 -3EVN. BlackRock also supported a climate change resolution at Occidental Petroleum. BlackRock, "Supporting a Shareholder Proposal Following Lack of Response to Prior Engagement," May 12, 2017, https:// perma.cc/4N3S-U3CJ.

49. Ross Kerber, "Amid Business Ties, Some Fund Firms Eased Proxy Pressure: Study," Reuters, April 18, 2017, http://perma.cc/AY3N-V86G; Investopedia, s.v. "An Introduction to Sovereign Wealth Funds," http://www.investopedia.com/articles/economics/08/sovereign-wealth-fund.asp; Christopher Balding, *Sovereign Wealth Funds: The New Intersection of Money and Politics* (New York: Oxford University Press, 2012), chap. 4.

50. See Neil O'Hara, "The Multiple Strategies of Hedge Funds," *Forbes,* November 22, 2013, https://perma.cc/TKU5-UGTH.

51. Aswath Damodaran, *Applied Corporate Finance,* 3rd edn. (Hoboken, N.J.: Wiley, 2011), 47.

52. Some scholars have argued for the application of fiduciary duties to some shareholders, particularly for hedge fund activists, vis-à-vis other shareholders. See Iman Anabtawi and Lynn Stout, "Fiduciary Duties for Activist Investors," *Stanford Law Review* 60 (2008): 1255.

53. Lisa Lindsley, LinkedIn; Lisa Lindsley, telephone interview, April 6, 2016; Sum of Us, About Us, http://perma.cc/4LVB-TN99.

54. Jena McGregor, "These Business Titans Are Teaming up for Better Corporate Governance," *Washington Post,* July 21, 2016, http://perma.cc /ZJD8-6YZY. See also "Commonsense Corporate Governance Principles," http://perma.cc/37CK-PMDG.

55. David H. Webber, "Big Corporations Are Trying to Silence Their Own Shareholders," *Washington Post,* April 13, 2017, https://perma.cc/XV8S -37LG.

56. 50 / 50 Climate Project, https://perma.cc/EM3T-Y653.

57. "Richard Ferlauto," *Washington Post,* May 10, 2017, https://perma.cc /666P-3257.

58. Stephen Foley, " 'The Bull's-Eye Is on Their Backs': US Investors Hit the Mark on Executive Excess," *The Independent,* June 17, 2006, http://perma .cc/DJ6R-CA49; SEC Office of Investor Education and Advocacy, "Investor Bulletin: Say-on-Pay and Golden Parachute Votes," March 2011, https:// perma.cc/3T6D-SDKW.

59. SEC Office of Investor Education and Advocacy, *Investor Bulletin: Say-on-Pay and Golden Parachute Votes*, March 2011, https://perma.cc/3T6D-SDKW.

60. Rich Ferlauto, interview, April 20, 2016; "The Directors' Remuneration Report Regulations 2002," Statutory Instrument, no. 1986, 2002, http://perma.cc/Q5YX-TVEF.

61. Rich Ferlauto, interview, April 20, 2016.

62. Ibid.; Rich Ferlauto, e-mail correspondence, February 23, 2017; Home Depot, DEF 14A filings for 2007, http://perma.cc/Y9CJ-NLXQ; 2008, http://perma.cc/7BUR-3E7X; 2009, http://perma.cc/KY9T-4H5A; 2010, http://perma.cc/KKK3-Y6CY; Countrywide, DEF 14A filings for 2006, http://perma.cc/FGR4-U98P; response, http://perma.cc/KX3R-EAZX; 2007, http://perma.cc/D2X7-BD32.

63. Home Depot, 10-Q (Quarterly Report), May 4, 2008, http://perma.cc/ZY22-T86F; Home Depot, 10-Q, May 3, 2009, http://perma.cc/TP8N-BRKE; Home Depot, 10-Q, May 2, 2010, http://perma.cc/6MSH-TVJC; Home Depot, 8-K, May 20, 2010, http://perma.cc/ZQW6-BZW8; Countrywide, 10-Q, June 30, 2006, http://perma.cc/UTJ7-DHEJ; Countrywide, 10-Q, June 30, 2007, http://perma.cc/YRP3-W9VW. For Home Depot, the votes were, by year: 2007, 43%; 2008, 42%; 2009, 44%; 2010, 36%. For Countrywide, the votes were, by year: 2006, 44%; 2007, 35%.

64. S. 1074, Shareholder Bill of Rights of 2009, Senate, U.S. Congress, http://perma.cc/KP7G-CNEB.

65. See, e.g., Anna Snider, "Shareholder Bill of Rights," Corporate Secretary, September 1, 2009, http://perma.cc/5BQT-VVFB, and Chuck Schumer, "Schumer, Cantwell Announce 'Shareholder Bill of Rights' to Impose Greater Accountability on Corporate America," press release, May 18, 2009, http://perma.cc/GC3Z-KHE5; Nell Minow, ValueEdge Advisors, https://perma.cc/Y3QP-CWYA.

66. Business Roundtable, businessroundtable.org, https://perma.cc/WC7R-CCHX.

67. J. Robert Brown, "Wachtell, Lipton and the Opening Salvo against the Shareholder Bill of Rights (The Criticisms)," TheRacetotheBottom.org, May 15, 2009, http://perma.cc/TP95-DDZT; Dan Eggen, "Opponents of 'Shareholder Bill of Rights' Reach out to Sen. Schumer," *Washington Post,* April 30, 2009, http://perma.cc/5KEN-TBEA; Victoria McGrane, "Consumer Bill Worries Business," Politico, May 26, 2009, http://perma.cc/YH4Z-CYEK; Business Roundtable, businessroundtable.org; "Excessive Executive Pay: What's the Solution?" Working Knowledge, Harvard Business School,

September 21, 2009, http://perma.cc/5G8G-WZRC; Andy Borowitz, "Clinton Campaign Accuses Sanders of Trying to Win Nomination," *New Yorker,* April 11, 2016, http://perma.cc/UQU9-YMBA.

68. S. 1074, Shareholder Bill of Rights of 2009.

69. H.R. 4173, S. 951, Dodd-Frank Wall Street Reform and Consumer Protection Act, U.S. Congress, http://perma.cc/MS7T-3CFV.

70. Dominic Rushe, "Citigroup Shareholders Reject CEO Vikram Pandit's Pay Package," *The Guardian,* April 17, 2012, http://perma.cc/WDC2-QVLS; David Enrich, Suzanne Kapner, and Dan Fitzpatrick, "Pandit Is Forced Out at Citi," *Wall Street Journal,* October 17, 2012, http://perma.cc/86J4-L99W; Caleb Melby, "Abercrombie Wages Charm Offensive after Revolts on Pay," Bloomberg, May 27, 2014, http://perma.cc/Q6HF-EDPL; Paul Hodgson, "Why Oracle Shareholders Keep Rejecting the Company's Executive Pay," *Fortune,* November 25, 2015, http://fortune.com/2015/11/25/oracle-shareholders-executive-pay/; Ashlee Vance, "End of an Era: Larry Ellison Steps Down as Oracle's CEO," Bloomberg, September 18, 2014, http://perma.cc/D7LZ-8C57; Semler Brossy, "Eight Additional Companies Fail Say on Pay," June 7, 2017, https://perma.cc/BG37-6E8A; Semler Brossy, "2016 Year-End Report: Failure Rate at Lowest Level Since 2011," February 2, 2017, https://perma.cc/PFK2-YKMV; Semler Brossy, "Annual Russell 3000 Say on Pay Results as of 07.27.16," July 27, 2016, https://perma.cc/8FVE-9NBJ.

71. "Data from Nasdaq: Stock Market News for January 19, 2017," NADAQ, January 19, 2017, http://perma.cc/6KXX-VEET.

72. See, e.g., Proxy Insight, UK Remuneration Review 2015, http://perma.cc/32QW-XF8C.

73. Paul Hodgson, "Surprise, Surprise: Say on Pay Seems to Be Working," *Fortune,* July 8, 2015, http://perma.cc/8HQ6-U3KF.

74. "Evaluating Pay for Performance Alignment," ISS, http://perma.cc/5AGA-L75F.

75. Dino Grandoni, "The Energy 202: What the Dodd-Frank Rollback Could Mean for Energy Companies," *Washington Post,* June 9, 2017, https://www.washingtonpost.com/news/powerpost/paloma/the-energy-202/2017/06/09/the-energy-202-what-the-dodd-frank-rollback-could-mean-for-energy-companies/5939899be9b69b2fb981dcb1/?utm_term=.7d19695b6ade.

76. H.R. 4173, S. 953, Dodd-Frank Wall Street Reform and Consumer Protection Act; "SEC Adopts Rule for Pay Ratio Disclosure."

77. Ferdman, "The Pay Gap between CEOs and Workers"; Lawrence Mishel and Alyssa Davis, "Top CEOs Make 300 Times More Than Typical

Workers," Economic Policy Institute, June 21, 2015, http://perma.cc/MP6M -KXSF.

78. Michael Passante, interview, August 17, 2016.

79. "A Special Interview with Heather Slavkin Corzo, New Director of the AFL-CIO Office of Investment," Heartland Capital Strategies, September 17, 2014, http://perma.cc/L63G-JGES; Heather Slavkin Corzo, personal conversation, April 14, 2011; Dan Pedrotty, LinkedIn, http://perma .cc/W58D-K4LC.

80. H.R. 4173, S. 953, Dodd-Frank Wall Street Reform and Consumer Protection Act; "Our Collective Strength," *AFL-CIO Equity Index Fund Newsletter,* October 2014, http://perma.cc/D8TA-EEJZ; "Implementing the Dodd-Frank Wall Street Reform and Consumer Protection Act," SEC, November 14, 2016, http://perma.cc/YM2R-WGV7; "This Fund Is Important. Here's Why," *AFL-CIO Equity Index Fund Newsletter,* April 23, 2015, http://perma.cc/H2US-V4GR; Heather Slavkin Corzo, "Big News to Report on the CEO-to-Worker Pay Ratio Disclosure Rules," AFL-CIO, July 14, 2015, http://perma.cc/V2AV-GKJQ; "SEC Passes Rule on CEO Pay Ratio," CNBC, August 5, 2015, http://perma.cc/DH8M-FLFC; Raúl Grijalva to Mary Jo White, March 17, 2015, https://perma.cc/YX5P -BB7F.

81. Senator Elizabeth Warren to Mary Jo White, June 2, 2015, https:// perma.cc/6VK5-SCMR.

82. "More Than 165,000 Petition Signers Demand SEC Finalize Rule Requiring CEO-to-Worker Pay Ratio Disclosure," press release, AFL-CIO, July 14, 2015, http://perma.cc/CF87-XXRM; Heather Slavkin Corzo, interview, July 27, 2016; Sarah Anderson, "This Is Why Your CEO Makes More Than 300 Times Your Pay," *Fortune,* August 7, 2015, http://perma.cc /MUZ3-99JC; Heather Slavkin Corzo, "Pay Ratio Rule Gives Shareholders Better Exec Comp Info," CFO.com, October 1, 2015, http://perma.cc /7WMZ-QG4J.

83. "SEC Adopts Rule for Pay Ratio Disclosure."

84. Grijalva to White, March 17, 2015; Heather Slavkin Corzo, interview, July 27, 2016.

85. "Surprise ISS Survey Results Reveal That Investors Intend to Use Pay Ratio Disclosures," Skadden Memorandum, September 25, 2017, https://www.skadden.com/insights/publications/2017/09/surprise-iss -survey-results.

86. Michael Piwowar, "Dissenting Statement at Open Meeting on Pay Ratio Disclosure," U.S. Securities and Exchange Commission, August 5, 2015, http://perma.cc/ZR8V-NHPL.

87. Division of Corporation Finance Guidance on Calculation of Pay Ratio Disclosure, U.S. Securities and Exchange Commission, September 21, 2017, https://perma.cc/DS44-YXPH; Broc Romanek, "The Big News! SEC Won't Delay Pay Ratio!" TheCorporateCounsel.net, September 18, 2017, https://perma.cc/M5SA-ZNE6.

5. The People's Lobbyists versus Private Equity

1. Louis D. Brandeis, *Other People's Money and How the Bankers Use It* (N.p.: N.p., 1913), 92.

2. See SEC, "What We Do," https://perma.cc/FL3W-5F6H.

3. Frank H. Easterbrook and Daniel R. Fischel, "Mandatory Disclosure and the Protection of Investors," *Virginia Law Review* 70 (1984): 669; Gretchen Morgenson, "Private Equity's Free Pass," *New York Times,* July 25, 2014, https://perma.cc/Q9KX-HPM2.

4. Heather Slavkin Corzo, interview, July 27, 2016; Preqin, "The 2016 Preqin Global Private Equity and Venture Capital Report," 2016, https://perma.cc/9TA3-47MQ, 5; Ben Protess, Jessica Silver-Greenberg, and Rachel Abrams, "How Private Equity Found Power and Profit in State Capitols," *New York Times,* July 14, 2016, https://perma.cc/9Q96-KCTJ; Peter Lattman, "Private Equity Makeover Effort Starts with Trade Group," *New York Times,* September 14, 2010, https://perma.cc/2EYF-HAHE; "Private Equity Growth Capital Council Updates Mission; Changes Name to American Investment Council," press release, American Investment Council, May 10, 2016, https://perma.cc/PXU7-AVJW.

5. Investopedia, s.v. David Allison, "Learn the Lingo of Private Equity Investing," https://perma.cc/PQR8-P4AQ; "Private Equity," *The Economist,* June 22, 2009, https://perma.cc/2PK5-XPJ5; Alan J. Patricof, "Close My Tax Loophole," *New York Times,* August 26, 2016, https://perma.cc/6FCK-FDJL.

6. Victor Fleischer, University of San Diego School of Law, https://perma.cc/N2XB-HN5C; "Wyden Announces Tax Leadership Team," U.S. Senate Committee on Finance, July 20, 2016, https://perma.cc/C3P3-URPD; Victor Fleischer, "Two and Twenty: Taxing Partnership Profits in Private Equity Funds," *New York University Law Review* 83 (2008): 1. "Two and Twenty" is a reference to private equity management fees, which are 2 percent off the top and 20 percent of profits.

7. Hedge Clippers, "Closing Wall Street's Lucrative Loophole: How States Can Raise Billions by Taxing Carried Interest," Hedge Papers no. 27, 2016, http://perma.cc/CPA9-ZYQR.

8. Ryan Ellis, "Senator Ron Wyden Endangers Tax Reform with Hire of Radical Partisan Victor Fleischer," *Forbes,* August 1, 2016, http://www.forbes.com/sites/ryanellis/2016/08/01/senator-ron-wyden-endangers-tax-reform-with-hire-of-radical-partisan-victor-fleischer/#78e794cd4dfd.

9. "Bottom Line Nation," *New York Times,* http://perma.cc/HQ3V-NWQX; Danielle Ivory, Ben Protess, and Kitty Bennett, "When You Dial 911 and Wall Street Answers," *New York Times,* June 25, 2016, http://perma.cc/XE4D-2DBL; Jennifer Daniel et al., "This Is Your Life, Brought to You by Private Equity," *New York Times,* December 24, 2016, http://perma.cc/5LY3-GEJQ; "From Plans to Pavement: How a Road Is Built," Michigan Department of Transportation, http://perma.cc/5FFY-7FWC; "How a Road Gets Built," North Carolina Department of Transportation, http://perma.cc/7SFU-DAZH; "Private Roads, Public Costs: The Facts about Toll Road Privatization and How to Protect the Public," *In the Public Interest,* U.S. PIRG Education Fund Frontier Group, April 1, 2009, http://perma.cc/4W58-894X; Protess, Silver-Greenberg, and Abrams, "How Private Equity Found Power and Profit in State Capitols"; John B. Goodman and Gary W. Loveman, "Does Privatization Serve the Public Interest?" *Harvard Business Review,* November–December 1991, http://perma.cc/Z8MU-WJ9T.

10. Heather Slavkin Corzo, interview, July 27, 2016; Heather Slavkin Corzo, LinkedIn, https://perma.cc/YNW2-HTVL; David L. Goret et al., "Dodd-Frank Bill Moves towards Passage: Highlights of the Investment Adviser Registration Requirements, Accredited Investor Standard and the Volcker Rule," Lowenstein Sandler PC, July 14, 2010, http://perma.cc/T6HM-AV52.

11. PE Lobbying Reports, OpenSecrets, 2010, http://perma.cc/9T5U-8YFQ; 2011, http://perma.cc/92XB-JSJZ; 2012, http://perma.cc/MLH6-8S4U; "Restoring Oversight and Accountability to the Financial Markets," Americans for Financial Reform, July 10, 2009, http://perma.cc/6BNL-LLTD; "Americans for Financial Reform Launch Campaign to Clean up Wall Street, Protect Your Pocketbook," press release, Americans for Financial Reform, June 2009, http://perma.cc/2NT9-4FPA; Heather Slavkin Corzo, interview, July 27, 2016; "Join Our Coalition," http://ourfinancialsecurity.org/about/our-call-to-action/; Ed Mierzwinski, "CFPB Turns 5 Years Old, PIRG Celebrates Accomplishments, Warns of Ongoing Threats," press release, U.S. PIRG, July 21, 2016, http://perma.cc/68TP-VMPC; David Corn, "Elizabeth Warren: Passed Over for CFPB Post, but . . . ," *Mother Jones,* July 17, 2011, http://perma.cc/QSV9-GBMN. See also http://ourfinancialsecurity.org/2009/06/launch-sidebare/.

12. Gretchen Morgenson, "Pension Funds Can Only Guess at Private Equity's Cost," *New York Times,* May 1, 2015, https://perma.cc/64HD-PZKT; "America's Biggest Pension Fund Just Revealed What It Pays Its PE Money Managers," Reuters, November 15, 2016, http://perma.cc/Q8UM-JBWJ; Beth Healy, "State Pension Fund Paid Private Equity Firms $1.5B over 5 Years," *Boston Globe,* November 30, 2016, http://perma.cc/Y3HY-9XE9; Goodman and Loveman, "Does Privatization Serve the Public Interest?"; Ivory, Protess, and Bennett, "When You Dial 911 and Wall Street Answers."

13. I recognize that there is substantial disagreement over who qualifies as working class versus middle class. I do not use those terms here to make a specific argument about where to draw that line. Job title, level of education, salary, benefits, and dozens of other attributes are all factors. I paint with a broad brush in using both terms to describe the workers who invest in pension funds. What should be clear is that none of the people who invest in pension funds can be described as upper class or one-percenters. Or if they are, it's not because of their jobs but because of wealth accumulated elsewhere. That stands in sharp contrast to the CEOs, hedge fund managers, and private equity fund managers they confront throughout this book.

14. Eileen Appelbaum, "Private Equity and the SEC after Dodd-Frank," Center for Economic and Policy Research, January 2015, http://perma.cc/BXL6-7266; "What the Law Does: Wins and Losses," Americans for Financial Reform, http://perma.cc/W3PV-YV6E.

15. Andrew J. Bowden, "Spreading Sunshine in Private Equity," speech, SEC, May 6, 2014, http://perma.cc/SY6S-AQCP; emphasis added.

16. Ibid.

17. "SEC Announces Enforcement Results for FY 2016: Increase in Actions Involving Investment Advisers, FCPA Violations; Most Ever Whistleblower Money Distributed in a Single Year," press release, SEC, October 11, 2016, https://www.sec.gov/news/pressrelease/2016-212.html; SEC, "Private Equity Fund Advisor Settles with SEC for Failing to Disclose Its Fee Allocation Practices," Administrative Proceeding, file no. 3–17491, August 24, 2016, https://perma.cc/2MLN-XUG7; Chase Peterson-Withorn, "What You Need to Know about Commerce Secretary Pick Wilbur Ross, Trump's Billionaire Pal," *Forbes,* November 29, 2016, https://perma.cc/3HAE-D9HT; *In the Matter of WL Ross & Co.,* LLC, Admin. Proc. file no. 3–17491, "Order Instituting Cease-and-Desist Proceedings Pursuant to Section 203(K) of the Investment Advisers Act of 1940, Making Findings, and Imposing a Cease-and-Desist Order," August 24, 2016, https://perma.cc/H7SJ-8N5Q.

18. Michael Pineschi, "Leonard Green and Partner's March 2016 ADV Discloses Changes to Private Jet Billing Policy," press release, UNITE HERE, April 2016, https://perma.cc/L8JP-7SD3.

19. See https://www.pecloserlook.org/.

20. Katherine Buccaccio, "Legal Special: GPs and the Unions," *Private Funds Management,* April 1, 2016, https://perma.cc/6QA7-RDBF; Jack Marco telephone interview, November 25, 2013.

21. Josh Eidelson, "Who's the Boss? Union Organizers Target Private Equity Owners," Bloomberg, October 19, 2017, https://perma.cc/46WA-S4LS.

22. Preqin, "Public Pension Funds Investing in Alternative Assets," 2015, https://perma.cc/N4FT-6R64, estimates that 29% of PE capital comes from public pension funds. Antonia López-Villavicencio and Sandra Rigot, "The Determinants of Pension Funds' Allocation to Private Equity," Social Science Research Network, November 30, 2013, http://dx.doi.org/10.2139/ssrn.2363356, estimates that between 2001 and 2011, public and private pension funds made up 43% of capital invested in private equity.

23. "Largest US Pension Fund CalPERS in Talks with BlackRock to Outsource Business, Source Says," Reuters, September 7, 2017, https://perma.cc/WR9D-5Y7H.

24. Josh Kosman, "Under Pressure KKR Poised to Take Pension Money Deal," *New York Post,* September 14, 2017, https://perma.cc/JC22-R6ER.

25. David H. Webber, "The Use and Abuse of Labor's Capital," *New York University Law Review* 89 (2014): 2106.

6. The New Sheriffs of Wall Street

1. "He's Making Hay as CEOs Squirm," *Businessweek,* January 15, 2007, http://perma.cc/9GRZ-8X36; Eliot Spitzer, "Erik Lie," *Time,* May 3, 2007, http://perma.cc/354F-FPAS; Erik Lie, "On the Timing of CEO Stock Options Awards," *Management Science* (May 2005): 802–12, http://perma.cc/VPF7-PGLL.

2. Charles Forelle and James Bandler, "The Perfect Payday," *Wall Street Journal,* March 18, 2006, http://perma.cc/S8X6-FAKB.

3. Ibid.

4. For a comprehensive account of stock options pricing, see David I. Walker, "Evolving Executive Equity Compensation and the Limits of Optimal Contracting," *Vanderbilt Law Review* 64 (2011): 611.

5. Although backdating stock options undermines the purpose of incentivizing future performance, it is not in and of itself illegal. What's illegal is not being transparent about it, that is, claiming you grant stock options in the usual way and then secretly backdating them.

6. Forelle and Bandler, "The Perfect Payday"; Charles Forelle and James Bandler, "Five More Companies Show Questionable Options Pattern," *Wall Street Journal,* May 22, 2006, http://perma.cc/9TAL-RWP5.

7. Stewart J. Schwab and Randall S. Thomas, "Realigning Corporate Governance: Shareholder Activism by Unions," *Michigan Law Review* 96 (1998): 1018, 1024: "We suspect that unions are less able than other institutional shareholders to exercise influence through informal, behind-the-scenes discussions."

8. Most of the litigation costs are assumed by the law firms themselves, because these cases are brought on a contingency-fee basis. But there are still some costs to being the named lead plaintiff on behalf of the class, including personnel time devoted to litigation rather than other tasks.

9. David Dayeen, "What Are Good Hedge Funds?" *American Prospect,* April 25, 2016, http://perma.cc/K8B3-HVG2; Paul Vizcarrondo Jr., "Liabilities under the Federal Securities Laws," Wachtell, Lipton, Rosen, and Katz, http://perma.cc/9GY4-SUY6.

10. Adam B. Badawi and David H. Webber, "Does the Quality of the Plaintiffs' Law Firm Matter in Deal Litigation?" *Journal of Corporate Law* 101 (2015): 113; New Issue Brief Outlines Public Pension Investment Process," National Institute on Retirement Security, 2012, http://perma.cc/EEG7 -4XA9; "Mutual Funds," Financial Industry Regulatory Authority, http:// perma.cc/4Q4C-3MEA; Investopedia, s.v. Dan Barufaldi, "Hedge Funds: Funds of Funds," http://perma.cc/B93U-CKD7; Fred Imbert, "Should You Invest Like a Pension Fund?" CNBC, September 11, 2015, http://perma.cc /262R-DAUG; David H. Webber, "Private Policing of Mergers and Acquisitions: An Empirical Assessment of Institutional Lead Plaintiffs in Transactional Class and Derivative Actions," *Delaware Journal of Corporate Law* 38 (2014): 907, 942, 941; Bobby Deal, personal conversation, June 3, 2010. Deal is assistant police chief and chairman of the Board of Trustees of the Jacksonville Police and Fire Pension Fund. See David H. Webber, "Is Pay-to-Play Driving Public Pension Fund Activism in Securities Class Actions? An Empirical Study," *Boston University Law Review* 90 (2010): 2031, 2071.

11. David H. Webber, "The Plight of the Individual Investor in Securities Class Actions," *Northwestern University Law Review* 106 (2012): 157, 166, 167nn46, 47; C. S. Agnes Cheng et al., "Institutional Monitoring through Shareholder Litigation," *Journal of Financial Economics* 95 (2010): 356, 357–58; Michael Perino, "Institutional Activism through Litigation: An Empirical Analysis of Public Pension Fund Participation in Securities Class Actions," *Journal of Empirical Legal Studies* 9 (2012): 368, 369–70; Badawi and Webber, "Does the Quality of the Plaintiffs' Law Firm Matter in Deal Liti-

gation?"; "Fiduciary Responsibilities," U.S. Department of Labor, http://perma.cc/YD6N-2LK2. There are several good reasons for this. Pension funds are comparatively large investors that have significant investments at stake. Although their investments in any particular company may be small relative to the overall size of their portfolios, they may still be many millions of dollars. The funds have some economic incentive to monitor the class-action lawyers to make sure the lawyers are skillfully litigating the case in their interests and that of other investors. Compared to most investors, pension funds are also comparatively sophisticated, run by fiduciaries with access to legal counsel, and are therefore better skilled at monitoring litigation. This combination of skin in the game and legal sophistication may explain why their leadership of class actions correlates with better outcomes for shareholders. It may be another reason why mutual funds and hedge funds do so little in the face of fraud. They can participate quietly in class actions that are ably led by pension funds. Given this litigation landscape, it was hardly surprising that working-class shareholders stepped forward to take action against McGuire and UnitedHealth.

12. Docket case no. 0:06CV01216, U.S. District Court, (D. MN), "Lead Plaintiffs' Amended and Consolidated Verified Derivative and Class Action Complaint," *In re UnitedHealth Group Incorporated Shareholder Derivative Litigation,* Civ. no. 06-1216 (JMR), 2006 WL 2791649 (D.Minn. Sept. 21, 2006). See also "UnitedHealth CEO McGuire Resigns over Backdated Stock Options," KHN Morning Briefing, June 11, 2009, http://perma.cc/W58H-GMVX.

13. "What Is Derivative Litigation?" Federman & Sherwood, http://perma.cc/3GBV-SBZY; "Lead Plaintiffs' Amended and Consolidated Verified Derivative and Class Action Complaint." See also Eric Dash and Milt Freudenheim, "Chief Executive at U.S. Health Insurer Forced Out," *New York Times,* October 15, 2006, http://perma.cc/86G9-W4DL.

14. *In re UnitedHealth Group Inc. PSLRA Litig.,* no. 06-1691-JMR-FLN, Order (D. Minn. Sept. 14, 2006).

15. Cases, Robbins, Geller, Rudman & Dowd, Frequently Asked Questions, http://perma.cc/7675-EJVK.

16. Kevin Lindahl, telephone interview, January 17, 2017.

17. "Lead Plaintiffs' Amended and Consolidated Verified Derivative and Class Action Complaint," ¶88; Kevin M. LaCroix, "UnitedHealth Derivative Settlement 'Largest Ever,;" D&O Diary, December 6, 2007, http://perma.cc/3M2H-4HM2.

18. "Lead Plaintiffs' Amended and Consolidated Verified Derivative and Class Action Complaint," ¶131, 132.

19. Ibid., ¶34, 285.

20. Ibid., ¶93: "The option price . . . shall not be less than 100% of the fair market value of the Common Shares at the date of grant of such option . . . and . . . the fair market value of the Common Shares . . . shall not be less than the closing price of the stock on the date for which fair market value is being determined as reported on any national securities exchange on which common shares are then traded."

21. That little can be discussed about what transpired between the filing of the complaint and settlement of the case speaks to a larger social problem, one in which lawsuits get brought and then settled, even for sums that go a long way toward curing the harm, but with all documents produced under confidentiality agreements. Rather than expend large sums of money litigating disclosure of documents and other evidence relevant to plaintiffs' claims, companies and plaintiffs will often enter into confidentiality agreements under which the companies agree to turn over the evidence without much of a fight in exchange for plaintiffs and their lawyers agreeing to maintain their confidentiality. From the perspective of both parties, such a deal makes sense. The companies are protected from embarrassing disclosures, the plaintiffs get the documents they need to make their case. True, those documents could become public at trial, but since 96 percent of the time these cases settle, they will never see the light of day. It's the public that gets hurt by these arrangements, because these lawsuits get settled without a full airing of the facts. This is the legal status quo.

22. Wikipedia, s.v. "Most Expensive Divorces of All Time," http://perma .cc/8M3Y-XP2W; Eric Dash, "Former Chief Will Forfeit $418 Million," *New York Times,* December 7, 2007, http://perma.cc/U8P3-N6TF.

23. 2008-04-29-Schedule 14A Definitive Proxy Statement.pdf, 13, 67, http://perma.cc/5G8L-MR37: "Our Board has adopted a related-person transactions approval policy regarding the review, approval and ratification of related-person transactions by our Audit Committee. . . . Under the policy, the following 'related-person' transactions are prohibited unless approved or ratified by the Audit Committee: Any transaction or series of transactions directly or indirectly involving a director, executive officer or five-percent shareholder of the Company or any of their respective immediate family members, in which the Company or its subsidiaries is directly or indirectly a participant and the amount involved exceeds $1.00" (13).

24. Ibid., 13: "Our Board has adopted a clawback policy that allows the Company to recover cash incentive compensation and equity awards from senior executives in the event of fraud."

25. Forelle and Bandler, "The Perfect Payday"; Gretchen Morgenson, "Sharper Claws for Recovering Executive Pay," *New York Times,* December 9, 2007, https://perma.cc/5LTX-DN7N. See also Dash, "Former Chief Will Forfeit $418 Million," which notes the role of pension funds and quotes their attorney.

26. Paul Blake, "Timeline of the Wells Fargo Accounts Scandal," ABC News, November 3, 2016, http://perma.cc/6FXN-7L64.

7. The Law of Fiduciary Duty and the Risk of Capture

The background for the legal analysis contained in this chapter was initially advanced in the *New York University Law Review.* See David H. Webber, "The Use and Abuse of Labor's Capital," *New York University Law Review* 89 (2014): 2106. I am indebted to the reporting of Martin Braun and William Selway of Bloomberg News for the story on Rick Thorne, Carol Sanders, and pension fund investments in Aramark.

1. Aramark provides more than five hundred school districts with services such as food service management, custodial services, and maintenance.

2. Martin Z. Braun and William Selway, "Pension Fund Gains Mean Worker Pain as Aramark Cuts Pay," Bloomberg, November 20, 2012, https://perma.cc/58US-FCGW; Rick Thorne, telephone interview, November 18, 2013; Industries, School Districts, Aramark, https://perma.cc/UHJ8-LNNZ; David H. Webber, "Protecting Public Pension Investments," *Washington Post,* November 20, 2014, https://perma.cc/3H3Z-AWKY; Martin Z. Braun, public finance reporter, Bloomberg News, telephone interview, August 7, 2013.

3. Webber, "The Use and Abuse of Labor's Capital," 2106; Braun and Selway, "Pension Fund Gains Mean Worker Pain as Aramark Cuts Pay."

4. Webber, "The Use and Abuse of Labor's Capital," 2106.

5. 29 U.S.C. § 1104(a)(1)(A).

6. 29 C.F.R. § 2509.08–1 (2008); emphasis added.

7. James D. Hutchinson and Charles G. Cole, "Legal Standards Governing Investment of Pension Assets for Social and Political Goals," *University of Pennsylvania Law Review* 128 (1980): 1340, 1370; 29 C.F.R. § 2509.08–1 (2013); Webber, "The Use and Abuse of Labor's Capital," 2106, 2112.

8. John H. Langbein and Richard A. Posner, "Social Investing and the Law of Trusts," *Michigan Law Review* 79 (1980): 72. The authors argue that consideration of the jobs impact of investments is a form of socially responsible investing—which they view as unacceptable under trust law—even

while noting that considering jobs "may provide some pecuniary offset to the financial cost of departing from conventional investment strategy."

9. Ibid. A note here about chronology. Many of these investments took place before the Bush DOL interpretation. That's because that Bush-era guidance encapsulated a view that had existed before it and that persists. I am not arguing that these investments have been justified only with reference to that Bush DOL guidance. In fact, Louisiana Teachers is a public pension fund that doesn't have to abide by DOL interpretations, for reasons described in the text.

10. 29 U.S.C. § 1104(a)(1)(A).

11. Webber, "The Use and Abuse of Labor's Capital," 2106, 2112.

12. Ibid., 2106, 2169, 2159, 2149.

13. *Brock v. Walton,* 794 F.2d 585 (11th Cir. 1986); *Bandt v. Board of Retirement, San Diego County Employees Retirement Association,* 136 Cal. App. 4th.

14. Webber, "The Use and Abuse of Labor's Capital," 2106, 2112; Brief for the Appellant Secretary of Labor, *Brock v. Walton,* 794 F.2d 586 (11th Cir. 1986) (No. 85-5641) (on file with author).

15. *Bandt v. Board of Retirement,* 136 Cal. App. 4th 140 (Jan. 30, 2006) (review denied May 10, 2006).

16. See *McLaughlin v. Rowley,* 698 F. Supp. 1333, 1338 (N.D. Tex. 1988), holding that below market rate loans violated duty of prudence for numerous reasons; *Donovan v. Mazzola,* 716 F.2d 1226, 1233–34 (9th Cir. 1983), holding that a loan made at made at below-market rates violated the exclusive purpose rule; *Withers v. Teachers' Ret. Sys. of N.Y.C.,* 447 F. Supp. 1248, 1259 (S.D.N.Y. 1978), rejecting the claim that trustees violated their fiduciary duties by investing in low-rated, unmarketable New York City bonds to protect the health of the fund; and *Blankenship v. Boyle,* 329 F. Supp. 1089, 1106 (D.D.C. 1971), holding that pension fund investments that benefited a union and not the fund violated fiduciary duties.

17. See "New York City Fire Department Pension Fund Statement of Investment Policy for Responsible Contractor Policy," section 7, https://perma.cc/WB29-VVVS. (The fire department policy is the same as those of the other NYC funds.) See also OPERS, "Private Equity Policy," 2016, 4, https://perma.cc/J6S6-R8B2.

18. CalSTRS, "Teachers' Retirement Board Policy Manual," 2014, M-12, https://perma.cc/953N-3AF5. The policy applies "in circumstances where the investment vehicle is working with a state, local or municipal agency to establish public-private partnerships ('PPPs') or to bid on public offers for the sale, lease or management of public assets."

19. CalPERS, "Statement of Investment Policy for Restricting Private Equity (PE) Investments in Public Sector Outsourcers," July 22, 2014, https://perma.cc/NZR5-G9U7.

20. "DOL Issues Guidance on Economically Targeted Investments," Pension Analyst Compliance Bulletin, Prudential, November 2015, https://perma.cc/FQJ2-UELQ; "Interpretive Bulletin Relating to the Fiduciary Standard under ERISA in Considering Economically Targeted Investments," Employee Benefits Security Administration, Federal Register, October 26, 2015, https://perma.cc/76F8-D964.

21. See Retirement Plans and ERISA FAQs, Employee Benefits Security Administration, U.S. Department of Labor, https://perma.cc/T2FS-X7R9.

22. Webber, "The Use and Abuse of Labor's Capital," 2106, 2188–89 (appendix), 2121; "An Impulse to Help," *Pensions and Investments,* December 24, 2012, https://perma.cc/AB5Q-TVC3.

23. See, e.g., *Village of Barrington Police Fund v. Department of Ins.,* 570 N.E.2d 622, 626 (1991):"Given the lack of Illinois case law construing the relevant portions of the Pension Code, we look for guidance to analogous provisions of . . . ERISA, and the federal case law construing ERISA."

24. Robert H. Sitkoff, "Trust Law, Corporate Law, and Capital Market Efficiency," *Journal of Corporate Law* 28 (2003): 565, 572. See also Webber, "The Use and Abuse of Labor's Capital," 2106, 2164.

25. "Sustainable Investing and Bond Returns," Barclays Research, 2016 https://perma.cc/U55U-RZRC: "The findings show that a positive ESG tilt resulted in a small but steady performance advantage." Gunnar Friede, Timo Busch, and Alexander Bassen, "ESG and Financial Performance: Aggregated Evidence from More Than 2,000 Empirical Studies," *Journal of Sustainable Finance and Investment* 5, no. 4, (2015), https://perma.cc/9HWY-CE65: "The results show that the business case for ESG investing is empirically very well founded." Amy O'Brien, Lei Liao, and Jim Campagna, "Responsible Investing: Delivering competitive performance," TIAA Global Asset Management, April 2016, https://perma.cc/K4M7-5YBP: "A TIAA analysis of leading RI equity indexes over the long term found no statistical difference in returns compared to broad market benchmarks, suggesting the absence of any systemic performance penalty."

26. Matteo Tonello, "Corporate Investment in ESG Practices," Harvard Law School Forum on Corporate Governance and Financial Regulation, August 5, 2015, https://perma.cc/48KW-AV2W; Christophe Revelli and Jean-Laurent Viviani, "Financial Performance of Socially Responsible Investing (SRI): What Have We Learned? A Meta-Analysis," *Business*

Ethics: A European Review 24, no. 2 (April 2015), https://perma.cc/J5SP
-K876: "The results indicate that the consideration of corporate social responsibility in stock market portfolios is neither a weakness nor a strength
compared with conventional investments." Frank J. Fabozzi, K. C. Ma,
and Becky J. Oliphant, "Sin Stock Returns," *Journal of Portfolio Management*
35, no. 1 (Fall 2008): 82–94, https://perma.cc/Y6FM-P5N2: "The financial performance that underlies social responsibility has generated an obvious interest on the part of investors, but the empirical evidence that supports investment performance is far from conclusive."

27. Bahar Gidwani, "The Link between Sustainability and Brand Value,"
The Conference Board, October 2013, https://perma.cc/62C3-6T77, finds
a positive connection between sustainability performance and brand value.
"2012 Corporate ESG / Sustainability / Responsibility Reporting. Does It
Matter? Analysis of S&P 500 Companies' ESG Reporting Trends and Capital Markets Response, and Positive Association with Desired Rankings &
Ratings," Governance and Accountability Institute, December 2012,
https://perma.cc/C8CR-HU32: "Overall, our findings show that companies who measure, manage, and ultimately disclose more and engage in
structuring reporting on their Sustainability or ESG issues enjoy considerable advantage when compared to their non-reporting peers."

28. Jeroen Derwall, Kees C. G. Koedjijk, and Jenke Ter Horst, "A Tale
of Values-Driven and Profit-Seeking Social Investors," *CFA Digest* 41, no. 3
(August 2011), argues that SRI is more than just value-driven and can be
used to help investors meet their financial goals. "Report on US Sustainable, Responsible, and Impact Investing Trends 2014," U.S. SIF: The Forum
for Sustainable and Responsible Investment, November 20, 2014, https://
perma.cc/R2EH-GJD8.

29. Indrani De and Michelle R. Clayman, "The Benefits of Socially Responsible Investing: An Active Manager's Perspective," *Journal of Investing*
24, no. 4 (Winter 2015): 49–72, https://perma.cc/558F-CWRT; "Investment Governance and the Integration of Environmental, Social and Governance Factors," OECD, 2017, https://perma.cc/A6CD-YFD8.

30. Preqin, "Public Pension Funds Investing in Alternative Assets," fact
sheet, 2015, https://perma.cc/N4FT-6R64, estimating that 29% of PE capital comes from public pension funds. Antonia López-Villavicencio and
Sandra Rigot, "The Determinants of Pension Funds' Allocation to Private
Equity," 2013, https://perma.cc/JLK3-5XJC, estimating that between 2001
and 2011, public and private pension funds made up 43% of capital invested
in private equity. See also Chapter 5.

31. Amir Tibon, "Maryland Governor Signs Order Denying Contracts to Firms That Boycott Israel," Haaretz, October 23, 2017, https://perma.cc/TJR4-QSA6.

32. "Pensions and Investments / Willis Towers Watson 300 Analysis: Year End 2015," Willis Towers Watson, September 5, 2016, section 10, https://perma.cc/CU6J-6KVR; "2016 Governors and Legislators," MultiState Associates Incorporated, https://perma.cc/4XTQ-4BT2.

33. "The World's 300 Largest Pensions," Willis Towers Watson, September 2016, https://perma.cc/CU6J-6KVR; "Pensions and Investments"; "2016 Governors and Legislators."

34. Leigh Ann Caldwell, "Senate Democrats Propose $1 Trillion Infrastructure Plan," NBC News, January 24, 2017, https://perma.cc/4ZGG-U79G; Melanie Zanona, "Trump's Infrastructure Plan: What We Know," The Hill, January 13, 2017, https://perma.cc/T3QF-JU2T.

35. Vonda Brunsting, LinkedIn, https://perma.cc/6HVF-JZXX.

36. Vonda Brunsting, telephone interview, February 6, 2017.

37. Team, Unitarian Universalist Common Endowment Fund, https://perma.cc/GT8U-LDNB; Vonda Brunsting, CFA Society Boston, https://perma.cc/P49Y-UYPL; Vonda Brunsting, telephone interview, February 6, 2017. See also Chapter 2.

38. Vonda Brunsting, telephone interview, February 6, 2017; Yves Smith, "Hedge Fund Industry Gets Critical Trustee Defeated in Election," Naked Capitalism, February 9, 2017, https://perma.cc/X4WY-RYMN. Smith notes the sometimes adversarial dynamic between pension staff and trustees.

39. Vonda Brunsting, telephone interview, February 6, 2017; Trustee Leadership Forum, Initiative for Responsible Investment, https://perma.cc/4428-DM7P; David Wood and Erin Shackelford, telephone interview, February 14, 2017; Labor and Worklife Program, Annual Report, June 2007, part 1, Report of Activities, http://www.law.harvard.edu/programs/lwp/LWPAnnualReport2007.pdf; National Conference on Public Employee Retirement System, Trustee Educational Seminar (TEDS), https://perma.cc/L8Y8-9J77.

40. Trustee Leadership Forum, Initiative for Responsible Investment; Vonda Brunsting, telephone interview, February 6, 2017.

41. David Wood and Erin Shackelford, telephone interview, February 14, 2017; Vonda Brunsting, telephone interview, February 6, 2017.

42. Treasurer Kurt Summers, Office of the City Treasurer, City of Chicago, https://perma.cc/F4ZA-KGNY. See also Meaghan Kilroy, "Chicago Treasurer to Launch Database to Facilitate Aggregate Fees for City Pension

Funds," *Pensions and Investments*, September 1, 2015, https://perma.cc/PT2W
-F6FH.

43. Simon Lack, *The Hedge Fund Mirage: The Illusion of Big Money and Why
It's Too Good to Be True* (Hoboken, N.J.: Wiley, 2012); Elizabeth Parisian
and Saqib Bhatti, "All That Glitters Is Not Gold: An Analysis of US Public
Pension Investments in Hedge Funds," https://perma.cc/EV72-Y5J9;
American Federation of Teachers, "The Big Squeeze: How Money Man-
agers' Fees Crush State Budgets and Workers' Retirement Hopes,"
May 2017, https://perma.cc/6B4J-G8DQ.

8. The Retirement "Crises" and the Future of Labor's Capital

1. Americans for Prosperity, AFP Labor Issues, http://perma.cc/R2UJ
-F5WZ; LJAF Pension Reform, http://perma.cc/V8GA-2BBA.

2. LJAF Pension Reform [http://perma.cc/V8GA-2BBA].

3. Tyler Bond, "Michigan Weakens the Retirement Security of Its
Public School Employees," National Public Pension Coalition, July 14,
2017, https://perma.cc/XL9V-YA5M; Michigan Public School Employees
401(k), https://perma.cc/Z43W-4d5J.

4. "My Retirement Paycheck," National Endowment for Financial Education, http://perma.cc/N3NS-2RNM; "Which Is Better? Defined Contribution vs. Defined Benefit Pensions," Pension Retirement, http://perma
.cc/V9EW-3CRX.

5. See U.S. Bureau of Labor Statistics, Employment Level, https://perma
.cc/JVT7-JEPR; U.S. Bureau of Labor Statistics, Defined Benefit Estimate,
https://perma.cc/5ZVU-HWKL. See also Pension Benefit Guarantee Corporation, "Who We Are," http://perma.cc/8PYD-H8NW.

6. U.S. Census Bureau, "2016 Survey of Public Pensions: State and Local
Data," https://perma.cc/R789-U7SV; Mark Miller, "The Vanishing
Defined-Benefit Pension and Its Discontents," Reuters, May 6, 2014, http://
perma.cc/N4XP-22C5.

7. Frances Denmark, "A Hitchhiker's Guide to Taft-Hartley," *Institutional Investor,* March 11, 2010, http://perma.cc/5K96-SS35.

8. Investopedia, s.v. Matt Lee, "Who Bears the Investment Risk in 401(k)
Plans?" http://perma.cc/HTY3-MFU3; Pension Retirement, "Which Is
Better?"

9. Investopedia, s.v. "Defined-Contribution Plan," http://perma.cc/6K7Y
-N6TG; Lydia DePillis, "401(k)s Are Replacing Pensions. That's Making
Inequality Worse," *Washington Post,* September 3, 2013, https://www
.washingtonpost.com/news/wonk/wp/2013/09/03/401ks-are-replacing
-pensions-thats-making-inequality-worse/?utm_term=.43f684b82bee. See

also Timothy W. Martin, "The Champions of the 401(k) Lament the Revolution They Started," *Wall Street Journal,* January 2, 2017, http://perma.cc /GX4Z-8YMU.

10. Martin, "The Champions of the 401(k) Lament the Revolution They Started."

11. See Teresa Ghilarducci and Tony James, "The Retirement Savings Plan," Teresa Ghilarducci Blog, 2017, https://perma.cc/FHL8-ZEG8; Monique Morrissey, "401(k)s Are an Accident of History," Economic Policy Institute, Working Economics Blog, January 4, 2017, https://perma.cc/NJB7 -4RB9; and Alicia H. Munnell et al., "How Has the Shift to 401(k) Plans Affected Retirement Income?" Center for Retirement Research, Boston College, March 2017, https://perma.cc/8YKX-N4QY. By contrast, see Jack VanDerhei et al., "What Does Consistent Participation in 401(k) Plans Generate? Changes in 401(k) Account Balances, 2007–2012," EBRI Issue Brief, no. 402, July 2014, https://ssrn.com/abstract=2474684, and Jack Van-Derhei, "Reality Checks: A Comparative Analysis of Future Benefits from Private-Sector, Voluntary-Enrollment 401(k) Plans vs Stylized, Final-Average-Pay Defined Benefit and Cash Balance Plans," EBRI Issue Brief, no. 387, June 2013, https://ssrn.com/abstract=2286849.

12. Ian Ayres and Quinn Curtis, "Beyond Diversification: The Pervasive Problem of Excessive Fees and 'Dominated Funds' in 401(k) Plans," *Yale Law Journal* 124, no. 5 (March 2015): 1345–1835, http://perma.cc/B94R -B27F; James Kwak, "Improving Retirement Savings Options for Employees," *University of Pennsylvania Law Review* 15, no. 2 (2013): 484; Carla Fried, "5 Ways to Protect Your Retirement if the Market Tanks," *Time,* March 21, 2016, http://perma.cc/HJ2P-2UUA; Anne Tergesen, "Is There Really a Retirement-Savings Crisis," *Wall Street Journal,* April 23, 2017, https://perma.cc/BUW8-VHLE; "Retirement Crisis: The Great 401(k) Experiment Has Failed for Many Americans," CNBC.com, March 23, 2015, https://perma.cc/W7MU-LMQJ.

13. See U.S. Bureau of Labor Statistics, Employment Level; U.S. Bureau of Labor Statistics, Defined Contribution Estimate. See also Pension Benefit Guarantee Corporation, "Who We Are."

14. "Why Do Employers Prefer Defined Contribution Retirement Plans?" Extension, October 23, 2012, http://perma.cc/PJ9X-JL85; Michael A. Fletcher, "401(k) Breaches Undermining Retirement Security for Millions," *Washington Post,* January 15, 2013, http://perma.cc/99VJ-DVTX.

15. Patricia Cohen, "Limit on 401(k) Savings? It's about Paying for Tax Cuts," *New York Times,* October 28, 2017, https://perma.cc/4KJ7 -XTFV.

16. "Comprehensive Annual Financial Report for Fiscal Year Ended June 30, 2015," CalPERS, https://perma.cc/T9PW-NDE5. But see also "Facts at a Glance," CalPERS, http://perma.cc/4AJQ-4J4S, which states that total assets were around $289 billion.

17. Brian Nelson, "Stocks vs Mutual Funds in a Brokerage Account," Bright Hub, December 31, 2010, http://perma.cc/CLN9-BNHD; Steven Davidoff Solomon, "Grappling with the Cost of Corporate Gadflies," *New York Times,* August 19, 2014, http://perma.cc/QQG3-T7YG.

18. Gretchen Morgenson, "Your Mutual Fund Has Your Proxy, Like It or Not," *New York Times,* September 24, 2016, http://perma.cc/5R6C-364V; As You Sow, About Us, http://perma.cc/856K-SE68.

19. "Americans for Prosperity Urges State to Fix Pension Crisis," Americans for Prosperity, June 11, 2015, http://perma.cc/Z8M4-B37W; Josh B. McGee, "Creating a New Public Pension System," LJAF, January 15, 2012, http://perma.cc/2X3B-XYNW; Josh McGee and Paulina S. Diaz Aguirre, "A Boomtown at Risk: Austin's Mounting Public Pension Debt," LJAF, November 2016, http://perma.cc/SK8F-576U; U.S. Census Bureau, "Annual Survey of Public Pensions: State- and Locally-Administered Defined Benefit Data Summary Brief: 2015," https://perma.cc/D45M-YQBP; "What's an Average Pension?" New Hampshire Retirement System, December 5, 2016, https://perma.cc/XQV5-NZ78; Jennifer Baker, telephone interview, September 28, 2016. See also "Political Empire: Pension Reform Group Pulls Rally Switcheroo," *Press Enterprise,* May 9, 2011, http://www.pe.com/articles/budget-597893-negrete-group.html.

20. This search was run on May 26, 2017.

21. Ayres and Curtis, "Beyond Diversification"; Andrew Biggs, "Are State and Local Government Pensions Underfunded by $5 Trillion," *Forbes,* July 1, 2016, http://perma.cc/W23R-D9U9; Jennifer Burnett, "3 Questions on State Bankruptcy," Council of State Governments, January 2017, http://perma.cc/WB8W-EAPZ. See also "Americans for Prosperity–Iowa Applauds State Legislature for Passing Collective Bargaining Reform," Americans for Prosperity, February 16, 2017, http://perma.cc/4G4U-G4VT.

22. Jennifer Baker, interview, September 28, 2016; Voter Empowerment Act of 2016, http://perma.cc/YPM2-MWW4; Los Angeles Fire and Police Pensions, "Pension Reform Initiatives for 2016," http://perma.cc/K4GE-5PCC; Dave Low, "Reed's State Pension Reform Measure Would Be Financial Disaster," *Mercury News,* August 26, 2015, http://perma.cc/865B-R936.

23. "CalPERS vs. Voters," *Wall Street Journal,* August 12, 2015, https://perma.cc/manage/create; Voter Empowerment Act of 2016; Los Angeles

Fire and Police Pensions, "Pension Reform Initiatives for 2016"; Jennifer Baker, interview, September 28, 2016.

24. Marianne Levine, "Enron Billionaire Frets about Public Pensions' Solvency," Politico, December 13, 2014, http://perma.cc/H4X7-M3KW; Jon Ortiz, "Chuck Reed Sues California Attorney General Kamala Harris over Summary of Pension Initiative," *Sacramento Bee,* February 7, 2014, http://perma.cc/CMJ9-79TC.

25. See, e.g., George Skelton, "Public Pensions Are Protected in Constitution," *Los Angeles Times,* November 14, 2011, https://perma.cc/E5U7-MDYU; Sasha Volokh, "The 'California Rule' for Public-Employee Pensions: Is It Good Constitutional Law?" *Washington Post,* February 4, 2014, https://perma.cc/J7CL-B4CC; Amy B. Monahan, "Statutes as Contracts? The 'California Rule' and Its Impact on Public Pension Reform," *Iowa Law Review* 97 (2012), http://perma.cc/YX2K-5NNU.

26. Michael Hiltzik, "Count the Bad Ideas in California Pension Overhaul Proposal," *Los Angeles Times,* August 15, 2015, http://perma.cc/39KT-HFWM.

27. "John Arnold," in "Forbes 400," *Forbes,* http://perma.cc/TLH6-SG78.

28. Bethany McLean and Peter Elkind, *The Smartest Guys in the Room: The Amazing Rise and Scandalous Fall of Enron* (New York: Portfolio Trade, 2003). I was directed to this source by Matt Taibbi's article, "Looting the Pension Funds," *Rolling Stone,* September 26, 2013, http://perma.cc/N457-JYES.

29. Levine, "Enron Billionaire Frets about Public Pensions' Solvency." See also Kristen Hays, "Enron Settlement: $7.2 Billion to Shareholders," *Houston Chronicle,* September 9, 2008, http://perma.cc/J7HC-D4YT. There is no allegation or evidence that Arnold was involved in the fraud.

30. Tim Reid, "Exclusive: Former Enron Trader Arnold May Launch National PR Push to Reform Pensions," Reuters, April 10, 2015, http://perma.cc/Y4ZV-3YZ3; David Sirota, "The Plot against Pensions," Institute for America's Future, September 26, 2013, http://perma.cc/HW86-DX88; LJAF Pension Reform, http://perma.cc/2R5Q-VW4Z.

31. Levine, "Enron Billionaire Frets about Public Pensions' Solvency"; Alicia Munnell, Jean-Pierre Aubry, and Mark Cafarelli, "Defined Contribution Plans in the Public Sector: An Update," Center for Retirement Research, Boston College, no. 37, April 2014, https://perma.cc/S4VA-9ADT.

32. David H. Webber, "The Use and Abuse of Labor's Capital," *New York University Law Review* 89 (2014): 2106; Braun and Selway, "Pension Fund Gains Mean Worker Pain as Aramark Cuts Pay."

33. Erica Jedynak, "Pension Reform Is at a Crossroads in New Jersey," *Forbes,* July 12, 2016, http://perma.cc/A8TH-T4NK. The author was the New Jersey state director of Americans for Prosperity. See also Robert Steyer, "New Jersey Pension Contribution Amendment Doesn't Make November Ballot," *Pensions and Investments,* August 9, 2016, http://perma.cc/S9QL -W488; Julia Crigler and David From, "A Tale of Two State Pension Crises," The Hill, August 16, 2016, http://perma.cc/UJP9-GCDE; and Brent Gardner and Andy Koenig, "AFP Stands against Taxpayer Bailouts of Underfunded Pensions in Letter," Open Letter to Chairman Orrin Hatch (R-Utah) and Ranking Member Ron Wyden (D-Ore.) of the Senate Finance Committee, Americans for Prosperity, September 21, 2016, https://americansforprosperity .org/afp-stands-taxpayer-bailouts-underfunded-pensions-letter/.

34. Legal Scholarship Network of the Social Science Research Network, e-mail, August 31, 2016, announcing December 1–2, 2016, "George Mason Law and Economics Center Workshop for Professors on Public Pensions."

35. Keith Brainard and Paul Zorn, "The 80-Percent Threshold: Its Source as a Healthy or Minimum Funding Level for Public Pension Plans," NASRA, January 2012, http://perma.cc/U2TC-D3W6; Alicia H. Munnell and Jean-Pierre Aubry, "The Funding of State and Local Pensions: 2015–2020," Center for Retirement Research, Boston College, no. 50, June 2016, http://crr.bc.edu/wp-content/uploads/2016/06/slp_50-1.pdf; Meaghan Kilroy, "Corporate Pension Funds Reverse Funding Decline in July—2 Reports," *Pensions and Investments,* August 2, 2017, http://www.pionline.com/article /20170802/ONLINE/170809967/corporate-pension-funds-reverse -funding-decline-in-july-8212-2-reports; John Klingner, "Taxpayers Bear the Brunt of Increasing Pension Costs," Illinois Policy, https://perma.cc /533T-3RCB. See also Alejandra Cancino, "How Tax Breaks Are Costing Illinois Billions in Lost Revenue," *Daily Herald,* October 21, 2016, http://www .dailyherald.com/article/20161021/news/161029748/.

36. National Association of State Retirement Administrators, "NASRA Issue Brief: State and Local Government Spending on Public Employee Retirement Systems," April 2017, https://perma.cc/BX9P-RYRJ.

37. See, e.g., Elizabeth Campbell, "S&P, Moody's Downgrade Illinois to Near Junk, Lowest Ever for a U.S. State," Bloomberg, June 1, 2017, https://perma.cc/HBH2-XE68, and Kate King, "S&P Global Downgrades New Jersey's Bond Rating," *Wall Street Journal,* November 14, 2016, https:// perma.cc/UP7Q-WHFN.

38. See Helena Smith, "A Year after the Crisis Was Declared Over, Greece Is Still Spiraling Down," *The Guardian,* August 13, 2016, https://perma.cc /W72W-476U. See also "Eurozone Crisis Live: Spanish Borrowing Costs

Hit 7% after Double Downgrade," *The Guardian,* June 14, 2012, https://perma.cc/TVR6-N738.

39. "Myths and Realities about State and Local Pensions," in Alice H. Munnell, "State and Local Pensions: What Now?" Brookings Institute, 2012, http://perma.cc/Y2W9-JPGT.

40. Steven Malanga, "Covering up the Pension Crisis," *Wall State Journal,* August 25, 2016, http://perma.cc/VG99-EJPK.

41. Mary Williams Walsh, "A Sour Surprise for Public Pensions: Two Sets of Books," *New York Times,* September 17, 2016, http://perma.cc/83FG-9ET8; Investopedia, s.v. "Risk-Free Rate of Return Definition," http://perma.cc/K8KA-NWUW; U.S. Treasury Yield Curve, http://perma.cc/2EML-CHV6.

42. "Myths and Realities about State and Local Pensions," emphasis added; "NYU Annual Returns on Stock," T.Bonds and T.Bills: 1928—Current, http://perma.cc/34CD-GSK6; Randy Diamond, "High-Return Era Ends for Many Big Public Pension Funds," *Pensions and Investments,* August 10, 2015, http://perma.cc/LE6T-266L.

43. Ryan O'Donnell, "Why You May Not Want to Save for College," *Wall Street Journal,* September 10, 2017, https://perma.cc/D7P4-J235.

44. George Mason Law and Economics Center, "Program on the Economics and Law of Public Pension Reform," http://perma.cc/THJ2-W8VR; Law and Economics Center Public Policy Conference on Solving the Public Pension Crisis for Law Professors, https://perma.cc/X5QR-J4JJ; Tina Reed, "Students Sue George Mason over Koch Brother Donation Records," *Washington Business Journal,* February 10, 2017, http://perma.cc/6KQ2-BBNP.

45. George Mason Law and Economics Center, "Program on the Economics and Law of Public Pension Reform"; George Mason Law and Economics Center, "LEC Workshop for Professors on Public Pensions—$1,000 Honorarium," http://perma.cc/B9W2-B4L8; Law and Economics Center Public Policy Conference on Solving the Public Pension Crisis for Judges and Attorneys General, http://perma.cc/Y5U2-5CLA, emphasis added.

46. "The Illinois Capitulation," *Wall Street Journal,* June 20, 2017, https://www.wsj.com/articles/the-illinois-capitulation-1498000268?nan_pid=1861008930.

47. Beermann has written about the legal aspects of pension reform. See Jack Beermann, "The Public Pension Crisis," *Washington and Lee Law Review* 70 (2013): 3.

48. American Legislative Exchange Council, "Pension Reform," http://perma.cc/W9E9-RZ6U; "The Big Money behind State Laws," *New York Times,* February 12, 2012, http://perma.cc/P4FE-CCGK.

49. American Legislative Exchange Council, "Pensions Funding and Fairness Act," http://perma.cc/9R82-8ZJK.

50. See Jeffrey Keefe, "Eliminating Fair Share Fees and Making Public Employment 'Right to Work' Would Increase the Pay Penalty for Working in State and Local Government," Economic Policy Institute, October 13, 2015, http://perma.cc/EJ93-M9XC.

51. Ibid.; "Supreme Court Denies Friedrichs Petition for Rehearing," Center for Individual Rights, June 28, 2016, http://perma.cc/FFH3-U36G.

52. Adele M. Stan, "Who's Behind Friedrichs?" *American Prospect,* October 29, 2015, http://perma.cc/4G2Y-MADL; "Where We Stand on Teacher's Retirement," California Teachers Association, http://perma.cc /6SUY-2C87.

53. Amy Howe, "Union Fees in Jeopardy: In Plain English," SCOTUS Blog, January 11, 2016, http://perma.cc/9LJJ-EUPY; *Knox v. Service Employees International Union,* 567 U.S. 298 (2012).

54. Howe, "Union Fees in Jeopardy"; Stan, "Who's Behind Friedrichs?"; Matt Ford, "A Narrow Escape for Public-Sector Unions," *The Atlantic,* March 29, 2016, http://perma.cc/R3C8-QUWW; *Friedrichs v. California Teachers Association,* Docket 14–915 (2016), Transcript, Oral Argument of Donald B. Verrilli, Jr., for the United States, as Amicus Curae, Supporting the Respondents, at 69–70. Justice Scalia commented, "The problem is that it's not the same as a private employer, that what is bargained for is, in all cases, a matter of public interest. And that changes the—that changes the situation in a way that—that may require a change of the rule [established forty years prior in *Abood* allowing for the payment of fair-share fees]. It's one thing to provide it for private employers. It's another thing to provide it for the government, where every matter bargained for is a matter of public interest."

55. "The New Friedrichs Case: *Janus v. AFSCME,*" California PERB Blog, January 17, 2017, http://perma.cc/M3L5-FCC3.

56. Robert Samuels, "Walker's Anti-Union Law Has Labor Reeling in Wisconsin," *Washington Post,* February 22, 2015, http://perma.cc/8AZE -LNYX; Justin Miller, "Janus: A New Attack Presents Old Challenges for Unions," *American Prospect,* October 24, 2017.

57. "SWIB Announces 2015 Wisconsin Retirement System Preliminary Returns," press release, State of Wisconsin Investment Board, January 13, 2016, https://perma.cc/Y6YH-KVZN; Brigham R. Frandsen, "The Effects of Collective Bargaining Rights on Public Employee Compensation: Evidence from Teachers, Fire Fighters, and Police," Brigham Young University, January 31, 2014, https://perma.cc/6V4M-BT8G; Michael Garland, telephone interview, January 18, 2017.

58. Levine, "Enron Billionaire Frets about Public Pensions' Solvency."

59. Bailey Somers, "CalPERS Named Lead Plaintiff in UnitedHealth Suit," LAW 360, September 17, 2006, http://perma.cc/EHG3-353J.

60. Christian E. Weller, "Your Money, Your Future: Public Pension Plans and the Need to Strengthen Retirement Security and Economic Growth," Testimony before the Joint Economic Committee of Congress, July 10, 2008, http://perma.cc/Q3AT-GWG6.

61. Ghilarducci and James, "The Retirement Savings Plan."

62. Josh Eidelson, "AFL-CIO Dismissing Staff amid Declines in U.S. Union Membership," Bloomberg, February 23, 2017, https://www.bloomberg.com/news/articles/2017-02-23/afl-cio-dismissing-staff-amid-declines-in-u-s-union-membership.

63. Ed O'Keefe and Steven Mufson, "Senate Democrats Unveil a Trump-Size Infrastructure Plan," *Washington Post,* January 24, 2017, http://perma.cc/L44W-AVTH; Mike Hall, "Labor Hits $10 Billion Goal for Clinton Global Initiative Jobs and Infrastructure Investment," AFL-CIO, June 25, 20014, http://perma.cc/SZJ7-NLPA; Bill Lockyer, Randi Weingarten, and Deborah Wince-Smith, "Jump-Starting America's Workforce," Clinton Foundation, April 3, 2014, http://perma.cc/3GSV-4A74; David A. Lieb, "America's Infrastructure Needs Repair," *US News and World Report,* September 19, 2016, http://perma.cc/H3RG-CVSR; Imogen Rose-Smith, "Pension Funds Ride to the U.S. Economy's Rescue," *Institutional Investor Magazine,* January 2, 2012, http://perma.cc/KD84-ZB8E.

64. "About ULLICO," http://www.ullico.com/about-ullico; Brian Hale, telephone interview, March 1, 2017.

65. Brian Hale, telephone interview, March 1, 2017.

66. Monte Tarbox, telephone interview, February 27, 2017; Yves Smith, "CalPERS Board Uncomfortable with Staff's 'Fire, Aim, Ready' Plan to Create Unaccountable Private Equity Vehicle," Naked Capitalism, July 24, 2017, https://www.nakedcapitalism.com/2017/07/calpers-board-uncomfortable-with-staffs-fire-aim-ready-plan-to-create-unaccountable-private-equity-vehicle.html.

67. New York City Fire Department Pension Fund, "Statement of Investment Policy for Responsible Contractor," https://comptroller.nyc.gov/services/financial-matters/pension/initiatives/responsible-contractor-policy/.

68. John Adler, interview, September 18, 2017; Dan Pedrotty, interview, September 11, 2017.

69. Dan Pedrotty, interview, September 11, 2017.

70. "Blackstone's Infrastructure Business Adopts Responsible Contractor Policy to Promote Fair Wages and Benefits for Workers on Infrastructure Projects," press release, Blackstone, September 5, 2017, https://perma.cc /FX3W-M8KY.

71. Ibid.

72. Anne Tergesen, "Lawmakers Try to Stop State-Sponsored Retirement Plans," *Wall Street Journal,* February 8, 2017, https://www.wsj.com /articles/lawmakers-try-to-stop-state-sponsored-retirement-plans -1486580352; Hank Kim, "The Secure Choice Pension," Pension Rights Center, http://www.pensionrights.org/what-we-do/events/re-imagining -pensions/secure-choice-pension.

73. Greg Iacurci, "Congress Seeks to Kill DOL Rules on State, City Auto-IRA Programs: House Republicans Introduce Bills to Block Labor Department Rules Promoting Creation of Retirement Plans for Private-Sector Employees," Investment News, February 8, 2017, http://www .investmentnews.com/article/20170208/FREE/170209912/congress -seeks-to-kill-dol-rules-on-state-city-auto-ira-programs.

74. Tergesen, "Lawmakers Try to Stop State-Sponsored Retirement Plans."

Acknowledgments

First and foremost, thank you to the activists I wrote about in these pages. If the book leaves readers sharing any of the enthusiasm I feel for the work that you do, it will have succeeded.

I still think of my first meeting with Thomas LeBien at Harvard University Press as one of the best conversations I have had about this project. Thomas, from the beginning, your counsel on all aspects of the work has proved unerring. It has immensely improved the experience of writing this book. Thank you. Thank you also to Margaret Hogan for copyediting the manuscript, to Louise Robbins for shepherding the manuscript through the editing process, to Sonya Bonczek, and to everyone else at the Press for being so helpful and enthusiastic about this project.

Frank Partnoy, thank you for many conversations, both related and not related to this book, and for proposing a different title than the one that wound up on the jacket.

At various stages of work on this project, I have benefited from the aid and counsel of Mehrsa Baradaran, Jack Beerman, Keith Brainard, Peter Conti-Brown, Jason Cooper, Jim Fleming, Tamar Frankel, Teresa Ghilarducci, Alan Gotthelf, Kent Greenfield, Marcel Kahan, Roy Kreitner, Pnina Lahav, Nell Minow, Nancy Moore, Moran Ofir, Barak Orbach, Kristen Queenan, Roy Shapira, Fred Tung, David Walker, Allison Webber, Mayris Webber, Robert Webber, Kathryn Zeiler, and three anonymous peer reviewers. Thanks to all of you. Thank you to Dean Maureen O'Rourke for enabling me to work on this project. Thank you also to the Boston University School of Law Faculty Workshop and the National Business Law Scholars Conference for tolerating early drafts of this work. And thank you to the Interdisciplinary Center Herzliya for tolerating a late draft of it, when I had run out of excuses.

This book benefited from the excellent research assistance of Elizabeth Driscoll, Connor Flaherty, Lauren Geiser, Aria Mahboubi, Beatrice Maidman, Garrett Miller, Dayna Mudge, Caitlin Tompkins, and Brandon Winer. Thank you all.

Irit Tau-Webber, this book would never have happened without your love and support. Boaz, Noam, and Eliane would not have happened without your love and support either. Thank you!

Index

Pedrotty, Dan: Blackstone and, 249; on hedge funds, 85–91, 93–101, 107–108; Responsible Contractor Policy promoted by, 247–248; Slavkin Corzo succeeds, 146; in Trustee Leadership Forum, 208

Pension Funding and Fairness Act (proposed), 234–235

pension funds: boards of trustees of, 9; class-action lawsuits by, 56–57, 302–303n11; current stability of, 40–41; defined-benefit versus defined-contribution, 214–235; in Detroit bankruptcy, 128–131; duty of loyalty and investments by, 184–201; during financial crisis, 128; hedge fund investments of, 79, 83–84, 90, 108–110; investments of, 8; litigation by, 171–172; private equity fund investments of, 157, 161, 301n22, 308n30; shareholder campaign against Safeway by, 22–30; for teachers, 89–95; in UnitedHealth case, 179. *See also* public pension funds

Petry, John, 88

Phoenix (Arizona), 224–225

Pitt, Harvey, 50

Piwowar, Michael, 150

political issues, 68–69

portfolio managers, 198

Preqin (hedge fund database), 90

private equity funds, 95–97, 153–155; public pension funds invested in, 301n22, 308n30; regulation of, 155–158; SEC on, 158–160; unions and, 161–163; UNITE HERE investigations of, 160–161

Private Securities Litigation Reform Act (1995), 56

privatization of public services, 190–191, 196, 200–201

Protégé Partners (hedge fund), 81

proxy access, 46–58, 240; Business Roundtable and U.S. Chamber of Commerce suit on, 58–63; as fundamental right of shareholders, 73–74; SEC on, 137; shareholder proposals on, 277n50; Stringer and Boardroom Accountability Project strategy on, 65–72; studies of, 72–73

proxy fights, 47

Public Employees' Retirement Fund (PERF), 32

public pension funds, 8; assets of, 202; attempts to break up, 214; Council of Institutional Investors of, 55, 94; ERISA not applicable to, 193; female beneficiaries of, 69; future of, 241–255; in hedge funds, 84, 90, 108, 109; largest, 202–203; myth of crisis in, 40; political power of, 203–204; political threats to, 213, 242; in private equity funds, 161, 162, 301n22, 308n30; Private Securities Litigation Reform Act on, 56; securities fraud class action suits by, 172; shareholder litigation by, 179; underfunding of, 284n33; as universal owners, 52; workers covered by, 8

public sector workers, 8; agency fees paid by, 235–241; compensation of, 228; covered by defined-benefit plans, 215; investments in pension funds by, 36–37; investments in privatization by, 190–191, 196, 200–201; stability of pension funds for, 40–41; teachers as, 89–95; threats to collective bargaining by, 213; women and minorities among, 69

Quinn, Randall, 60, 71

Quirk, Paul, 208

Raimondo, Gina, 225

Rauner, Bruce, 93

Raymond, Lee, 126

Reagan, Ronald, 59

real estate investment trusts (REITs), 102–103

Reed, Chuck, 223

Reed, Jack, 156

regulation: Brandeis on, 152; of private equity funds, 153, 155–158

access suit of, 58–63; on say-on-pay, 139; on Secure Choice Pensions, 252; as special-interest group, 140

Vanguard (mutual fund), 14, 53–55, 133, 293–294n48
Vermeule, Adrian, 59–60
Vermont, 252
Verrilli, Donald, 237
Vickers, Suzanne, 248
Voices for Working Families (organization), 117
Voter Empowerment Act (proposed, California), 222–223
Voya (mutual fund), 214

Walberg, Tim, 252
Walker, Scott, 127
Wall Street Journal: on backdated stock options, 165–167, 179; Lindsley attacked by, 115–116; on SEC on proxy access, 57–58, 71, 240
Wall Street Walk, 177
Wal-Mart (firm), 31–35
Walt Disney Company (Disney), 12–14
Warren, Elizabeth, 156–157; on CEO-worker pay ratios, 147, 149–150, 252; on Consumer Financial Protection Bureau, 179

Washington Mutual (bank), 118
Washington State Investment Board (WSIB), 7, 22
Waters, Maxine, 146–147
Weingarten, Randi, 90–95, 98–99, 101, 107–108
Welch, Jack, 6
Weldon, Bill, 126
Wells Fargo (bank), 179–180
Westly, Steve, 4
West Virginia, 225
White, Mary Jo, 147, 149–150
Winter, Scott, 291n23
Wisconsin, 127, 238
withhold vote campaigns, 13–14
WL Ross LLC & Company, 159–160
women: in public pension funds, 69; as teachers, 94–95
Wood, David, 208
working class, defined, 8, 300n13
WorldCom (firm), 49
Wyden, Ron, 154, 155

Young, Beth: on JPMorgan and Dimon, 120–121; on proxy access, 49–50, 52; on say-on-pay voting, 137, 138
Youngdahl, Jay, 208

Zuccotti Park (New York), 97, 99–100